DYNAMICS OF NEW PANCHAYATI RAJ SYSTEM IN INDIA

Volume VII : FINANCIAL STATUS OF PANCHAYATS

Dynamics of New Panchayati Raj System in India

Vol.	I	:	Select States
Vol.	II	:	Select States
Vol.	III	:	Select States
Vol.	IV	:	Empowering Women
Vol.	V	:	Panchayati Raj and Multi-level Planning
Vol.	VI	:	Capacity Building
Vol.	VII	:	Financial Status of Panchayats
Vol.	VIII	:	Panchayati Raj and Common Property Resource Management
Vol.	IX	:	Participatory and Direct Democracy : Gram Sabha
Vol.	X	:	Panchayati Raj and Empowerment of Dalits
Vol.	XI	:	State-Local Body Relationship
Vol.	XII	:	Panchayati Raj and Socio-Political and Economic Transformation
Vol.	XIII	:	Leadership in Panchayati Raj Institution
Vol.	XIV	:	Thinkers Framework on Panchayati Raj
Vol.	XV	:	Theoretical Nuances of Local Bodies

About the Editor

Prof. Ganapathi Palanithurai, Coordinator in Rajiv Gandhi Chair, Department of Political Science and Development Administration, in Gandhigram Rural University, Tamil Nadu. He is also associated with Centre Planning Commission, State Planning Commission of Tamil Nadu, Population Foundation of India, Ford Foundation, UNICEF, Rajiv Gandhi Foundation, CAPART, Ministry of Rural Areas and Employment and DANIDA (Danish-Indo Development Agency) in specific areas of activities in connection with empowerment of people.

Prof. Palanithurai has to his credit fifty-eight books and one hundred and twenty seven articles on three major areas, namely, legislative behaviour, ethnicity and Panchayati Raj System. He was recipient of Fellowship from Shastri Indo-Canadian Institute, New Delhi and World Academy of Art and Science, USA. He is the Chairman of the Tamil Nadu Council for Sustainable Livelihoods. He was a visiting fellow in the McGill University, Canada in 1989. He is a member of the expert committee constituted by the Government of Tamil Nadu to monitor the training programme for local body leaders.

DYNAMICS OF NEW PANCHAYATI RAJ SYSTEM IN INDIA

VOLUME VII
Financial Status of Panchayats

Edited by
G. PALANITHURAI

CONCEPT PUBLISHING COMPANY PVT. LTD.
NEW DELHI-110 059

ISBN-13: 978-81-8069-672-5 (Vol. VII)
ISBN-13: 978-81-7022-910-0 (Series)

First Published 2010

Published and Printed by

Concept
Since 1974

Concept Publishing Company Pvt. Ltd.
Regd. Office:
A/15-16, Commercial Block, Mohan Garden
New Delhi-110059 (India)
Phones : 25351460, 25351794, *Fax* : 091-11-25357109
Email : publishing@conceptpub.com,
Website: www.conceptpub.com

Editorial Office:
H-13, Bali Nagar, New Delhi-110 015, India.

Cataloging in Publication Data-- *Courtesy:* D.K. Agencies (P) Ltd. <docinfo@dkagencies.com>

Dynamics of new panchayati raj system in India / edited by
G. Palanithurai. v. 7. cm.
Contributed articles.
Includes bibliographical references.
Includes indexes.
Contents: v. 7. Financial status of panchayats.
ISBN 13: 9788170229100 (set) ISBN 13: 9788180696725 (v. 7)

1. Panchayat--India. 2. Local government--India. I. Palanithurai, G. (Ganapathy), 1953-

DDC 320.840 954 22

TO

THE DIVINE MOTHER

(In India) one should begin with the old panchayat system in the villages and the work upto the top. The panchayat system and the guilds are more representative and they have a living contact with people, they are the parts of the people's ideas.

— *Sri Aurobindo*

The village Republic will be managed by a panchayat which will be living political force and entity. Panchayats will be united in a free and voluntary association by "ever widening circle of village republics". It will not be an "apex sustained by the bottom" but an oceanic circle where centre will be the individual always ready to perish for the village, the latter ready to perish for the circle of villages and so on, sharing the majesty of the oceanic circle which they are parts.

— *Mahatma Gandhi*

We trust the people

We have faith in the people

It is the people who must

determine their own destinies

and the destiny of the Nation

To the people of India, let us

ensure maximum democracy and

maximum devolution. Let the

people be empowered.

— *Rajiv Gandhi*

PREFACE

The degree of autonomy of Local Bodies is determined on the basis of the demarcated responsibilities, powers, functions, finance and functionaries devolved to each tier of governance in Local Bodies. Of all the indicators, finance that too the untied funds to local bodies indicate the autonomy of the local bodies. In India we witnessed during 1970s and 1980s, local bodies were de-established effectively only through the reduction of resources devolved to them. Moreover, the local bodies were not given due recognition in mobilising resources on their own. The tax domain of the local bodies is very limited. In the well established local body system in any country one will find that 50 per cent of the total expenditure is met from internal resources and in such a way taxation power is given to local bodies. But India is always a paradox. It has created a vibrant local body system through the Constitution of India. But they are allowed to suffer for want of resources. Near about 30 lakh representatives are in position. And of them, 10 lakh are women. Hence, it has been made as a vibrant body.

But while seeing the financial position of local bodies in India, one would wonder why such a hype is created through the Constitution. Many countries look towards India for guidance to establish local body system in their countries. Even some countries have created local bodies through executive orders or legislative decisions, provincial legislations have allocated at least not less than 10 per cent of the total expenditure. In India, local body finance is around 4 per cent only.

Having realized the implications, in anticipation, the federal government through the amendment has created a State Finance Commission which will see the financial feasibility for the sustainability of the Panchayati Raj System. Yet barring a few States, the formation of State Finance Commission became a ritual. Even to constitute a committee pressure has to be exerted. The committees have to submit the reports; State governments have to accept the recommendations; and the accepted recommendations have to be implemented in letter and spirit. These are all fulfilling constitutional obligations.

Further, the local bodies have to be given powers to mobilize resources internally. For this the tax reform is to be introduced. A few States are setting example for other States as role model. But many of the States, local body finance is in a very bad shape. There is yet another question, whether the local bodies are having enough capacity to mobilize resources. Still arguments are projected that local governance institutions are not having well laid financial system to mobilize resources and spend the same. But generally one major proposition has been developed that the Local Bodies are spending institutions. Instead of mobilizing resources, they are interested in spending resources. Of all the issues of the Local Bodies, local finance is a major issue to be seen in proper perspective. Against this background, an initiative has been taken to edit a volume on Panchayat Finance. The articles in this volume have been drawn from scholars narrating the experiences in their respective States. They are being compiled.

To complete any task in life, one would require the support of many. For any academic work, we need a team. I am a believer in team work. I have several teams in my department. One team is looking after action research and capacity building. Another team is working in support structure to extend helping hand to the Panchayat leaders who are in struggle. There are academics taking responsibility in running academic programmes in Development Administration, Governance and Development as they do in Panchayati Raj. Apart from our team, there are many individuals and institutions who are constantly helping us to carry out our academic research and outreach programmes. Working with the marginalized and women in the domain of local governance is a very difficult job. We are always with the disadvantaged. All our activities in the Rajiv Gandhi Chair for Panchayati Raj studies are related to the strengthening of the Local Bodies. We are always swimming against the current. Hence, it is my duty and responsibility to express my sincere thanks to my colleagues working with me to carry out academic activities, research activities and outreach activities. Equally my family members deserve my appreciation and I express my special thanks to them also.

G. PALANITHURAI

CONTENTS

LIST OF THE CONTRIBUTORS

Fahimuddin
Fellow,
Giri Institute of Development Studies,
Sector 'O', Aliganj,
Lucknow

M. Devendra Babu
Assistant Professor
Economics Unit,
Institute for Social and Economic Change,
Nagarbhavi,
Bangalore - 560 072

T.M. Thomas Issac
Minister for Finance
Government of Kerala
Room No. 118, First Floor,
North Block, Govt. Secretariat,
Thiruvananthapuram - 1

P. Shaheena
Assistant Professor,
College of Co-operation,
Banking and Management,
Kerala Agricultural University,
KAU (P.O.), Vellanikkara,
Thrissur, Kerala

S.K. Singh
National Institute of Rural Development,
Rajendra Nagar,
Hyderabad - 500 030

C. Pratheep
Lecturer in Economics,
Mulamana VHSS, Anakudy,
Thiruvananthapuram, Kerala

B. Mohanan
Professor,
Dept. of Politics and International Studies,
Pondicherry University,
Pondicherry

Dilip Kumar Ghosh
Senior Research Officer,
State Institute of Panchayats and Rural Development (SIPRD),
Kalyani, Nadia - 741 235

G. Palanithurai
Professor and Head,
Department of Political Science and Development Administration,
Gandhigram Rural University,
Gandhigram - 624 302
(Tamil Nadu)

O.P. Bohra
National Institute of Public Finance and Policy,
18/2, Satsang Vihar Marg,
Special Institutional Area,
New Delhi - 110 067

D. Bandyopadhyay
Council for Social Development,
Sangha Rachana,
53, Lodi Estate,
New Delhi - 110 003

INTRODUCTION

Finance in Panchayati Raj is crucial for institutionalization of the Panchayats at the grassroots. It is to be noted that while analyzing the reasons for the decline of the Local Bodies in India in 1970s and 1980s, it was argued that financial constraints made the local institutions defunct and people also lose their interest in the local bodies as they are unable to attend to the felt needs of the people. A country with a size of a continent with diversified issues and problems requires decentralized solutions and actions which would ultimately strengthen the Central and State governments. Local governments are the first level governments nearer to the people responding to the problems of the communities in a responsive and responsible way. When Tsunami struck the entire coastal regions, the first-two days the communities themselves managed the affairs on their own. Other agencies came to the help only after two days. It was strange that Panchayat did not have untied funds or emergency funds with them to meet emergencies like Tsunami. People themselves contributed money to manage the affairs. Even today in villages, there is a common good fund for conducting temple and cultural festivals. They are created with the mobilization of resources from the people. Mostly, the funds are managed in transparent ways. They have general bodies also called "*Oor Sabha*". Totally the funds are pooled and they are untied. But the Gram Panchayat funds are tied. Thus Panchayats should require untied funds to meet the emergency needs. Unfortunately there is no provision for the untied funds. In the absence of untied funds, Panchayat presidents are not in a position to explain to the people. Somehow or other they have to attend to the works. Hence one will find all kinds of manipulations in Panchayat funds. The local governments should have more freedom and flexibility to take decisions to meet the immediate and urgent needs of the communities. They should have reasonably a good resource base at their disposal. The whole functioning of the Panchayats and their sustainability and stability depend on the flow of funds to the Panchayats and their power to generate resources from the community. In this country there is a tendency to develop a peculiar line of perception that the Central management thinks that the fiscal management of the centre is fine but it is not fine enough in State government and in the same way, State government feels that financial management of the State government is reasonable but the financial management of the local government is poor. This kind of tendency hinders the whole process of decentralization.

With regard to the financial conditions of the local bodies in developed countries, no uniformity could be found. There are good examples. In some Nordic countries, local income taxes form a sound and buoyant economic base. It is to be understood that the purpose for which the local governance is designed will decide the quantum of resources to be devolved to grassroots institutions and powers to be devolved to raise resources through tax. It is clear from the available literature that the western developed countries use decentralized framework as a cost-effective mechanism in delivery of services whereas the others use it either as support to consolidate the central power or as a response to or as an antidote to inefficiencies and ineffective government delivery of local public goods. Though we cannot follow the model of the West, we can derive some important lessons from the West for adaptation. It is to be noted that the finance of the local bodies of the West ranges between 7.5 per cent and 25 per cent of the total expenditure.

It is also clear that around 50 per cent of the total expenditure is met from the resources raised by the local bodies. Thus local bodies are given fund raising and spending authority. Whereas in the case of the developing countries tax autonomy is limited and expenditure autonomy is a far cry from tax autonomy. In terms of expenditure in developing countries the per cent of the GDP ranges from 3 per cent to 6 per cent. In terms of total expenditure developing countries' local bodies expenditure ranges between 13 per cent and 22 per cent. A few other developing countries in the world provide good lessons to India. The status of Panchayats in India in terms of the observation of the chairperson of the second Administrative Reform Commission is that "I was recently told about the observation of a visiting European who wondered how India is able to function without any local government worthy of the name. His bafflement is understandable. We have allowed the local bodies to atrophy and starve them to funds to such an extent that while local government revenues accounted for 15 per cent of the total government revenues in the USA in the year 2001, the corresponding figure in India was just 3 per cent. Even after passing of the 73rd and 74th Constitutional Amendments, the transfer of funds, functions and functionaries has been nominal in most States with notable exceptions such as Kerala." Finance is a neglected aspect in the whole of devolution exercise in India. It is true that part IX of the Constitution extensively deals with devolution of powers more on structural empowerment of the Panchayati Raj Institutions. Specifically Articles 243C, 243D, 243E, 243G and 243K deal with those aspects. But the real strength lies in the delivery of services to the people but it is linked with the financial devolution which included power to the Panchayats to generate resources from within. Generally in India, Panchayati Raj Institutions receive funds from various sources. They are:

1. Grants from Central Government, based on the recommendation of the Central Finance Commission as per article 280 of the Constitution.
2. Devolution from the State government based on the recommendations of the State Finance Commission as per Article 243-I.
3. Loans and grants from the State government.
4. Programme-specific allocation under centrally sponsored schemes and additional central assistance.
5. Internal resource mobilization (tax and non-tax revenues).

Across the country, States have not given adequate attention to fiscal devolution towards the Panchayats. There is a strong argument put up by some of the States. Primarily devolution refers power-shift from the top to bottom. So it has to flow from Centre to States and from States to the local bodies. In India, an argument is projected that power devolution is from State to local bodies. The

States are facing a series of crisis and their powers are curtailed through centrally sponsored schemes and the recommendations of the Central Finance Commission. Literally, the States are under the control of the Centre. Hence, Centralization takes place in this country. In this context, while looking at power devolution, many of them argue that the present package of devolution is set to disturb the State governments. When this perception gains momentum how can one devolve powers? Moreover Panchayat's own resources are already meagre. This is partly due to this tax domain of the Panchayat. Further even if the tax domain is enlarged the Panchayats are reluctant to collect such tax revenues. Further Panchayats do not get adequate untied funds from the Centre and the State governments. Major portion of the grants from both governments is scheme-specific.

Since the State governments are facing financial crisis, they are not in a position to devolve adequate resources to the Panchayats. Further on many of the subjects mentioned in the 11th Schedule, State governments are directly spending money and hence they are not devolving resources to the Panchayats. In order to strengthen the resource base of the Panchayats recommendations have always been made on the following ways: (1) potential for taxation; (2) fixation of realistic tax rates; (3) widening of tax base and (4) improved revenue collection.

Basically, the State Finance Commission was incorporated in the Constitution with a view to avoid the danger of weakening the Panchayats by reducing the resource base. However, this new provision has not been very successful. In many of the States, State Finance Commissions were constituted as a matter of official requirement. There is no congruence between the time frame of the State Finance Commissions and Central Finance Commission. Some of the State Finance Commissions have done their exercises seriously but their valid recommendations have not been accepted.

Many of the accepted recommendations of the State Finance Commissions have not been implemented. From the constitution of the State Finance Commission, and implementation of the recommendations of the State Finance Commission, pressure has to be exerted on the State governments. The centralized drive for resource devolution is considered as a major issue in the Centre-State relations. There are four States which are appreciated with regard to the effective devolution of resources as per the recommendations of the State Finance Commissions. Kerala is the only State which has implemented all the recommendations of all the three State Finance Commissions. Maharashtra is a pioneering State in creating a Panchayati Raj window for expenditures. From the creation of such a Panchayati Raj window for expenditure, one can easily understand how much money comes through the line departments and how much of money being spent directly by the Panchayats. In a way it is a kind of demystification of administration and governance. Managing finances for development at grassroots is a complicated subject. State governments have adopted several models by which the process is handled. There is yet another issue of raising resources from the people for the services delivered by the local bodies. It is pay and use as in the West. But in the rural areas allocating money for the services delivered by the department is very difficult.

Based on all the experiments and experiences in financial devolution in Panchayati Raj Institutions, the Second Administrative Reform Commission has made some broad recommendations:

1. A comprehensive exercise needs to be taken up regarding broadening and deepening of the revenue base of local governments. This exercise will have to simultaneously look into four major aspects of resources mobilization, viz (i) potential for taxation; (ii) fixation of realistic tax rates; (iii) widening of tax base; and (iv) improved collection. Government may incorporate them as one of the terms of reference of the Thirteenth Finance Commission.
2. All common property resources vested in the village Panchayats should be identified, listed and made productive for revenue generation.
3. State governments should by law expand the tax domain of Panchayats. Simultaneously it should be made obligatory for the Panchayats to levy taxes in this tax domain.

4. At the higher level, the local bodies could be encouraged to run/manage utilities such as transport, water supply and power distribution on a sound financial basis and viability.
5. The expanded tax domain could initially include levies on registration of cattle, restaurants, large shops, hotels, cyber cafes, tourist buses etc.
6. The role of State governments should be limited to prescribing a band of rates for these taxes and levies.
7. Panchayats should be given a substantial share in the royalty from minerals collected by the State governments. This aspect should be considered by the SFCs while recommending grants to the Panchayati Raj Institutions.
8. State governments should consider empowering PRIs to collect cess on the royalty from mining activities. In addition they should also be given power to impose and collect additional/special surcharges from such activities (mines/minerals/plants).
9. Innovative steps should be taken by the State and the PRIs to augment their resources and be rewarded by linking the grants of the Central Finance Commission and the State Finance Commissions to such measures. States may reward better performing PRIs through special incentives.
10. In the tax domain assigned to PRIs, village Panchayats must have primary authority over taxation. However, where such taxation has inter-Panchayat ramifications, the local government institutions at higher levels—intermediate Panchayats and District Panchayats—could be given concurrent powers subject to a ceiling. Whenever a tax or fee is imposed by the higher tier, such taxes should be collected by the concerned village Panchayats.

In this connection, the experiences of the different States are enumerated in this volume.

Fahimuddin has analysed the revenue and expenditure pattern of the village Panchayats in Uttar Pradesh in his article entitled "Revenue Mobilisation, Financial Devolution and Expenditure by Village Panchayats in UP". He brought to light the potentials of the

Panchayats in mobilizing the resources through tax and non-tax revenue legitimized through law. He has looked at the financial position in the backdrop of the entrustment of responsibilities to the Gram Panchayats. He has analysed the financial status of the village Panchayats from 1990-91 to 1993-94. Similarly, the expenditure patterns have also been analysed, from 1990-91.to 1997-1998. The scholar has concluded that the Village Panchayats have not fully utilized the potentials of mobilizing the internal resources.

T.M. Thomas Issac and P. Shaheena's article entitled "Fiscal Devolution and State Finance Commission in Kerala" highlighted the financial autonomy enjoyed by the local bodies of Kerala. It is a well-known fact that Kerala is a model for implementation of the 73rd Amendment to the Constitution of India. Kerala is the only State to have implemented all the recommendations of all the three State Finance Commissions.

The authors have highlighted that Kerala enjoyed traditionally such levels of fiscal autonomy and hence the State Finance Commission could not make substantial recommendations, and yet, the State Finance Commission made recommendations to enhance the revenue-raising powers of the Local Self Governments. Further the arbitrary fiscal transfers have been streamlined. The new responsibilities, assigned to the Local Bodies and the new assets created and transferred to the Local Bodies enabled the Local Bodies to put up new demands for enhanced grant transfer from the State. The people's planning campaign made further demand, namely the untied funds for the local bodies to fulfil the needs of the people. But at the same time tax collection is a problem wherein people could be involved as they are involved in the plan preparation.

Pratheep and Mohanan in their article "Rural, Peri-Urban Contrast in Financial Management: A Study with Special Reference to Gram Panchayats in Kerala" made an attempt to study the financial position of Gram Panchayats in contrast to peri-urban Gram Panchayats. The scholars have selected five Panchayats each from Kozhikode district and Thiruvananthapuram district. With the collected primary and secondary data from 1998-99 to 2002-2003, analysis has been made. They brought out the marked difference between peri-urban and rural local bodies in revenue generation and expenditure. Though Panchayats are called self-governing institutions, the Kerala Gram Panchayats are heavily dependent on the State government for funds. The peri-urban Gram Panchayats are far better in terms of their resources than the rural Gram Panchayats. In order to reduce the dependency of the Panchayats for grants from the State government, alternative resource mobilization has to be thought of. Moreover the resource-base of the Panchayats has to be expanded. Internal resource mobilization has to be strengthened.

Karnataka is one of the pioneering States in devolution of powers but it moves back and forth. Devendra Babu in his article "Rural Local Governments: A Study of Fiscal Position in Karnataka" made an attempt to critically evaluate the fiscal position of Panchayati Raj Institutions in Karnataka. It specifically analyses the revenue raising powers of the Panchayati Raj Institutions. The pattern of grants in aid to Panchayati Raj Institutions are extremely limited. At the same time revenue transfer from the higher level government concerned the Panchayati Raj Institutions are mere spending institutions. It is the practice everywhere that the lowest unit, namely Gram Panchayats will have taxation powers. Other two tiers entirely depend on the State and Central government grants. But the Gram Panchayats are not serious in mobilising resources by using the powers conferred on them. Since the Central Finance Commission fixed internal resource mobilization is one of the criteria for Central Finance Commission grants, many of the State governments including Karnataka could not get adequate grants.

Panchayat Finance: The Case of West Bengal written by Dilip Kumar Ghosh brings an overall picture about the financial position of the Panchayats in West Bengal. He has three major objectives: (a) to present an overview of the resource mobilization scenario in the Panchayats; (b) to examine the utilization pattern of own resources mobilised; and (c) to explore the extent of untied funds provided to the Panchayats. He has analysed the financial conditions of West Bengal Panchayats from 1997 to 2003. Functions are assigned to Panchayats without sufficient support of functionaries and funds. When fund flows to the Panchayats, conditionalities are attached and it underlies the fact that State government believes that local bodies are only implementing agencies. Whenever the State Finance Commissions are consitituted meaningful recommendations have to be implemented by the State government. In order to make the local bodies self-governing institutions, their own tax base has to be expanded. Internal resource mobilization power has to be given. Further the Panchayats should have more of untied funds by which people needs have to be met and thereby people's participation in the development activities can be ensured. Unless the Panchayats are equipped with adequate resources, the Panchayats cannot be strengthened.

G. Palanithurai's article "Status of Panchayat Finance in Tamil Nadu" has analysed the process of devolution of financial powers in Tamil Nadu in the backdrop of the powers devolved to Panchayats. It is logical that responsibilities have to be devolved to Panchayats. To fulfil the responsibilities, powers have to be devolved. Commensurate with responsibilities, functionaries and resources have to be devolved. In Tamil Nadu Panchayat responsibilities have been increased but commensurate with responsibilities, resources have not been devolved. Though there were three commissions constituted for Panchayat finance, Panchayats have not improved their finances significantly. Panchayats have been made to face financial crisis. Panchayats have been looked at as only an agency to implement the schemes and programmes of the government. The royalty which is due to Panchayat based on minerals and other natural resources has not been realized. It is interesting to note that all the three State Finance Commissions have made moderate recommendations. But even these moderate recommendations have not been fully accepted. Only a limited number of recommendations have been accepted and of them only a few have been implemented. The State Finance Commissions were not given the respect they deserve. While releasing the grants to the local bodies, amounts will be adjusted against the dues of the Panchayats. Deductions are made even in statutory grants given to the local bodies. Panchayats do not have adequate untied funds. They do not have even emergency fund at their disposal. The author has presented the full scenario of the Panchayats' finance in Tamil Nadu in his report.

S.K. Singh in his write up entitled "Internal Resource Mobilisation by Panchayats: The Case of Madhya Pradesh" has analysed the tax and non-tax revenues of the Panchayats. The trend and patterns of expenditure have been described in this work. The three levels of resource mobilization has been captured and analysed. He has analysed the period form 1992-93 to 1997-98. The author has concluded that the financial structure of Panchayats in the State experience similar rhetoric of dependency syndrome and grant culture. It is extremely fragile and it is a matter of concern. In the process of democratic decentralization augmentation of internal resources is crucial. It largely depends on the political will of the leadership. He has made an extensive anlaysis in all the three tiers of the Panchayats.

O.P. Bohra in his article "Improving Finances of Panchayats through Central Finance Commission Transfers" brought to light the international scenario of revenue sharing among the Centre, State and local governments. Against this backdrop he has highlighted the national perspectives of resource devolution to local bodies. He has taken the 10th, 11th and 12th Central Finance Commissions' allocation of grants to the local bodies for analysis. Global and national trends of resource sharing have been covered in this article. He has highlighted the efforts made by the Central Finance Commissions towards strengthening the resource base of the local bodies and yet he has made it clear that the criteria used by the Central Finance Commission for the devolution of grants to the local bodies seem to be ineffective. Based on the criteria used by the Central Finance Commission for the devolution of resources only five States have claimed the major share of allocation. Hence, he has made an observation that the Thirteenth Central Finance Commission should evolve more scientific criteria for need-based and equitable distribution of resources.

D. Bandyopadhyay in his article "Guiding Role of Central Finance Commission Regarding State Counterparts" brought to light the present position and status of the State Finance Commission had enjoyed in the State government in terms of the status of the recommendations and their acceptability. He has also highlighted the linkage between the Central Finance Commission and State

Finance Commissions in terms of the framework of transactions carried out by them to make local bodies vibrant in terms of its financial autonomy. The Eleventh Finance Commission has fixed devolution index and left it to the State. He has indicated the erroneous approaches of the Central Finance Commissions and suggested that the Thirteenth Finance Commission should develop a workable objective and rational a devolution index and it should move further to guide the State Finance Commission by evolving a suitable framework for their activities.

From the analysis of a few States one will come to a conclusion that the financial devolution is a crucial task. Despite provisions in the Constitution, many of the States are reluctant even to constitute State Finance Commissions. After constituting the State Finance Commission, they have not been allowed to submit the recommendations. If the Commissions had submitted recommendations, their recommendations are not accepted. Even if some of the provisions are accepted, they have not implemented. This is the picture that one gets about the financial empowerment of the local bodies in India.

Only a few States are committed sincerely towards in financial devolution. They are pioneers in devolving powers. But many of the States leave the Panchayats under the mercy of the State governments. In some of the States, taxation powers have been given to the Panchayats but the Panchayats have not exercised their powers. Thus totally Panchayat finance is a crucial and problematic area. An array of steps is to be taken to improve the financial position of the local bodies.

REFERENCES

Amba, Agarwal, *Fiscal Decentralisation: Financing of Panchayati Raj Institutions in India*, New Delhi: Serial Publications, 2005.

Bardhan, P. and D. Mookerjee (eds), *Decentralization and Local Governance in Developing Countries: A Comparative Perspective*, New Delhi: Oxford University Publications, 2007.

Konrad Adenauer Foundation, *Local Government Finance in India*, New Delhi: Manohar, 1998.

Omamen, M.A. "Rural Fiscal Decentralisation in India : A Brief Survey of Literature", in L.C. Jain (ed), *Decentralisation and Local Governance*, Hyderabad: Orient Longman Private Limtied, 2005.

Roy, Bahl. *The Rules of Fiscal Decentralisation*, Georgia: Georgia State University, 1999.

Sethi, Gee. *Fiscal Decentralisation to Rural Governments in India*, New Delhi: Oxford University Press, 2005.

Shah, Anwar. "Fiscal Decentralisation in Developing Countries and Transitive Economies: An Overview", in L.C. Jain (ed), *Decentralisation and Local Governance*, Hyderabad: Orient Longman Private Limited, 2005.

Second Administrative Reform Commission, *Local Governance : An Inspiring Journey into the Future*, New Delhi: Government of India, 2007.

The World Bank, *Overview of Rural Decentralisation in India,* Vols. I, II and III, Washington D.C: The World Bank, 2000.

1

REVENUE MOBILISATION, FINANCIAL DEVOLUTION AND EXPENDITURE BY VILLAGE PANCHAYATS IN U.P.

FAHIMUDDIN

The financial resources of the Panchayati Raj Institution (PRI) have to be considered in the context of the Seventy Third Constitution Amendment Act which became effective from 24th April, 1993. The financial resources contemplated for the PRIs have been laid down in Article 243-H of the amendment and the institutional arrangement to review the financial position is provided in Article 243-I which empowered the Government of a State to constitute a Finance Commission at the commencement of 73rd Amendment and every fifth year to review the financial position of the PRIs and make recommendations to improve it. These provisions are very crucial to strengthen the PRIs to enable them to function as grassroots democratic institutions. In this article, an attempt has been made to review the revenue mobilisation pattern of village Panchayats in U.P. Besides, the analysis of expenditure status, the financial devolution that has happened after the amendment of the PRIs Act in U.P., in the light of 73rd Amendment, has also been examined.

Revenue Mobilisation : The Past Scenario

The U.P. Panchayati Raj Act, 1947 empowered the village Panchayats to levy a surcharge on land revenue besides various non-taxes, fees and user's charges. It was observed that village Panchayats could not exploit the potential of various taxes and non-taxes. For example, in the total revenue generated by village Panchayats in U.P. during 1992-93, the share of land revenue was 0.90 per cent, which declined to 0.52 per cent in 1997-98. The per capita revenue mobilisation was negligible to such a extent that village panchayats were not in a position to take up any development work at their discretion.

Amendment in Tax and Non-Tax Powers

The village panchayats in U.P. have been empowered under Section 37 of the U.P. Panchayati Raj Act to levy a surcharge on land revenue not less than twenty-five paise but not exceeding fifty paise in a rupee on the amount of land revenue. It is the only obligatory taxation power entrusted to village panchayats in U.P. in the old as well as new Panchayati Raj Legislation. Besides, there are provisions of some discretionary taxation and fee imposition powers. These are tax on theatre, cinema or similar entertainment, tax on animals and vehicles other than mechanically propelled vehicles, a tax for cleaning private latrines and drains and a tax for cleaning and lighting of streets and sanitation. Fees are to be imposed on the registration of animals sold in the market, fees for the use of slaughter houses and encamping groups, water charges where water is supplied by the village panchayats for domestic use and an irrigation tax where water for irrigation purpose is supplied by the village panchayats. A comparative list of tax and non-tax revenue powers of village panchayats as assigned in old act and amended after 73rd Amendment is as shown in Table 1.1:

Table 1.1: Amendment in Tax and Non-tax Revenue Powers of Village Panchayats in U.P.

U.P. Panchayati Raj Act, 1947 Amended in April, 1994 as per Seventy Third Constitutional Amendment

1. OBLIGATORY	*1. OBLIGATORY*
(i) In areas where the right, title and interest of intermediaries have been acquired under the Zamindari Abolition and Land Reforms Act, 1956 or the Kumaun and Uttara Khand Zamindari Abolition and Land Reforms Act, 1960, a tax on land not less than twenty-five paise in a rupee on the amount of land revenue payable or deemed to be payable therefore. Provided that where the land is in the actual cultivation of a person other than the person by whom the land revenue therefore is payable the tax shall be payable by the person in actual cultivation.	(i) In areas where the right, title and interest of intermediaries have been acquired under the Zamindari Abolition and Land Reforms Act, 1956 or the Kumaun and Uttara Khand Zamindari Abolition and Land Reforms Act, 1960, a tax on land not less than twenty-five paise in a rupee on the amount of land revenue payable or deemed to be payable therefore. Provided that where the land is in the actual cultivation of a person other than the person by whom the land revenue therefore is payable the tax shall be payable by the person in actual cultivation.
(ii) In areas other than those referred to in clause (1) a tax on the land revenue not less than twenty-five paise but not exceeding fifty paise in a rupee on the amount of land revenue by a tenant, by whatever name called, under the law in force relating to land tenures. Provided that where the land is in the actual cultivation of the person other than the person liable to pay land revenue therefore the tax shall be payable by the person in actual cultivation of such land.	(ii) In areas other than those referred to in clause (1) a tax on the land revenue not less than twenty-five paise but not exceeding fifty paise in a rupee on the amount of land revenue by a tenant, by whatever name called, under the law in force relating to land tenures. Provided that where the land is in the actual cultivation of the person other than the person liable to pay land revenue therefore the tax shall be payable by the person in actual cultivation of such land.
2. DISCRETIONARY	*2. DISCRETIONARY*
(i) A tax on Theatre, Cinema or similar entertainment temporarily stationed in the area of Gram Panchayat not exceeding five rupees per diem.	(i) A tax on Theatre, Cinema or similar entertainment temporarily stationed in the area of Gram Panchayat not exceeding five rupees per diem.
(ii) A tax payable by the owner thereof on animals and vehicles other than mechanically propelled vehicles kept within the area of Gram Panchayat and	(ii) A tax payable by the owner thereof on animals and vehicles other than mechanically propelled vehicles kept within the area of Gram

Contd.....

Table 1.1: *Contd.*

2. DISCRETIONARY	*2. DISCRETIONARY*
plied for hire at the rate: - In the case of animals not exceeding three rupees per animal per annum. - In the case of vehicles, not exceeding six rupees per vehicle per annum.	Panchayat and plied for hire at the rate: - In the case of animals not exceeding three rupees per animal per annum. - In the case of vehicles, not exceeding six rupees per vehicle per annum.
(iii) A tax on persons exposing goods for sale in markets/haats or melas belonging to or under the control of the Gram Panchayat concerned.	(iii) A tax on persons exposing goods for sale in markets/haats or melas belonging to or under the control of the Gram Panchayat concerned.
(iv) Fees on the registration of animals sold in any market or place belonging to or under the control of the Gram Panchayat.	(iv) Fees on the registration of animals sold in any market or place belonging to or under the control of the Gram Panchayat.
(v) Fees for the use of slaughter-houses and encamping grounds.	(v) Fees for the use of slaughter-houses and encamping grounds.
(vi) A water rate where water for domestic consumption is supplied by the Gram Panchayat.	(vi) A water rate where water for domestic consumption is supplied by the Gram Panchayat.
(vii) A tax for cleaning private latrines and drains payable by the owners or occupiers of the house to which the private latrine or drain is attached where such cleaning is done through the agency of the Gram Panchayat.	(vii) A tax for cleaning private latrines and drains payable by the owners or occupiers of the houses to which the private latrine or drain is attached where such cleaning is done through the agency of the Gram Panchayat.
(viii) A tax for cleaning and lighting of streets and sanitation	(viii) A tax for cleaning and lighting of streets and sanitation.
(ix) An irrigation rate where water for irrigation purposes is supplied by the Gram Panchayat from any small irrigation project constructed or maintained by it.	(ix) An irrigation rate where water for irrigation purposes is supplied by the Gram Panchayat from any small irrigation project constructed or maintained by it.
(x) Any other tax which the State Legislature has the power under the Constitution including Article 277 thereof, to impose in the State and of which imposition by the Gram Panchayat has been authorised by the State Government.	(x) Any other tax which the State Legislature has the power under the Constitution including Article 277 thereof, to impose in the State and of which imposition by the Gram Panchayat has been authorised by the State.

Source: U.P. Panchayati Raj Act, 1947 and the Amended Act, 1994.

A review of the amendment indicates that there was hardly any change in the list of taxes and non-taxes. It could be so because the list was already exhaustive and there was no scope to add or delete the items of revenue mobilisation.

Changes in Tax Rates

The rate structure of taxes and fees to be imposed by the village panchayats in U.P. has been provided in Section 37 of the U.P. Panchayati Raj Act. In case of most of the taxes and fees, rates have not been fixed in the Act rather it has been left to the discretion of concerned village panchayats to decide the rate of various taxes and fees. Only in case of tax on property and surcharge on land revenue, there are provisions of maximum and minimum rates. There are also provision of maximum rates of taxation on vehicles, entertainment, animals and imposition of minimum level of fine by the Village Panchayats. Surprisingly, the rate structure of taxes, fees and fines could not be raised over the years even after the 73rd Amendment. It indicated that as the imposition of most of the taxes, fees and fines by the Village Panchayats is still discretionary, their rates are also discretionary. Therefore, unless tax and non-tax powers of Village Panchayats are made obligatory and rates are determined and revised over the years, the financial position of Village Panchayats is difficult to be improved. The details of rate structure of taxes, fees and user charges as prevalent in U.P. over the years has been presented in Table 1.2.

Financial Status of Village Panchayats

The total revenue generated by village panchayats consisted of own tax, i.e. surcharge on land revenue levied by village panchayats, various grants-in-aid from the State as well as Central Government, State Finance Commission devolved fund and TFC grant. All this items of revenue added together provided an income of Rs. 40,01,980 thousand in 1990-91 which increased to Rs. 73,28,122 thousand, indicating a simple growth of around 8 per cent per annum only. Besides, if 4 per cent of the net proceeds of State taxes devolved

Table 1.2: Pattern of Rate Structure of Taxes, Fees and User Charges Levied by the Village Panchayats in U.P.

Items	*1992-93*		*1993-94*		*1994-95*		*1995-96*		*1996-97*		*1997-98*		*1998-99*	
	Min	*Max*	*Min*	*Max*	*Min*	*Max*	*Min*	*Max*	*Min*	*Max*	*Min*	*Max*	*Min*	*Max*
TAXES/USER CHARGES														
(i) Property (Rs.)	12	2000	12	2000	12	2000	12	2000	360	6000	360	6000	360	6000
(ii) Vehicle (Rs.)	0	6	0	6	0	6	0	6	0	6	0	6	0	6
(iii) Agriçultural Land (Rs.)	25	50	25	50	25	50	25	50	25	50	25	50	25	50
(iv) Entertainment (Rs.)	0	5	0	5	0	5	0	5	0	5	0	5	0	5
(v) Animals (Rs.)	0	3	0	3	0	3	0	3	0	3	0	3	0	3
(vi) Cleaning and Lighting of Streets and Sanitation					Not Fixed									
FEES, FINES ETC.														
(i) Fairs and Festivals					Not Fixed									
(ii) Fines and penalties (Rs.)														
(a) For infringement of the Provisions (Rs.)	Not fixed	10	Not fixed	10	Not fixed	10	Not fixed	500	Not fixed	500	Not fixed	500	Not fixed	500
(b) For tampering with the Gram Panchayat's property (Rs.)	Not fixed	50	Not fixed	50	Not fixed	50	Not fixed	1000	Not fixed	1000	Not fixed	1000	Not fixed	1000
(iii) Fees														
(a) Registration of animals					Not Fixed									

Contd.....

significant in view of high rate of inflation and population growth in the State. Besides, the degree of dependency of Village Panchayats on grants-in-aid has been quite high which is to be minimised in future if Village Panchayats are really to act as a grassroots democratic unit of planning and development. The trend in the financial status of Village Panchayats in U.P. from 1990-91 to 1997-98 has been shown in Table 1.3.

Revenue of Village Panchayats from Different Sources

The total revenue accruing to village panchayats in U.P. came through different sources. The major part was provided by the district administration including DRDA which contributed 91 to 98 per cent of total revenue for 1990-91 to 1995-96. Since 1996-97 to 1998-99, revenue available from district administration declined substantially. The grant from the department of rural development was second important source of revenue. Its share in total revenue was 7.70 per cent in 1990-91 which declined to 3 per cent in 1995-96. The Tenth Finance Commission grant given to Gram Panchayats through rural development increased the share of rural development department. Similarly, the amount devolved to Village Panchayats on the basis of State Finance Commission recommendations becomes the important source of revenue to Village Panchayats in U.P. Its share in total revenue was 25.61 per cent in 1997-98 which increased to 28.58 per cent in 1998-99. It becomes evident here again that the Village Panchayats in U.P. have meagre revenue generation from their own tax and non-tax sources of revenue as reflected from the Table 1.4.

Devolution of Grants-in-Aid and Shared Taxes

The grants-in-aid have been the major source of revenue to the Village Panchayats in U.P. The total amount which Gram Panchayats received as grants-in-aid was Rs. 39,68,760 thousand in 1990-91 which increased to Rs. 59,56,265 thousand in 1998-99. Despite this phenomenal growth in the quantum of revenue, the trend over the years has been quite unsteady as reflected from the Table 1.5. It became evident that while the revenue of grants-in-aid

Table 1.3 : Total Revenue of Village Panchayats in U.P.: 1990-91 to 1997-98

Source	*1990-91*		*1991-92*		*1992-93*		*1993-94*	
	AM	*PC*	*AM*	*PC*	*AM*	*PC*	*AM*	*PC*
I. OWN TAX								
(i) Surcharge on Land Revenue	33220 (0.84)	–	34969 (0.84)	5.26	38665 (0.91)	10.57	52307 (0.92)	35.28
2. SHARED REVENUE								
(i) State Finance Commission	–	–	–	–	–	–	–	–
3. GRANTS-IN-AID FROM STATE								
(i) General Purpose Grant	279510 (6.98)	–	239755 (5.78)	– 14.22	–	–	–	–
(ii) Specific Purpose Grant	950 (0.02)	–	617 (0.01)	– 35.05	1700 (0.04)	175.53	1525 (0.03)	– 10.29
(iii) Grant for Development Purpose	27786 (0.69)	–	17470 (0.43)	– 37.13	30999 (0.73)	77.44	47744 (0.84)	54.02
4. TFC Grants	–	–	–	–	–	–	–	–
5. Centrally Sponsored Scheme	3660514 (91.47)	–	3851746 (92.94)	5.22	4180559 (98.32)	24.11	5564099 (98.21)	33.09
TOTAL	4001980 (100.00)	–	4144557 (100.00)	3.56	4251923 (100.00)	2.59	5665675 (100.00)	33.25

Contd.....

Table 1.3: *Contd.*

Source	*1994-95*		*1995-96*		*1996-97*		*1997-98*	
	AM	*PC*	*AM*	*PC*	*AM*	*PC*	*AM*	*PC*
I. OWN TAX (i) Surcharge on Land Revenue	48426 (0.89)	–7.42	40629 (0.63)	–16.10	23119 (0.43)	–43.10	38213 (0.52)	65.29
2. SHARED REVENUE (i) State Finance Commission	–	–	–	–	–	–	1876880 (25.61)	–
3. GRANTS-IN-AID FROM STATE (i) General Purpose Grant	–	–	99500 (1.56)	–	–	–	–	–
(ii) Specific Purpose Grant	1135 (0.02)	–25.57	1328 (0.02)	17.00	1288 (0.02)	–3.01	–	–
(iii) Grant for Development Purpose	48598 (0.89)	1.79	91061 (1.42)	87.38	497357 (9.19)	446.18	364484 (4.97)	–26.72
4. TFC Grants	–	–	–	–	1519040 (28.07)	–	1519040 (20.73)	–
5. Centrally Sponsored Scheme	5335566 (98.20)	–4.11	6173488 (96.37)	15.70	3369879 (62.29)	–45.41	3529505 (48.17)	4.79
TOTAL	5433725 (100.00)	–4.09	6406006 (100.00)	17.89	5410683 (100.00)	–15.54	7328122 (100.00)	35.44

Note: AM - Amount (Rs. thousand); PC - Percentage Change. Figures in brackets indicate Percentage.
Source: Directorate of Panchayati Raj, Government of U.P., Lucknow.

Table 1.4: Total Revenue Receipts of the Village Panchayats in U.P. from Different Sources/Agencies : 1990-91 to 1998-99

Source	*1990-91*	*1991-92*	*1992-93*	*1993-94*	*1994-95*	*1995-96*	*1996-97*	*1997-98*	*1998-99*
1. Own Source	33220 (0.84)	34969 (0.84)	38665 (0.91)	52307 (0.92)	48426 (0.89)	40629 (0.63)	23119 (0.43)	38213 (0.52)	41926 (0.50)
2. State Government	–	–	–	–	–	–	–	1876880 (25.61)	2400000 (28.58)
3. District Administration including DRDA	3660514 (91.46)	3851746 (92.94)	4180559 (98.32)	5564099 (98.21)	5331966 (98.13)	6173488 (96.37)	3369879 (62.28)	3127937 (42.69)	3692005 (43.96)
4. Rural Development	308246 (7.70)	257842 (6.22)	32699 (0.77)	49269 (0.87)	53333 (0.98)	191889 (3.00)	2017685 (37.29)	2285092 (31.18)	2264260 (26.96)
Total	4001980 (100.00)	4144557 (100.00)	4251923 (100.00)	5665675 (100.00)	5433725 (100.00)	6406006 (100.00)	5410683 (100.00)	7328122 (100.00)	8398191 (100.00)

Note: Figures in brackets indicate percentages.

Source: Department of Panchayati Raj, Government of U.P., Lucknow.

Table 1.5: Devolution of Grants-in-Aid and Shared Taxes to Gram Panchayats in U.P. : 1990-91 to 1997-98

(*Rs. Thousand*)

Year	*Grants-in-Aid*		*Shared Taxes*	
	Amount	*Percentage Change*	*Amount*	*Percentage Change*
1990-91	3968760	–	–	–
1991-92	4109588	3.55	–	–
1992-93	4213258	2.52	–	–
1993-94	5613368	33.23	–	–
1994-95	5385299	–4.06	–	–
1995-96	6365377	18.20	–	–
1996-97	5387564	–15.36	–	–
1997-98	5413029	0.47	1876880	–
1998-99	5956265	10.04	2400000	27.87

Source: Department of Panchayati Raj, Government of U.P., Lucknow.

experienced growth of only 3.55 per cent and 2.52 in 1991-92 and 1992-93 respectively as against previous years, it showed a growth of 33.23 in 1993-94 over 1992-93. It showed a negative growth of 4.06 per cent in 1994-95 while in next year, it registered a growth of 18 per cent. During the last three years of 1996-97, 1997-98 and 1998-99, the trend was fluctuating. As far the shared taxes are concerned, it is a new source of revenue to the Village Panchayats because the Village Panchayats in U.P. for the first time received the funds after the acceptance of SFC's recommendation of devolution of net proceeds of taxes to PRIs in U.P. The other point is to be noted that in grants-in-aid, share of general purpose grants have been relatively larger in total grants-in-aid revenue of Village Panchayats. Thus, an account of erratic pattern of grants-in-aid, the State Finance Commission, therefore, recommended that present system of grants-in-aid to rural local bodies is to be done away with and more or less the same amount or somewhat more amount with assured annual compound growth rate be given to them by way of their share in the net proceeds of taxes, duties, tolls and fees leviable by the State government. This will enable the Village Panchayats to know right in the beginning of each financial year what amount they will get by way of their share in net proceeds of State taxes etc. They can then plan their programme accordingly keeping in view also their own resources. It will be clear in their mind that this is what they will get from the State government and that the balance of their requirements have to be arranged by them through better enforcement and collection of their own tax and non-tax revenues and by better exploitation of their tax and non-tax potential.

Per Capita Revenue of Gram Panchayats

The per capita revenue of Gram Panchayats in U.P. from different sources was calculated which has been presented in Table 1.6. The table revealed that Rs. 36 per capita was the revenue of village Panchayats from all sources in the years 1990-91, 1991-92 and 1992-93. It varied between Rs. 47 to Rs. 45 in 1993-94 and 1994-95 respectively. It increased to Rs. 51 in 1995-96 but declined to Rs. 42 in 1996-97. The per capita income became highest, i.e. Rs. 56 in 1997-98 and this increase could come due to SFC recommended devolution of funds. As per the pattern of revenue generation, the per capita revenue from own sources always remained less than Rs.1 during the years 1990-91 to 1997-98. The per capita income from the centrally sponsored schemes was highest. It also reflected that in the year 1997-98 when SFC recommended funds were provided and TFC grant was given to Village Panchayats in U.P., the per capita availability of revenue improved significantly.

Expenditure of Gram Panchayats

The Gram Panchayats in U.P. made a total expenditure to the tune of Rs. 40,25,580 thousand in 1990-91 which increased to Rs.78,33,842 thousand in 1997-98 showing a growth of around 12 per cent per annum. Such increase could be possible by substantial contributions received from TFC and SFC grants. On the whole, a review of the growth in expenditure pattern since 1990-91 to 1996-97 indicated that like revenue as observed in preceding section, the expenditure did not demonstrate any significant growth over the years except in 1993-94, when expenditure increased by 33 per cent over the previous year. The centrally sponsored schemes were

Table 1.6 : Per Capita Revenue of Gram Panchayats in U.P. 1990-91 to 1997-98

Source	*1990-91*	*1991-92*	*1992-93*	*1993-94*	*1994-95*	*1995-96*	*1996-97*	*1997-98*
I. OWN TAX								
(i) Surcharge on Land Revenue	0.39	0.31	0.33	0.44	0.40	0.33	0.18	0.29
2. SHARED REVENUE								
(i) State Finance Commission	–	–	–	–	–	–	–	14.37
3. GRANTS-IN-AID FROM STATE								
(i) General Purpose Grant	2.51	2.10	–	–	–	0.80	–	–
(ii) Specific Purpose Grant	0.01	0.01	0.01	0.01	0.01	0.01	0.01	–
(iii) Grant for Development Purpose	0.25	0.15	0.27	0.40	0.40	0.73	3.89	2.79
4. TFC Grants	–	–	–	–	–	–	11.89	11.63
5. Centrally Sponsored Scheme	32.83	33.77	35.83	46.62	43.71	49.44	26.38	27.01
Total	35.89	36.34	36.44	47.47	44.51	51.30	42.36	56.09

the major items of expenditure on which Village Panchayats spent 91 to 97 per cent of total expenditure since 1990-91 to 1995-96. The situation, somewhat changed in 1996-97 and 1997-98 when Village Panchayats received TFC and SFC funds. All this showed that the expenditure pattern of Gram Panchayats in U.P. after the 73rd Amendment has changed and Village Panchayats could spent the TFC and SFC funds on untied developmental items. In Table 1.7, the pattern of expenditure of Village Panchayats from 1990-91 to 1997-98 has been shown.

Expenditure on Various Functions

The expenditure incurred by the Village Panchayats in U.P. for performing various functions from 1990-91 to 1997-98 was obtained from the Department of Panchayati Raj, Government of U.P. and shown in Table 1.8. It is evident from the table that Village Panchayats made expenditure on thirteen (13) activities besides grant available equivalent to land revenue and funds devolved under SFC recommendations and TFC grants were untied which provided free hand to Village Panchayats to spend the amount on various activities according to their own priorities and needs. The works done under the Jawahar Rozgar Yojana (JRY) were the most important on which Village Panchayats spent 91 to 97 per cent of their total expenditure from 1990-91 to 1995-96. Thereafter, it declined to 61 per cent in 1996-97 and 42 per cent in 1997-98. The expenditure on street lighting was the next important item of expenditure on which around one per cent plus was spent. In 1996-97, expenditure structures somewhat changed to the earlier pattern because of the TFC grant. In this year, Village Panchayats spent 61.41 per cent on JRY works, 6.33 per cent on construction of Panchayat Bhawans, 2.67 per cent on village pavements and drainages and 27.68 per cent on activities sanctioned under TFC grant. On all other activities, less than one per cent of total expenditure was made. In the subsequent year of 1997-98, the same pattern of expenditure was evident. In this year, 25.24 per cent of total expenditure was also made on the activities approved under

Table 1.7 : Expenditure of Village Panchayats in U.P. : 1990-91 to 1997-98

	1990-91		*1991-92*		*1992-93*		*1993-94*	
Item	*AM*	*PC*	*AM*	*PC*	*AM*	*PC*	*AM*	*PC*
I. General Administration								
(i) Salary of Staff	1869 (0.05)	–	1828 (0.04)	–2.19	2306 (0.05)	26.15	2522 (0.04)	9.37
(ii) Maintenance of Assets and others	31351 (0.78)	–	33141 (0.79)	5.71	36359 (0.84)	9.71	49785 (0.87)	36.93
2. Expenditure on Obligatory Services								
(i) Street Lighting	23600 (0.59)	–	30700 (0.74)	30.04	63300 (1.47)	106.19	65300 (1.14)	3.16
(ii) Sanitation	–	–	–	–	–	–	–	–
3. Expenditure on Development Grants								
(i) Grants from State Government	307296 (7.63)	–	257225 (6.16)	–16.29	30999 (0.72)	–87.95	47744 (0.83)	54.02
(ii) Grants for Centrally sponsored schemes	3660514 (90.93)	–	3851746 (92.26)	5.22	4180559 (96.88)	8.54	5564099 (97.09)	33.09
(iii) TFC Grants	–	–	–	–	–	–	–	–
(iv) Grants of office bearers	950	–	617	–35.05	1700	175.53	1525	–10.29
4. Centrally Sponsored Scheme	(0.02)		(0.01)		(0.04)		(0.03)	
Total	4025580	–	4175257	3.72	4315223	3.35	5730975	32.81

Contd.

Table 1.7: *Contd.*

Item	*1994-95*		*1995-96*		*1996-97*		*1997-98*	
	AM	*PC*	*AM*	*PC*	*AM*	*PC*	*AM*	*PC*
I. General Administration								
(i) Salary of Staff	2751 (0.05)	9.08	3536 (0.05)	28.53	3956 (0.07)	11.88	4322 (0.06)	9.25
(ii) Maintenance of Assets and Others	45675 (0.83)	–8.25	37093 (0.57)	–18.79	19163 (0.35)	–48.34	33891 (0.43)	76.86
2. Expenditure on Obligatory Services								
(i) Street Lighting	67300 (1.23)	3.06	69300 (1.07)	2.97	77000 (1.40)	11.11	108400 (1.38)	40.78
(ii) Sanitation	–	–	–	–	–	–	397644 (5.07)	–
3. Expenditure on Development Grants								
(i) Grants from State Government	48598 (0.88)	1.79	190561 (2.94)	292.12	497357 (9.07)	160.10	364484 (4.65)	–26.71
(ii) Grants for Centrally Sponsored Schemes	5331965 (96.99)	–4.17	6173488 (95.34)	15.78	3369879 (61.41)	–45.41	3525581 (45.02)	4.62
(iii) TFC Grants	–	–	–	–	1519040 (27.68)	–	1519040 (19.39)	–
(iv) Grants devolved under SFC	–	–	–	–	–	–	1876880 (23.96)	–
4. Training of office bearers	1135 (0.03)	–25.57	1328 (0.02)	17.00	1288 (0.04)	3.01	3600	179.50
Total	5497424	–4.08	6475306	17.79	5487683	–15.25	7436198	42.75

Note: AM=Amount in Rs. thousand, PC=Percentage change. Figures in brackets indicate percentage.

Source: Directorate of Panchayati Raj, Government of U.P., Lucknow.

Table 1.8 : Expenditure on Various Functions by Village Panchayats in U.P. : 1990-91 to 1997-98

(In Thousands)

Function	*1990-91*	*1991-92*	*1992-93*	*1993-94*	*1994-95*	*1995-96*	*1996-97*	*1997-98*
1. Salary and other Emoluments of staff	1869 (0.5)	1828 (0.04)	2306 (0.05)	2522 (0.04)	2751 (0.05)	3536 (0.05)	3956 (0.07)	4322 (0.06)
2. General Administration	950 (0.02)	617 (0.01)	1700 (0.04)	1525 (0.03)	1135 (0.02)	1328 (0.02)	1288 (0.02)	3600 (0.05)
3. Village Pavements & Drainage	21124 (0.52)	Nil	15968 (0.37)	17025 (0.30)	15389 (0.28)	55487 (0.86)	146641 (2.67)	231664 (3.11)
4. Construction of Panchayat Bhawan	5668 (0.14)	13980 (0.33)	11717 (0.27)	27929 (0.49)	29190 (0.53)	33751 (0.52)	347334 (6.33)	132457 (1.78)
5. Upgradation of Rural Markets	Nil	Nil	384 (0.01)	604 (0.01)	2298 (0.04)	27 (0.01)	27 (0.01)	27 (0.01)
6. Incentive to Village Panchayats to Generation of Income	744 (0.02)	660 (0.02)	670 (0.02)	696 (0.01)	684	696 (0.01)	660 (0.01)	96 (0.01)
7. Residential Houses for Village Panchayat Adhikaris	Nil	Nil	88 (0.01)	Nil	Nil	1100 (0.02)	2695 (0.05)	240 (0.01)
8. Workshop of Panchayat Udyog	180 (0.01)	2790 (0.07)	1980 (0.04)	1440 (0.03)	1037 (0.02)	Nil	Nil	Nil

Contd...

Table 1.8 : *Contd.*

(*In Thousands*)

Function	*1990-91*	*1991-92*	*1992-93*	*1993-94*	*1994-95*	*1995-96*	*1996-97*	*1997-98*
9. Managerial Assistance of Panchayat Udyog	70 (0.01)	40 (0.01)	192 (0.01)	50 (0.01)	Nil	Nil	Nil	Nil
10. Sanitation	Nil	Nil	Nil	Nil	Nil	Nil	Nil	397644 (5.34)
11. Tenth Finance Commission	Nil	Nil	Nil	Nil	Nil	Nil	1519040 (27.68)	1519040 (20.42)
12. Work done under Jawahar Rojgar Yojana	360514 (90.93)	3851746 (95.25)	4180559 (96.87)	5564099 (97.08)	5331965 (96.99)	6173488 (95.33)	3369879 (61.41)	3127937 (42.06)
13. Street Light	23600 (0.58)	30700 (0.74)	63300 (1.47)	65300 (1.13)	67300 (1.22)	69300 (1.07)	77000 (1.40)	108400 (1.46)
14. Community Assets & Others	31351 (0.78)	33141 (0.79)	36359 (0.84)	49785 (0.87)	45675 (0.84)	37093 (0.57)	19163 (0.35)	33891 (0.45)
15. Grants Equivalent to own Revenue	279510 (6.94)	239755 (0.74)	Nil	Nil	Nil	99500 (1.54)	Nil	Nil
16. Funds Devolved under SFC	Nil	Nil	Nil	Nil	Nil	Nil	Nil	1876880
Total	4025580 (100.00)	4175257 (100.00)	4315223 (100.00)	5730975 (100.00)	5497424 (100.00)	6475306 (100.00)	5487683 (100.00)	7436198 (100.00)

Source: Department of Panchayati Raj, Government of U.P., Lucknow.

SFC grants. In this way, the pattern of expenditure on various functions made by the Village Panchayats in U.P. suggested that grants given for tied activities like JRY works remained the major activities on which most of the expenditure was being made. The TFC grant in 1996-97 and SFC grant in 1997-98 have improved the financial position of Gram Panchayats in U.P. and have provided considerable leverage in selection of activities on the basis of their priorities and felt needs to make expenditure on them.

Per Capita Expenditure of Village Panchayats

The per capita expenditure of Village Panchayats in U.P. which was Rs. 36.10 in 1990-91 showed increasing trend to Rs. 56.91 in 1997-98 except in two years of 1994-95 and 1996-97 when it became lower than the preceding years. The per capita expenditure on general administration and obligatory services remained less than Re. 1 in all the years considered here. Only the per capita expenditure on centrally planned schemes was largest. In general, the per capita expenditure was just only Rs. 57 in 1997-98 which was highest in all the years considered but it was very meagre amount to hire a unskilled labourer for two days. With this meagre per capita expenditure, what development works Gram Panchayats can do in U.P. Therefore, recommendations of the State Finance Commission to augment the resources of Gram Panchayats in U.P. need immediate consideration of the government. In Table 1.9, per capita expenditure by Village Panchayats in U.P. on different items from 1990-91 to 1997-98 has been shown.

Revenue and Expenditure Gap

The data furnished by the Department of Panchayati Raj, Government of U.P. regarding income and expenditure of Village Panchayats in U.P. showed that there remained a mismatch between the two, as Village Panchayats have made a slightly higher expenditure over their income during all the years from 1990-91 to 1997-98 as reflected from Table 1.10:

Table 1.9 : Per Capita Expenditure of Gram Panchayats in U.P. : 1990-91 to 1997-98

Function	*1990-91*	*1991-92*	*1992-93*	*1993-94*	*1994-95*	*1995-96*	*1996-97*	*1997-98*
1. General Administration								
(i) Salary of staff	0.02	0.02	0.02	0.02	0.02	0.03	0.03	0.03
(ii) Maintenance of Assets and others	0.28	0.29	0.31	0.42	0.37	0.30	0.15	0.26
2. Expenditure on Obligatory Services								
(i) Street Lighting	0.21	0.27	0.54	10.55	0.55	0.55	0.60	0.83
(ii) Sanitation	–	–	–	–	–	–	–	–
3. Expenditure on Development Grants								
(i) Grants from State Government	2.76	2.26	0.27	0.40	0.409	1.53	3.89	2.79
(ii) Grants from Centrally Sponsored Schemes	32.83	33.77	35.83	46.62	43.68	49.44	26.38	26.98
(iii) TFC Grants	–	–	–	–	–	–	11.89	11.63
(iv) Grants devolved under SFC	–	–	–	–	–	–	–	14.37
4. Training of Office Bearers	0.01	0.01	0.01	0.01	0.01	0.01	0.01	0.03
Total	36.10	36.61	36.99	48.02	45.03	51.86	42.96	56.91

Source: Directorate of Panchayati Raj, Government of U.P., Lucknow.

Table 1.10 : Total Revenue and Total Expenditure of Village Panchayats in U.P. : 1990-91 to 1997-98

Year	*Total Revenue*	*Total Expenditure*	*Surplus (+), Deficit (–) (Revenue - Expenditure)*
1990-91	4001980	4025580	–23600
1991-92	4144557	4175257	–30700
1992-93	4251923	4315223	–63300
1993-94	5665675	5730975	–65300
1994-95	5433725	5497424	–63699
1995-96	6406006	6475306	–69300
1996-97	5410683	5487683	–77000
1997-98	7328122	7833842	–505720

The scrutiny of different items on which Village Panchayats made expenditure as given in Table 1.9, revealed that there is one function, i.e. street lighting, on which some village panchayats have made expenditure even today though they have not received any grant from the State for this function. The State Finance Commission observed that grants for maintenance of public lamp posts in villages, routed through the Department of Rural Development have been discontinued over the years.* This expenditure which is reported to be still made by few Village Panchayats on street lighting has increased expenditure over income during all the years considered here. The State Finance Commission has also examined the income-expenditure pattern of Village Panchayats in U.P. The Commission could obtain income data in case of 7,344 Village Panchayats and expenditure data of 7,000 Village Panchayats out of the total 58,605 Gram Panchayats of the State, that too from 24 districts out of 68 districts**. With this limited data, the SFC found the surplus of income over expenditure of Village Panchayats in U.P., and based on this, projected the future income-expenditure scenario of Gram Panchayats in U.P. The SFC data related with 7,344 Village Panchayats also showed income of Village Panchayats from non-

*State Finance Commission (Panchayati Raj and Urban Local Bodies), Uttar Pradesh, Interim Report, December 1995, p. 82.

**State Finance Commission (Panchayati Raj and Local Bodies), Uttar Pradesh, Final Report, Vol. 1, December 1996, pp. 262-265.

tax sources while the data provided to us by the Department of Panchayati Raj, Government of U.P., Lucknow showed no such income from 1990-91 to 1997-98 from non-tax sources. Therefore, all such discrepancies between our analysis and SFCs are there. We feel that SFCs analysis has been based on the data of few Village Panchayats which supplied information to SFC directly. In our case, the Department of Panchayati Raj has provided income-expenditure data of all the 58,605 Gram Panchayats of U.P. Therefore, our analysis seems to be logically superior to the SFC interpretation of income-expenditure pattern of Gram Panchayats in U.P.

On the whole, Village Panchayats need to generate own resources more and more and some lessons can be learnt from the States like Karnataka where Village Panchayats have evolved several way to generate their own finances. The devolution of the State fund should largely be untied so that Village Panchayats could plan according to their own needs.

2

RURAL LOCAL GOVERNMENTS : A STUDY OF FISCAL POSITION IN KARNATAKA

M. DEVENDRA BABU

Introduction

The democratically elected Panchayati Raj Institutions (PRIs) to be called 'self-governments', should have, among others, fiscal autonomy. This means they should have freedom to take decisions on revenue raising and expenditure matters. Resource raising powers include own tax and non-tax and borrowing powers. Indirectly this implies that the local governments should not depend too much on higher level governments for their fiscal needs. They should be able to generate their own resources to carry out the entrusted regulatory and development functions. The resources available from different sources should match the functions and responsibilities entrusted. In the absence of this, the Local governments would become only the spending agencies always dependent upon the discretion of the State government in the devolution of grants. Besides, it is the responsibility of the government to adopt some objective criteria with proper weightage for distribution of grants between the Panchayats so as to take care of balanced development.

The past experience shows that the local elected bodies in India particularly the rural ones were deprived of resources. They were at the mercy of higher level governments for their financial needs (Government of India, 1954: 31; Government of India, 1963; Finance Department, 1971: 204; Finance Department, 1983: 12; Ministry of Rural Development, 1978: 1). Visualising the repetition of history, the policy makers provided some safeguards in the financial matters of the local bodies with the 73rd and 74th Constitutional Amendment Acts. Some broad fiscal measures have been highlighted in these Acts for consideration of State governments. Among these, Article 243(H) of the 73rd Amendment directs the States to bestow upon the PRIs authority to levy taxes, tax assignment and also to make grants-in-aid. Further, Article 243(I) of the same Act mandates every State to constitute a 'Finance Commission' once in five years. The functions of the State Finance Commission (SFC) are to determine, *inter alia*, distribution and assignment of taxes, duties, tolls and fees between the State and the local bodies; to recommend grants-in-aid from the Consolidated Fund of the State. Further, the responsibility of transferring resources to the local bodies has also been placed with the Union Finance Commission (UFC). The responsibility of UFC lies in the sub-clauses (bb) and (c) added to Article 280(3) of the Constitution which state that the UFC should take into account the recommendations of the SFCs in its resource devolution scheme. Thus the main objectives behind all these Constitutional provisions are: (a) to share the tax sources and revenues between the State and the local bodies; (b) to properly distribute resources between the panchayats; and (c) to evolve a stable fiscal decentralisation process in the country.

Objective of the Study

In the above background, this article makes an attempt to critically evaluate the fiscal position of PRIs in Karnataka. More specifically, it analyses the revenue raising powers of PRIs; growth and pattern of grants-in-aid to PRIs; the extent of mobilisation of own revenues;

and the criteria applied for horizontal distribution of resources. The analysis is based on quantitative and qualitative information. The former is based on secondary sources of information and the latter on the observations and discussions held with the functionaries of PRIs in the State. Further, information relating to resource mobilisation and composition of revenues collected from the eight sample Gram Panchayats (Babu, 1999) is also used in the analysis. It is a descriptive and analytical study.

PRIs System in Karnataka

When PRIs were declining in the country, the report of the Expert Committee (Ministry of Rural Development, 1978) came in handy for those leaders who were inclined to revive the local governance system. Karnataka was one of the few States in India, that had shown interest in, and initiated action towards establishing PRIs in the early 1980s. A three tier Panchayat system was established in the year 1987. The unique features of the system were: delegation of a large number of development functions and responsibilities; merging of DRDA (District Rural Development Agency) with Zilla Parishad; provision of administrative personnel; devolution of funds from the State government; constitution of Finance Commission and Performance Evaluation Committee.

In Karnataka elections were held in 2005 for these institutions for the third time after the 73rd Amendment was put into effect. The structure adopted is three-tier, namely the Gram Panchayat (GP) at the village level, Taluk Panchayat (TP) at the intermediate (taluk) level and Zilla Panchayat (ZP) at the district level. The organisational structure of Panchayats is presented in Chart 2.1. Presently there are 5,653 GPs, 176 TPs and 27 ZPs in the state. The Chairpersons of these bodies were accorded the status of 'Executive Heads'. The State has deputed nearly 3.43 lakh personnel from various departments to serve in the PRIs and the estimated cost on account of their salaries and other emoluments was Rs. 2,617 crores per annum (Government of Karnataka, 2000). Further, the PRIs have been entrusted with 399 plan and 255

Chart 2.1 : Organisational Structure of Three-Tier Panchayats in Karnataka

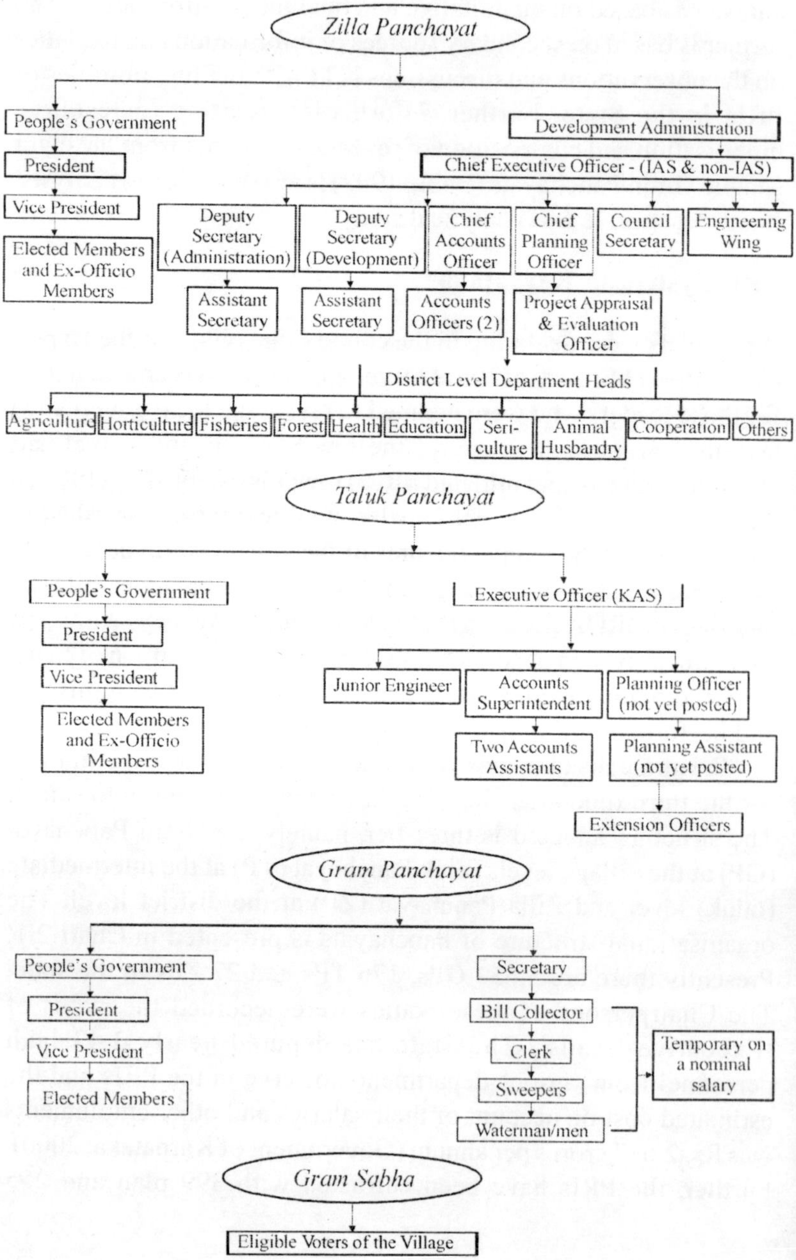

non-plan schemes totalling 654 in about 29 sectors. In order to give them greater flexibility to prioritise their needs, rationalisation of schemes was undertaken and this resulted in the reduction of schemes to 335 from the earlier 654 schemes [Rural Development and Panchayat Raj Department (RDPRD), 2004]. The total grants (plan and non-plan) allocated to these bodies in the State budget for the 2005-06 is Rs. 6,843 crores. Besides, the State government constituted a Finance Commission as per the Constitutional mandate in the year 1994. The Commission in turn submitted its report to the government in the year 1996. A Second Finance Commission (after 73rd Amendment) was constituted in the year 2000 and it submitted its report to the government in December 2003.

Fiscal Powers

As stated earlier, the PRIs should have tax and non-tax powers to generate own resources along with grants-in-aid from the higher level governments. If the Panchayats have their own income, they will be in a position to decide their priorities and needs and spend accordingly. In the absence of this, the Panchayats not only lose their independent decision-making power with regard to expenditures but also face severe fiscal imbalances. It may be observed that except GPs no other tier enjoys taxation powers.

Non-tax is another important source of revenue for the PRIs. Non-tax revenue consists of rent from the buildings, sale of assets, user charges for the services provided, auction of trees and fruits, sale of garbage and manure etc. In Karnataka all the three-tiers have been vested with powers to collect non-tax revenue from their own properties and assets and utilise the same for their own needs. However, they have no power to utilise the yield (user charges) from various departments and the same has to be credited to the State Consolidated Fund. The field experience reveals that the GPs, to some extent, mobilised revenues from non-tax sources, while it was negligible in the case of TPs and almost zero in the case of ZPs (Babu, 1999: 40).

Borrowings

Borrowings play an important role in development finance. In federal countries the Constitutions invariably provide for borrowings by the Central and State governments. In India also the Constitution provides for borrowings by both the Centre and the States (of course with certain conditions for the latter). In Karnataka, the Panchayat Raj Act, 1993, empowers all the three-tier Panchayats to raise loans for development purposes (Government of Karnataka, 1993). However, in spite of this statutory power, there is no evidence so far of any Panchayat in the State having made any attempt to borrow from financial institutions/agencies. Though the Act provides for raising loans by the PRIs, the process involved is not so smooth. The Panchayats seeking loans have to fulfil two conditions: the first is that any Panchayat seeking loan should obtain prior sanction and guarantee from the State government, and the second is that the Panchayat concerned should make arrangements to form a 'sinking fund' for timely repayment of the debt (Government of Karnataka, 1993). With regard to the first condition, the State is not keen to provide guarantee for any loan raised by the PRIs. As for the second condition, the PRIs, by and large, have no own resource raising powers and hence it is beyond their capacity to create a 'sinking fund' for the debt redemption later. Because of these constraints the Panchayats in the State have not made any attempt to raise loans.

Further, the State does not share individual taxes/duties (except the surcharge on stamp duty with TPs) with PRIs. Instead it shares its entire revenues minus loans.

The above information makes it clear that the two higher level Panchayats in the State have no taxation powers and, with the non-tax revenue being very negligible along with the inability to go for borrowings, they entirely depend upon transfers in the form of grants from the State and the Centre. The type and extent of grants received by PRIs is discussed in the proceeding paragraphs.

Grants-in-Aid

The main source of revenues for PRIs in the State, as elsewhere in

India, constitutes transferred resources in the form of grants-in-aid from the higher level governments. Broadly, the grants come from the State and the Centre. The State government grants consist of plan and non-plan funds. Whereas the Central transfers comprise of conditional and matching plan grants on the basis of Planning Commission's recommendations and non-plan grants on the basis of UFC's sharing method. The Tenth Finance Commission (1995-2000) provided *ad hoc* grants for PRIs on a matching basis for the first time. The Eleventh Finance Commission (2000-05) recommended specific purpose grants for the local bodies (Government of India, 2000: 79-80; Babu, 2002b: 1-17). The Twelfth Finance Commission (2005-10) recommended larger grants than the previous FC's recommended share. Further, it specified the purpose for which it should be used (Government of India, 2005).

Trends and Pattern of Grants-in-aid to PRIs

The grants provided to PRIs in Karnataka over the years brings out certain interesting features. As can be seen from Table 2.1, the quantum of grants allocated to PRIs has been increasing over the years. It was Rs. 917 crores during 1987-88, and Rs. 6,843 crores in the year 2005-06. However, a cursory look at the growth of grants brings out the fact that it is increasing in absolute terms but declining in percentage terms. The decline is noticed not only in the plan grants (State and Central share) but also in the grants from the State's own revenues (plan and non-plan grants). Under plan grants, the share of PRIs in the State's total plan outlay was 32 per cent during 1987-88 and the same has declined to 21 per cent in the year 2005-06. A study of the same across different periods of PRIs rule since 1987-88 reveals a gradual decline of grants in percentage as well as absolute terms. For instance, the annual average percentage share in the first period (1987-91) was nearly 37; whereas during administrators' control (1992-93) and the second period (1994-99), it was around 23; and in the latest period (2000-05) it was 17 per cent, a drop of 20 per cent in the last 14 years.

Table 2.1 : Trends in the Grants Devolved to PRIs (Three Tiers) in Karnataka

(Rs. Crores)

Year and PRIs Period	*Grants Allocated to PRIs*								
	Plan Grants (State & Centre)	*Non-Plan Grants (State)*	*Total Grants*	*State Plan Outlay*	*Share of PRIs in the State Plan Outlay*	*Per cent Share of PRIs in the State Plan Outlay*	*State's Own Tax and Non-Tax Revenue*	*Revenue Allocated to PRIs from State's Own Revenue*	*Per cent of State's Own Revenue Transferred to PRIs*
1987-88	364.84	551.73	916.57	1132	365	32.23	1850.08	772.73	41.77
1988-89	392.95	597.12	990.07	1152	393	34.11	2144.2	837.12	39.04
1989-90	444.82	697.06	1141.88	1306	445	34.06	2434.53	962.06	39.52
1990-91	545.28	694.22	1239.50	1366	645	39.92	2849.32	987.22	34.65
1991-92	675.04	837.95	1512.99	1937	675	34.85	3521.48	1194.95	33.93
Total of Ist Period	**2422.93**	**3378.08**	**5801.01**	**6893**	**2523**	**36.60**	**12799.61**	**4754.08**	**37.14**
1992-93	670.08	973.51	1643.59	2625	670	25.53	3900.35	1347.51	34.55
1993-94	739.61	1097.93	1837.54	3621	793	21.92	4545.91	1568.93	34.51
Total of Administrators Period	**1409.69**	**2071.44**	**3481.13**	**6246**	**1463**	**23.42**	**8446.26**	**2916.44**	**34.53**
1994-95	972.61	1213.05	2185.66	4175	973	23.30	5136.98	1751.05	34.09
1995-96	1100.31	1354.1	2454.41	4648	1100	23.67	6509.35	1974.10	30.33
1996-97	1272.84	1628.55	2901.39	5311	1213	23.97	7110.15	2360.55	33.20

Contd...

Table 2.1 : *Contd.*

(Rs. Crores)

Year and PRIs Period	*Grants Allocated to PRIs*								
	Plan Grants (State & Centre)	*Non-Plan Grants (State)*	*Total Grants*	*State Plan Outlay*	*Share of PRIs in the State Plan Outlay*	*Per cent Share of PRIs in the State Plan Outlay*	*State's Own Tax and Non-Tax Revenue*	*Revenue Allocated to PRIs from State's Own Revenue*	*Per cent of State's Own Revenue Transferred to PRIs*
1997-98	1419.74	2020.98	3440.72	5605	1420	25.20	7676.27	2752.98	35.86
1998-99	1447.03	2357.01	3804.04	6513	1447	22.22	8412.96	3089.01	36.72
1999-00	1527.82	2707.95	4235.77	7087	1528	21.56	9355.65	3499.95	37.41
Total of IInd Period	**7740.35**	**11281.64**	**19021.99**	**33339**	**7681**	**23.04**	**44360.03**	**15427.64**	**34.90**
2000-01	1696.96	2892.47	4589.43	8506	1697	19.95	10762.65	3854.83	36.02
2001-02	1834.30	2993.63	4827.93	9605	1834	19.09	10946.70	4076.63	37.24
2002-03	1241.20	3286.47	4527.67	9522	1241	13.03	11717.38	3903.47	33.31
2003.04	1302.27	3431.45	4733.72	9780	1302	13.31	16389.35*	4119.86	25.14
2004-05	1425.24	3468.18	4893.42	11741	1425	12.14	19444.31**	4238.18	21.80
2005-06	2880.29	3962.46	6842.75	13555	2880	21.25		5965.36	
Total of IIIrd Period	**10380.26**	**20034.66**	**30414.92**	**62709**	**10380.26**	**16.55**	**48235.71**	**15954.79**	**33.08**

Note: * Revised Estimate; * * Budget Estimate

Source: 1. *'Economic Survey 1997-98 and 2001-02', Government. of Karnataka;* 2. *Reserve Bank of India, 'RBI Bulletins'*, (various issues); 3. Government of Karnataka, *Budget Allotment for Zilla Panchayat Plan and Non-Plan* (various years)

The grants devolved to PRIs out of the State's own revenues show that the trend is slightly better compared to the position of plan grants. It was 37 per cent, 35 per cent and 31 per cent respectively in the first, second and third periods. Thus a marginal decline is noticed in the last 14 years compared to the first period. The ratio of State's transfers to PRIs in relation to State income (Gross State Domestic Product) reveals that it is around 4 per cent during 1990-91 to 1993-94 and from 1994-95 onwards it ranged between 3 and 3.5 per cent. The implications emerging from these trends are:

(i) the grants devolved to PRIs are not proportional to the growing revenues of the State;
(ii) the availability of developmental (plan) grants is declining which is reflected in the negligible allocations made to certain important sectors by the PRIs;
(iii) a general mismatch between the functions entrusted and resources available to the local governments; and
(iv) the commitment of the State towards fiscal decentralisation was greater in the first period (1987-91) than in the later periods.

Tied/Untied Grants

A related question that needs answer is: whether the grants given to PRIs by the higher level governments are tied or untied grants? This has become a focal issue in recent years in the country. The proponents of fiscal decentralisation advocate providing untied grants to the decentralised governments so that they will have freedom in spending according to their priorities. The study of the nature of plan grants devolved to PRIs in Karnataka, over the years, reveals that they are largely tied to the programmes/schemes entrusted to them from above (Aziz, 1993; Government of Karnataka, 1988, 1996: 129-130; Satishchandran, 2000). The Planning Department of Karnataka proclaims that it is providing lump sum plan grants to ZPs who have freedom to allocate across the sectors as per their priorities. But, the same department issues guidelines/norms for their utilisation. The broad guidelines issued are that the Panchayats should earmark grants for committed expenditure on salaries, minimum needs programmes, spill over works, ongoing schemes relating to scholarships, farms, hospitals, the State's share on centrally sponsored schemes etc. A large number of functionaries opine that after earmarking grants as per the above norms, there remains nothing to take up new projects/schemes of their choice. This position indicates that the PRIs are only spending agencies of the State rather than self-governing institutions. The Finance Commission (1996) of Karnataka, recognising the need for untied grants at the hands of PRIs, recommended 10 per cent of the PRIs plan outlay to be given without conditions (Government of Karnataka, 1996: 293). The functionaries of Panchayats in the State also feel the need for free outlay. In fact they exerted pressure on the State government to provide untied grants to them. The government responded, though belatedly, by making a provision for free outlay (namely development grant) in the 2001-02 budget.

Share of Three Tiers

The 73rd Constitutional Amendment has mandated all the major States to adopt three-tier Panchayat structure. Almost all the States adhered to this mandate and established three-tier Panchayats in different years. However, the powers, functions and resources devolved to the PRIs vary from State to State and from tier to tier within the State. The GPs occupy an important place among the three-tiers not only in providing basic amenities to the people but also in decentralised planning. Decentralised planning envisages that planning emanate from the grassroots (village) level and that the lowest tier of the Panchayat system ensure people's participation in such planning. The Central Government, of late, has taken initiatives to strengthen and empower the lowest tier of the panchayats functionally and financially (Sinha, 1999: 6-8). The other two higher level panchayats have been entrusted with infrastructure and sectoral development activities.

Further, the Karnataka Panchayat Raj Act demarcates the functions of PRIs in three different Schedules. Schedule-I contains 30 subjects, Schedule-II 27 functions and Schedule-III 28 functions to be carried out respectively by the GPs, TPs and ZPs. However, the subjects enshrined under Schedule-I are yet to be transferred to GPs. But, this does not mean that the GPs have no functions to perform at all. The GPs, in reality, have been entrusted with a large number of obligatory and discretionary functions other than what is stated under Schedule-I. It is the responsibility of GPs to provide, maintain and manage the basic services such as drinking water, streetlights, roads, drainage and sanitation, public properties etc. It is a daunting task for the GPs to provide these services at a reasonable level. The SFC observes that the GPs hardly get adequate funds even to maintain water supply works, streetlights etc. (Government of Karnataka, 1996: 240). To provide essential services at a normative level, the GPs require large resources. Thus, the lower tier assumes greater significance in terms of provision of services compared to the other two tiers.

The extent of grants devolved to the GPs (among the three-tiers) in the State has to be seen in the above perspective. A glance at the shares of the three tiers in the PRIs total plan grants unfolds their relative positions. This information is presented in Table 2.2. The table reveals that the ZPs and TPs get almost an equal share in the total grants till 2001-02. However, from 2002-03 the share of ZPs has been increasing at the cost of TPs. The position of GPs was very low till 2003-04. Its share hovers around 14 per cent. Fortunately, from the year 2004-05 GPs got importance among the three tiers and got around 33 per cent in the year 2005-06. The change in the shares of three tiers may be attributed to two reasons. One, the government initiated activity mapping of the Panchayat activities and this resulted in devolution of more functions to GPs. Second, during 2005-06 the State transferred around 150 schemes hitherto held by it to PRIs along with funds. In this the GPs have been entrusted with certain development functions such as watershed, minor irrigation, drinking water supply, rural energy, rural employment, housing etc.

It is worth stating that the SFC (1996), after studying the then existing shares of the three tiers, came to the conclusion that there existed a discrepancy in the allocation of grants across the tiers. To set right this anomaly the Commission recommended 40 per cent,

35 per cent, and 25 per cent respectively as the shares of ZPs, TPs and GPs in the PRIs total plan grants (Government of Karnataka, 1996: 241). However, the State government did not take any firm decision on this recommendation and only said that it will be achieved in course of time. It took almost nine years to set right the discrepancies in the availability of development funds among the three tiers. Besides scheme-wise grants, each GP receives a grant of Rs. 5 lakh annually which is considered as untied.

Table 2.2: Relative Shares of ZPs, TPs and GPs in the PRIs Plan Grants in Karnataka

(Rs. lakhs)

S. No.	*Year*	*Zilla Panchayats*	*Taluk Panchayats*	*Gram Panchayats*	*All Panchayats*
1	1995-96	46447.55 (42.21)	46068.62 (41.87)	17515.1 (15.920	110031.27 (100.00)
2	1996-97	51991.00 (40.85)	56651.53 (44.51)	18641.79 (14.65)	127284.32 (100.00)
3	1999-00	69037.85 (45.19)	67382.66 (44.10)	16361.28 (10.71)	152781.79 (100.00)
4	2000-01	72839.24 (42.92)	73818.99 (43.50)	23037.84 (13.58)	169696.07 (100.00)
5	2001-02	72554.8 (39.55)	79660.48 (43.43)	31221.33 (17.02)	183436.61 (100.00)
6	2002-03	70091.11 (56.47)	36302.39 (29.25)	17726.97 (14.28)	124120.47 (100.00)
7	2003-04	70318.44 (54.00)	37014.68 (28.42)	22894.34 (17.58)	130227.46 (100.00)
8	2004-05	70059.78 (49.16)	40894.93 (28.69)	31568.95 (22.15)	142523.66 (100.00)
9	2005-06	115180.21 (39.99)	76353.43 (26.51)	96495.59 (33.5)	288029.23 (100.00)

Note: Figures in parenthesis are percentages to the respective row totals.

Source: 1. For 1995-96 and 1996-97–Rural Development and Panchayat Raj Department, Government of Karnataka; 2. Government of Karnataka, *'Budget Allotment for Zilla Panchayat–Plan & Non-Plan' 1999-2000 to 2005-06.*

SFC and the Local Bodies

The SFC (1996) of Karnataka (first after the Constitutional Amendment) did not recommend any tax powers to Zilla and Taluk Panchayats. Similarly, it did not recommend any of the State's taxes/ duties to be assigned to PRIs. The reasons cited for not according tax powers to higher level tiers are: fragmentation of tax base; growth of district level bureaucracy in the name of tax collection machinery; additional avenues for tax evasion and conflict in regard to the taxation of inter-district mobile tax base; and unwillingness to collect adequate revenues by the elected representatives due to closeness to the tax payers (Government of Karnataka, 1996: 160). Instead, the Commission recommended a fixed annual share of 36 per cent of the State's own revenue for both rural and urban local bodies (ULBs). Of the 36 per cent, the share fixed for PRIs was 30.6 per cent and the remaining 5.4 per cent for ULBs. The State government accepted this recommendation and also implemented. But the quantum of grants transferred to PRIs during the year 2003-04 shows that it is less than the SFC's recommended share of 30.6 per cent. The second SFC submitted its report in December 2003 and its major recommendation was devolution of 40 per cent of the State's own revenue to the local bodies (PRIs and ULBs). Of this, the share fixed for PRIs was 32 per cent. But, unfortunately the State has not initiated any action on this report so far. The trends in the grants devolved by State out of its revenues shows that the PRIs were getting more than 32 per cent till 2002-03 but thereafter it has declined (Table 2.1).

Resource Mobilisation by PRIs

As mentioned elsewhere in this article, no tax powers have been given to the ZPs and TPs in the State. Only the GPs enjoy this power. Further, no worthwhile assets exist at the hands of TPs and ZPs to mobilise non-tax revenues. Such being the case, any discussion on the resource mobilisation by PRIs in the State confines to GPs only. Though, a large number of tax sources have been entrusted to the GPs, in reality, they could tap only a few of them as revealed from the sample study. The most exploited tax sources are house/building tax, water cess, streetlight cess and factory tax. The tax sources, which have not been tapped, are the entertainment tax, vehicle tax, tax on advertisement and hoardings. The important non-tax revenues collected are—licence fee, rent from shops and buildings, sale of sites, deposits, auction of trees, fruits and fish. The GPs have not made efforts to mobilise resources from a large number of non-tax sources such as bus/auto/tanga stand fee, garbage and manure, pilgrim/fairs fee, fee on cattle sheds and grazing lands (Babu, 1999: 33).

As against the above unsatisfactory performance, the GPs since 2003-04 are doing well in resource mobilisation due to the intervention of State's Rural Development and Panchayat Raj Department. The progress made in the tax mobilisation since then is very impressive. The revenue mobilised from different sources increased by about 146 per cent since the assessment of properties in the year 2003 (Table 2.3).

Table 2.3 : Impact of Property Tax Revision on Revenue Mobilisation by GPs in Karnataka

(Rs. crores)

Tax Source	*Before Revision*	*After Revision*	*% Change*
Number of Properties Assessed (in lakhs)	74.16	104.47	41.00
Property Tax	37.86	86.25	127.81
Health Cess	6.00	13.56	126.00
Education Cess	4.10	9.66	136.00
Library Cess	2.45	9.35	282.00
Water Cess	16.07	49.33	207.00
Street light Cess	7.01	19.23	174.00
Licence Fee	1.02	3.07	201.00
Other Taxes	6.45	8.53	32.25
Total	80.96	198.98	146.00

Source: Rural Development and Panchayat Raj Department, *'Annual Report-2003-04'*, Government of Karnataka.

Composition of Revenues of GPs

It would be relevant here to bring out the quantum of resources available to the GPs and their composition. The information on revenues of eight sample GPs is presented in Table 2.4. As can be seen from the table, the average revenue per GP per year from all sources was Rs. 3.28 lakh in mid-1990s. Since the State government has enhanced its grant from Rs. one lakh to Rs. five lakh in the year 2003-04, the average revenue per GP would go up to Rs. 7 lakh per annum (State's statutory grant, Central grant and own revenue). However, the average grant available per GP from 2005-06 work out to Rs. 17 lakh. The broad composition of revenues reveals that 20 per cent constitutes tax revenue, 3 per cent non-tax revenue and 77 per cent government grants. Thus, it is clear from the table that the resources available to GPs from own sources are less than one-quarter of the total revenues indicating that they too depend heavily upon grants from the higher level governments.

A disaggregated study of the revenues (Table 2.4) shows that property tax contributes around 43 per cent; water cess 25 per cent; street-light cess 10 per cent. Coming to the grants a major share of about 60 per cent constitutes Centre's JRY/SGRY grant, another 35 per cent constitutes State grants and the remaining 5 per cent accounts for UFC's grant. Another point to be noted from the table is that each of the GPs received on an average Rs. 86,955 from the State per annum instead of Rs. 1 lakh grant. This is because, the MPs/GPs over the years had accumulated huge arrears of electricity charges and were unwilling to clear them on their own. As such, the State government, while disbursing annual grants, deducted a portion of the grant to clear the electricity dues on their behalf. This policy of deduction from the grant has been discontinued. Now, the GPs receive the entire Rs. 5 lakhs grant directly from the government and they have been instructed to pay electricity dues from time to time by themselves.

Devolution Criteria

One of the objectives of inter-governmental transfers is to minimise horizontal fiscal imbalances. The same objective holds good for

Table 2.4: Pattern and Composition of Revenues of the Selected Gram Panchayats in Karnataka

(in Rs.)

Source of Revenue	*Year*				*Total of Four Years*	*Average Revenue Per GP/ Year*	*Percent to Sub-Totals*	*Per cent of Major Sources in the Total*
	1994-95	1995-96	1996-97	1997-98				
I. Tax Revenue								
1. House Tax	146902	337647	243806	367017	1095372	34230.38	51.49	–
2. Water cess	82207	158233	92311	87693	420444	13138.88	19.77	–
3. Electricity cess	12272	900	1387	1300	15859	495.59	0.75	–
4. Other Taxes	47050	187461	107513	253507	595531	18610.34	28.00	–
Total Tax Revenue	288431	684241	445017	709517	2127206	66475.19	100.00	20.26
II. Non-Tax Revenue								
1. Rents and Other Income from Own Property	35417	33356	62087	0	130860	4089.38	40.55	–
2. Licence Fee	16215	8365	5000	5200	34780	1086.88	10.78	–
3. Others	66850	33534	46397	10305	157086	4908.94	48.67	–
Total Non-Tax Revenue	118482	75255	113484	15505	322726	10085.19	100.00	3.07
III. Grants-in-Aid								
1. State Govt. Grant	616372	724943	764880	676351	2782546	86954.56	34.56	–
2. 10th FC Grant	0	0	0	423380	423380	13230.63	5.26	–
3. Central (JRY) Grant	1254834	1304092	1176034	1109974	4844934	151404.19	60.18	–
Total Grants	1871206	2029035	1940914	2209705	8050860	251589.38	100.00	76.67
Total Revenue	2278119	2788531	2499415	2934727	10500792	328149.75	–	100.00

Source: Annual Audit Reports of the concerned Gram Panchayats.

the State and the local level governments also. The developmental levels and the fiscal needs vary from one Panchayat to another. These differences have to be minimised gradually by adopting appropriate grant distribution policies. While distributing grants across the Panchayats, the government should adopt a broad set of criteria along with weightages. Keeping in view the importance of this objective, the State government adopted 12 and 5 criteria during 1987-88 for distribution of plan grants across Zilla Parishads and Mandal Panchayats (MPs) respectively. The criteria and weightages adopted are shown in Table 2.5. It is reportedly claimed that the same 12 criteria are being continued even now for the purpose of distribution of plan grants to Zilla Panchayats. But, this has not been applied from 1990-91 onwards. In its place an *ad hoc* method of hiking the grants by 5 to 10 per cent to the previous year's allocation is being adopted.

When the State implemented a three-tier structure of Panchayats in the year 1994, it made TP an active middle tier by devolving large number of functions and resources to them. For the purpose of distribution of grants across the TPs, the then 5 criteria used for distribution of grants to the MPs were replaced with six new criteria

Table 2.5: Criteria and Weightages adopted for the Distribution of Plan Grants to Zilla Parishads/Panchayats and Mandal Panchayats in Karnataka

Criteria	*Weightage (per cent)*
A. Zilla Parishads/Panchayats	
1. Population	50
2. Backwardness in agriculture as measured by the value of agricultural output per hectare	5
3. Backwardness in irrigation as measured by the proportion of irrigated area to net area sown	7
4. Backwardness as measured by the value of industrial output	5
5. Backwardness in communications as measured by road and railway mileage per 100 sq. km. and per lakh of population	5

Contd.

Criteria	*Weightage (per cent)*
6. Backwardness in financial infrastructure as measured by size of population served by each commercial and co-operative bank	2
7. Backwardness in medical and health facilities as measured by the number of hospitals per 1000 population/bed population ratio	5
8. Backwardness in power supply as measured by the proportion of villages electrified	5
9. Problems of weaker sections: (a) as measured by the proportion of SCs/STs in the total population (b) as measured by the proportion of landless agricultural labourers	 2 2
10. Special problems of malnad areas and drought prone areas: (a) as measured by the area under forest (b) as measured by the rural population of drought prone areas	 2 2
11. Literacy percentage	5
12. Performance in family planning programme	3
Total	*100*
B. Mandal Panchayats	
1. Population	50
2. Area of Mandal Panchayat	15
3. Dry Land Area	15
4. Agricultural Labour Population	10
5. Per capita Resources raised	10
Total	*100*

Source: Government of Karnataka, 'District Governments and Decentralised Planning', 1988.

as shown in Table 2.6, in the year 1998. Even in this case also there is no evidence of ZPs applying this criteria while distributing grants across the TPs. The field experience shows that the ZPs adopt some vague criteria in arriving at the development levels of various TPs and accordingly distribute the grants.

In the case of GPs the criterion followed since 1994 is to provide a fixed grant uniformly to each of the GPs as brought out elsewhere in this article.

Table 2.6: Criteria Adopted for Distribution of Grants between the Taluk Panchayats

Criteria	*Weightage (in %)*
1. Population	50
2. Area	10
3. Literacy	10
4. SC/ ST Population	10
5. Dry Land Area	10
6. Number of Agricultural Labourers	10
Total	100

Source: Rural Development and Panchayat Raj Department, 'GO - RDPR 46, DPD 98, 8-9-1998', Government of Karnataka.

Thus, no scientific and rational method is followed in the distribution of grants among the Panchayats within each tier. This does not augur well for the State in the present context where difficult conditions prevail in certain parts of the State due to widening regional disparities.

As against the above criteria, the SFC had recommended five criteria to be followed at all the three levels. The criteria and weightages recommended are:

(i) Proportion of population living in the Panchayat area (33.33%);
(ii) Proportion of area covered by the Panchayat (33.33%);
(iii) Illiteracy rate (11.11%);
(iv) Number of persons per bed (11.12%); and
(v) Length of roads (11.11%);

It would be apt to bring out here the major differences between the State and SFC criteria. Unlike the former, the SFC included 'area' as one of the criteria and for this it assigned a weight equal to that of population criterion. The State government, however, did not accept this criteria on some grounds (Babu, 2002c).

Distribution of Non-Plan Grants

Of the total grants devolved to PRIs, the share of non-Plan grants account for more than 55 per cent. Over the years it varies between 55 and 63 per cent. This grant is entirely given out of the State's own revenues. Bulk of this grant accounts for salary expenditure. For instance, during 1995-96 salary component accounted for 74 per cent. Allocations for salary component are made on the basis of actual requirements worked out by the ZPs. The allocation to other items such as repairs and maintenance of roads and buildings, purchase of medicines for hospitals etc. is made as per the norms fixed by the administrative departments concerned.

Summary and Suggestions

From the foregoing analysis it may be concluded that in general the resource raising powers of PRIs in the State are extremely limited, while revenue transfers from the higher level governments is high.

Besides powers and functions, the PRIs need to be endowed with adequate resources comprising own and devolved grants. Alongside they should have freedom to utilise the available resources according to their needs and priorities. Seen in this context, the picture that obtains in the State is not completely in conformity with this normative framework.

At the outset, it should be noted that of the three tiers only the lowest tier is entrusted with taxation powers. The higher two tiers almost entirely depend upon the State and the Central grants. The SFC also did not recommend any tax powers to TPs and ZPs. This kind of distribution of resources between the State and the PRIs will have different kind of impact on the latter. The impact is seen in: (a) loss of freedom for the third tier governments in the resource allocation matters; (b) high dependency on the higher level governments for resources; and (c) impact of UFC's devolution criteria on PRIs in different States. It may be noted here that the Eleventh Finance Commission (EFC) and the Twelfth Finance Commission of India, while determining the shares of PRIs in different States, had taken the extent of tax powers entrusted to local bodies by the States and resources mobilised on their own as criterias among others (Government of India, 2000: 81; 2005). Due to this criterion, many States including Karnataka could not gain much from the UFC's recommendation (Babu, 2002b). Strengthening of PRIs lies in making them fiscally strong and autonomous as far as possible. The Centre as well as the future UFCs' can consider the extent of decentralisation practised especially in fiscal matters while determining the needs of PRIs. Thus, there is need for rethinking on the part of State government and also the future SFCs in bestowing tax powers on the PRIs and also in making borrowings easy.

With regard to borrowings by the PRIs, the conditions imposed come in their way. There is a feeling among the functionaries of Panchayats that the State government may not give permission and guarantee for their loan venture. Secondly, the TPs and ZPs do not have their own revenue sources and as such forming a 'sinking fund' by them would be a formidable task. The latter problem could be eased to some extent if the higher two levels of Panchayats are vested with some statutory tax powers. Again, it is worthwhile to consider creation of an Apex Body to control and manage borrowings exclusively for rural and urban local bodies.

The PRIs in Karnataka are relatively getting larger transfers from the State government. However, it is declining in percentage terms since 1992-93 and in absolute terms from the year 2002-03. Certain policies like creation of Local Area Development Fund (LADF) Scheme for MLAs/MLCs in the year 2001-02 and channelling funds to certain parallel bodies is robbing the legitimate share of PRIs. This unhealthy development should be discontinued and the funds meant for rural development are routed through PRIs only. In addition to this, the grants given should have a fair amount of untied grants. The process started in recent years in this direction should continue.

Again, the criteria followed for horizontal distribution makes a mockery of sorts in the State. Bargaining by the districts/ZPs for more grants has crept into the system leading to further disparities across the regions. Thus there is a need for adopting a set of broad criteria along with weightages by the State for allocation of grants across the Panchayats. Alternatively, the SFC had suggested five criteria along with weightages to be applied at all the three levels and the State could adopt them directly and if need be with some modifications in the weightages.

Another disappointing feature observed is low resource mobilisation by GPs from their own tax and non-tax sources. Though many of the tax sources entrusted to the GPs are inelastic in nature, they have failed to make serious efforts to mobilise revenues even from the elastic sources. A large number of factors contributed to the inefficiency in revenue mobilisation by GPs. The important among these are: lack of knowledge on the part of functionaries about their tax and non-tax powers; the functionaries themselves being defaulters to their GPs; non-involvement of elected representatives with the tax collecting personnel; non-revision of tax rates for a long time; ignorance about the importance of people's contribution; lack of monitoring by the higher level Panchayats; unscientific method of fixing tax rates by the State; lack of incentive schemes. The GPs, instead of depending heavily on the higher level governments for resources, should think on how best the above hindrances in tax mobilisation could be overcome and resources raised optimally. As a first step the elected members should pay taxes to their GPs promptly, setting an example for others in the villages. The recent exercise of GPs in rationalising properties and putting greater efforts in tax mobilisation drive should not dampen the spirits and it should continue. The recent elections to GPs brought new members and they need training and skill upgradation on the ways and means of resource mobilisation.

It is also important that the State government give respect to the SFC Reports by implementing their important recommendations expeditiously,which can pave way for genuine fiscal decentralisation.

REFERENCES

Aziz, Abdul, 1993. *Decentralised Planning: The Karnataka Experience*, Sage, New Delhi.

Babu, M. Devendra, 1999. *Functional and Financial Devolution to PRIs: A Study in Karnataka* (Mimeo), Institute for Social and Economic Change, Bangalore.

Babu, M. Devendra, 2002a. 'Report of the Karnataka State Finance Commission: Status and Implications', *The Indian Journal of Economics*, Vol. LXXXII, No. 326.

Babu, M. Devendra, 2002b, 'Eleventh Finance Commission's Recommendations and the Local Bodies: Impact Across the States'. *Management in Government*, Vol. XXXIV, No. 2.

Finance Department, 1971, *Report of the Taxation Enquiry and Resource Committee*, Government of Punjab.

Finance Department, 1983, *Karnataka Taxation Review Committee, (Part-II, Report on Local Finances)*, Government of Karnataka.

Government of India, 1954, *Report of the Taxation Enquiry Commission*, 1953-54, Vol. I.

Government of India, 1963, *The Study Team on Panchayat Raj Finances*.

Government of India, 2000, *Report of the Eleventh Finance Commission*.

Government of India, 2005, *Report of the Twelfth Finance Commission*.

Government of Karnataka, 1988, *District Governments and Decentralised Planning*.

Government of Karnataka, 1993, *The Karnataka Panchayat Raj Act, 1993*.

Government of Karnataka, 1996, *Report of the State Finance Commission Relating to Rural Local Bodies*.

Government of Karnataka, 2000, *Salary Amount Allocated to Zilla Panchayats, Appendix Table-B, (Staff)*, 1999-2000.

Ministry of Rural Development, 1978, *Report of the Committee on Panchayati Raj Institutions, 1977-78*. Government of India.

Rural Development and Panchayat Raj Department, 2004, '*Annual Report-2003-04*', Government of Karnataka.

Satishchandran, T.R., 2000, *Karnataka*, in George Mathew (ed), 'Status of Panchayati Raj in the States and Union Territories of India - 2000', Institute of Social Sciences and Concept Publishing Co., New Delhi.

Sinha, Yashwant, 1999, *Budget Speech*, Government of India.

3

FISCAL DEVOLUTION AND STATE FINANCE COMMISSION IN KERALA

T.M. THOMAS ISSAC AND P. SHAHEENA

Introduction

The best summary index of the significance of the lower tiers of government in the governance structure is the ratio of their expenditure to the overall expenditure of the government. In 1990-91 the ratio of expenditure of Gram Panchayats constituted 3.32 per cent and that of the urban bodies 2.99 per cent of the State government expenditure. According to the estimate of Datta (1992) the share of local expenditure in the total government expenditure in India was 2.9 per cent for the rural local bodies and 3.5 per cent for the urban local bodies. The overall ratio of rural and urban local bodies in Kerala works out to be 6.3 against the national average of 6.4 per cent. The local bodies in the rural areas were relatively much stronger in Kerala when compared to rest of India.

A detailed analysis undertaken by Lekha (1997) also reveals that the share of local expenditure in the total government expenditure in the State had been rising during 1960s and 1970s and had tended to decline during 1990s. The expenditure ratio for Grama Panchayats rose from 1.76 per cent in 1960-61 to 4.74 per cent in 1981-82. Thereafter it has steadily tended to decline. However, from 1996-97 onwards there has been a sharp rise in the ratio of expenditure of Grama Panchayats to 9.1 per cent in

1998-99. District Panchayats and Block Panchayats came into existence in October 1995-96. It is seen from Table 3.1 that the relative expenditure of these rural local bodies as well as the municipal bodies significantly improved during the latter half of 1990s. As a result the ratio of expenditure of all Local Bodies to the State government expenditure rose to a record high of 16.6 per cent in 1998-99.

Table 3.1 : The Ratio of Expenditure of Local Self Governments to State Government Expenditure (1993-94 to 1998-99)

Year	Gram Panchayats	Block Panchayats	District Panchayats	Municipalities	Corporations	Total
1990-91	3.2	–	–	1.9	1.09	6.19
1993-94	3.4	–	–	1.8	1.1	6.30
1994-95	3.5	–	–	1.7	1.1	5.30
1995-96	3.3	1.4	.02	1.6	0.9	7.29
1996-97	5.4	1.4	.64	1.9	1.02	10.36
1997-98	4.9	2.1	1.16	2.0	1.05	11.21
1998-99	9.1	2.0	1.91	2.27	1.32	16.60

What factors have brought about the above transformation of the fiscal role of the Local Self-Governments (LSGIs) in Kerala within such a brief period. State Finance Commission (SFC) is the Constitutional body to review the financial situation of the LSGIs and make recommendations as to enhance their own revenue raising capacity or additional transfer of funds from the State government and the principles for the distribution among the LSGIs. The First State Finance Commission had submitted an Interim Report in October 1995 and the Final Report in February 1996. What role has the SFC played in this transformation? What are the new fiscal issues that have been thrown up by the dramatic turn around of the fiscal fortunes of the LSGIs?

To answer these questions it is important that we present an overview of the State of Local Body finances at the time of appointment of the first SFC. We address this task in Section I of this article where we discuss the fiscal problems of the LSGIs in early 1990s with a historical background of broad trends over the past decades. In Section II of the article, we summarise the major recommendations of the SFC, their implications and the action taken thereon by the State government. Section III of the article is devoted to an analysis of the post-SFC period when impulses from unexpected sources, quite outside the scope of SFC, gave an unprecedented thrust to the process of fiscal devolution in the State.

Before we go into a detailed analysis of the pattern of Local Body finance, certain important structural features of the Local Self Government system in the State may be taken note of. The first point to be noted is the absence of higher tiers at block and district levels until recently. District Councils had been constituted in 1990 but were soon rendered totally ineffective and reduced to an ornamental status by hostile attitude of the United Democratic Front Government, that had come to power in early 1991. Kerala never had intermediate tier. As we touched upon earlier the higher tiers of Panchayats were introduced only in 1996.

Another distinctive feature is the relatively larger size of the grassroots tier of LSGIs bodies in the rural areas—the Gram Pancahayats (GP). There were 991 GPs with an average population of 25,004 as per 1991 Census. The average area of a Panchayat is 37.5 sq. km. In contrast the municipalities in Kerala relatively were smaller in size with an average population of 52,058. There were 54 municipalities with an average area of 22.63 sq. km. Besides, there were three Municipal Corporations. The Urban bodies covered nearly 15 per cent of the State's population.

SECTION I

LOCAL BODY FINANCES ON THE EVE OF THE FIRST SFC

Pattern of Expenditure

The expenditure of the LSGIs would depend on the functions that is devolved to them. The Panchayat Act of 1960 had a comprehensive list of 62 functions. However, in actual practice the role of Panchayats had been confined to small-scale public works and basic civic functions. This has been reflected in the composition of the expenditure of the Panchayats. During the 1980s around 25-30 per cent of the expenditure is accounted for by the establishment charges. Around 25 per cent were accounted for by public works. Around 12-15 per cent of the expenditure was on education, drinking water and public works and streetlights. Around 35 to 40 per cent of the expenditure was classified as 'miscellaneous' that included expenditure on other development heads, social welfare activities and debt repayment.

Table 3.2 : Pattern of Expenditure of Gram Panchayats in Kerala

	Establishment Charges	*Public Works*	*Education*	*Water Supply, Drainage*	*Streetlights*		*Miscellaneous*	*Total*
1970-71	24.83	31.24	2.87	2.88	7.24	0.42	30.51	100.00
1974-75	31.23	18.34	2.27	3.11	9.32	0.27	35.45	100.00
1980-81	26.02	26.93	2.58	3.29	6.12	0.39	34.72	100.00
1985-86	31.56	22.03	1.19	2.23	10.78	0.97	31.24	100.00
1989-90	32.79	18.62	1.67	2.02	6.58	0.20	38.11	100.00
1990-91	25.85	24.78	2.26	3.26	5.69	0.39	37.76	100.00
1991-92	28.24	23.28	1.79	2.08	6.12	0.39	38.11	100.00
1992-93	26.78	25.58	1.69	2.52	6.58	0.23	36.62	100.00
1993-94	27.33	26.87	1.70	1.56	5.74	1.19	35.61	100.00
1994-95	26.47	28.19	1.62	2.29	5.14	0.30	35.98	100.00

Source: Administration Report of Panchayats (various issues).

Broadly, the same pattern holds good for the municipalities also. The major difference is with respect to debt servicing which constitute only around 2.0 to 2.5 per cent of the expenditure of the Gram Panchayats while it constitutes 7.5 to 9.5 per cent for the municipal bodies. Municipal bodies also have a higher share of civic services like street lighting, drinking water etc. The most important point to be noted is that the role of local bodies—both rural and urban—in material goods producing sectors such as agriculture, fisheries, animal husbandry was negligible. Even with respect to the civic amenities and public works only the rural local bodies supplemented departmental activities.

The LSGIs accounted for only negligible proportion of the plan expenditure of the State. The budgeting procedures of the LSGIs did not consider it to be significant enough to have a distinction between Plan and Non-Plan expenditure. The Plan expenditure of the LSGIs consisted of certain departmental schemes that were implemented through the former and, more importantly, a limited amount of untied funds, which were given as Plan grants. The most important source of plan resources was the public works, which were implemented as part of the centrally sponsored Poverty Alleviation programmes.

The expenditure of the LSGIs was not determined in a scientific manner in relation to the functions. The expenditure was not demand driven but supplied determined. We shall now turn our attention to the financial resources available to the LSGIs and their sources. After all, this aspect constitutes the main focus of the analysis and recommendations of the SFC.

The Level of Fiscal Autonomy

The relative income of the different tiers of LSGIs may be gauged from their average income for the year 1991. The average income of Gram Panchayat was Rs. 10.06 lakhs, municipalities Rs. 90.44 lakhs and corporations Rs. 936 lakhs. The real income of the LSGIs, even taking into account the inflation has tended to rise throughout the post-independence period, even though it tended to decelerate from the 1980s (Lekha, 1997). Even in per capita terms the Panchayats in Kerala belong to the highest strata (Oommen, 1995). An important point that arises in this context is the level of fiscal autonomy or the ratio of own revenue to the total income of the LSGIs. What are the sources of the own revenue and how well they have been exploited?

As can be seen from Table 3.3, 44 per cent of the total income of the Panchayats and 85 per cent of the income of the municipalities in 1990-91 were derived from their own tax and non-tax revenue sources. This indicates the high level of fiscal autonomy that the LSGIs in Kerala had traditionally enjoyed for various historical reasons. In other States also the municipalities have traditionally enjoyed high level of fiscal autonomy. As per the statistics provided by the Seventh Finance Commission the all States average of the ratio of own taxes and non-tax revenues of the municipalities to their total expenditure was 81.3 per cent. However, the ratio for the rural local bodies in India was only 10.8 per cent. In some of the States like West Bengal and Orissa the internal resource mobilisation of the Panchayats was only 3 per cent (Datta, 1992).

Table 3.3 : Share of Different Sources in Total Receipts of LSGIs (1990)

Item	*Panchayats*	*Municipalities and Corporations*
1. Tax Revenue	33	58
2. Assigned Taxed (Surcharge on Stamp Duty and Basic Tax)	22	4
3. Shared Tax (Motor Vehicles Tax)	3	5
4. Non-Tax Revenue	11	27
5. Grants	31	6
Total	*100*	*100*

Source: SFC Final Report (1996).

As can be seen from Table 3.4, but for exceptional years the own revenue sources of the Gram Panchayats accounted more than 50 per cent of the total receipts. The share ranged between 46 per cent in 1992-93 to 68 per cent in 1960-61. Even though the share of own revenues have tended to fluctuate the trend has been for the share to decline over time from around little less than 70 per cent in early 1960s to around 50 per cent during the early 1990s. As share of SDP, also the own tax and non-tax resources declined in the 90s. Their share has reached the lowest since the mid-70s, in the 90s. To understand the factors have been responsible for the erosion of the level of fiscal autonomy, we shall probe into the trends in tax revenues and non-tax revenues of the Panchayats.

Own Tax Revenues

The composition of tax revenue is presented in Table 3.5. As is revealed by the table, building tax accounted for lion's share of tax resources. The overall trends in tax resources to a great extent is dictated by the movements in building tax. The building tax as a percentage of own tax revenue has increased since 1980-81. The higher share of Building Tax could be attributed to the inflow of NRI remittances and the resultant construction boom. However, the rate at which taxes are levied points to the existence of considerable laxity in tapping the potential.

Table 3.4 : Composition of Revenue Resources of Gram Panchayats in Kerala

Year	*Tax*	*Non-Tax*	*Total Own Resources*	*Tax Transfers*	*Others*	*Grants*	*Loans*	*Total*
1960-61	45.16	23.68	68.84	15.43	NA	13.79	1.95	100.00
1965-66	38.61	20.67	59.28	13.48	NA	24.42	2.83	100.00
1970-71	38.73	21.98	60.71	21.44	NA	17.07	0.78	100.00
1975-76	42.69	17.49	60.18	2.08	NA	15.74	0.00	100.00
1980-81	31.51	22.71	54.22	22.32	7.59	15.46	0.41	100.00
1985-86	37.30	20.28	57.58	23.15	4.52	14.33	0.42	100.00
1990-91	29.22	21.00	50.22	13.50	4.50	29.53	0.34	100.00
1991-92	32.46	19.54	52.00	13.50	4.49	30.01	0.00	100.00
1992-93	28.06	18.18	46.24	15.38	4.01	29.81	0.06	100.00
1993-94	29.10	18.44	47.53	18.58	4.01	29.81	0.06	100.00
1994-95	32.67	19.66	52.33	16.80	4.89	25.56	0.41	100.00

Source: Computed from Administrative Reports of Panchayats, Directorate of Panchayat, Government of Kerala (Various Issues).

Table 3.5 : Composition of Tax Resources of Rural Local Bodies in Kerala

Year	*Building Tax*	*Professional Tax*	*Entertainment*	*Others*	*Own Tax*
1970-71	55.11	25.36	11.78	7.76	100.00
1975-76	36.05	23.45	12.80	27.70	100.00
1980-81	42.21	23.97	17.69	16.13	100.00
1985-86	44.71	27.74	14.62	12.94	100.00
1990-91	49.42	27.56	13.77	9.26	100.00
1991-92	50.42	31.50	9.65	8.43	100.00
1992-93	48.20	31.77	10.78	9.25	100.00
1993-94	52.84	28.25	9.76	9.15	100.00
1994-95	53.23	28.39	9.13	9.26	100.00

Source: Computed from Administrative Reports of Panchayats, Directorate of Panchayat Government of Kerala (Various Issues).

The rate of building tax is fixed by the Panchayats within the statutory limits set by the Government. The LSGIs had shown a tendency to fix the rates at the minimum levels. The Naha Commission had pointed out that out of the 1001 Panchayats then existing, around 703 were levying tax at the minimum rate of 6 per cent. Table 3.6 gives the distribution of Panchayats according to the rate of building tax. The report of the KSFC also reiterated the other deficiencies in the system like, large number of exceptions (by extending the concept of huts to the undeserving) and artificial restrictions. The estimated rental value, in the absence of a well developed rental market, is often arbitrary and not disclosed to the tax authorities.

Table 3.6 : Rate of Building Tax

Rate of Building Tax	*Year*	
	1985	1995
6	703 (70.2)	546 (56.3)
7	94 (9.4)	120 (12.4)
7.5	4 (0.4)	—
8	155 (15.5)	217 (22.4)
9	12 (1.2)	42 (4.3)
10	33 (3.3)	454 (4.6)

Source: Final Report, First SFC, 1997.

Profession Tax is the second most important component of tax resources. The tax share varied from 21 to 32 per cent. The full potential of this tax is yet to be realised. Major obstacle in the way of resource mobilisation was the absence of comprehensive list of assessees with the result that many escape the tax net. Too many slabs were also a stumbling block in the smooth execution of tax collection.

Entertainment tax, which is usually a State-tax is the prerogative of LSGIs in Kerala and ranks third position among the tax resources. This tax had the maximum share in 1977-78 when its share rose to 18.8 per cent. Since then it has been showing a gradual decline, reaching less than 10 per cent in mid-1990s. Like other sources of revenue this tax also suffers from under assessment. An estimation of potential tax at the lowest level of tax rate, by the SFC has brought out the abysmally small tax effort. Instances of tax rate even below the statutory minimum was also pointed out.

Apart from the above, the Panchayats in Kerala mobilise resources from a large number of minor taxes like show tax, surcharge on Show Tax, Service Taxes like Sanitary Tax, Water Tax, Lighting Tax, Drainage Tax, Vehicle Tax, Vessels Tax, Land Cess, Land Conversion Tax etc. Many of these sources are not exploited by most of the Panchayats. Proportion of Panchayats imposing these taxes in 1994-95 is given in the Table 3.7 below.

Table 3.7 : Tax Proportions of Panchayats

Service Tax	*Sanitary*	*Water Tax*	*Lighting Tax*	*Drainage*	*Show Tax*	*Advertisement Tax*	*Land Cess*	*Tax on Vessels*
1.79	8.11	4.74	11.89	1.05	76.84	33.26	3.47	4.42

Source: Final Report, SFC, 1997.

Non-Tax Revenue

Non-Tax revenue especially the long array of licence fees under the purview of LSGIs was a potential source of revenue. Licence fees, income from properties, fines, penalties, sale proceeds of trees, usufruct, river sand etc. form the non-tax revenue of the Panchayats. Composition of non-tax revenue is given in Table 3.8. Though miscellaneous income constitutes the highest source of revenue, more disaggregated details of this clubbed income is not available. It has been pointed out that there is good scope for improving the revenue from properties and licence fees. Quite a large number of license fees are underutilised and lack uniformity across Panchayats.

Tax Transfers

Tax transfers (duty on transfer of property) and Basic Tax (assigned tax) formed quite a substantial source of revenue for the rural LSGIs. The share rose from 16 per cent in 1960-61 to 27 per cent in 1987-88.

Table 3.8 : Composition of Non-tax Revenue

Year	*Property Income*	*Licence Fee*	*Miscellaneous*	*Total*
1970-71	17.65	8.78	73.56	100.00
1975-76	17.12	11.68	71.20	100.00
1980-81	11.20	5.89	82.90	100.00
1985-86	11.15	5.78	83.07	100.00
1990-91	7.57	3.77	88.66	100.00
1991-92	8.57	4.88	86.55	100.00
1992-93	8.30	9.55	82.15	100.00
1993-94	8.32	6.44	85.25	100.00
1994-95	7.99	4.32	87.69	100.00

Source: Computed from Administrative Reports of Panchayats, Directorate of Panchayat Government of Kerala (Various Issues).

Since then the share declined to 16 per cent in 1994-95 (see Table 3.4). Though in absolute amount the contribution from this source had increased, this has not corresponded to the increase in the value of property transferred. There is widespread under- valuation of property and avoidance of Stamp Duty through the devise of transferring effective ownership through the device of power of attorney (GoK, 1996). Another reason for the decline from this source is the avoidance of arrears by the Government of Kerala (GoK). Until 1987-88 the receipts from this source was exhibited in the State Budget and released to the local bodies through the Inspector General of Registration, during the corresponding financial year. The system was changed leading to huge arrears and the amounts were retained with the GoK themselves.

Grants

As for grants, though their share had been lower than own revenue all throughout, the share tended to increase by the early 90s (see Table 3.4). The introduction of untied grants would have contributed to this increase.

The grant-in-aid are broadly of two types–Specific Purpose and General Purpose. A remarkable feature of the grant-in-aid to the LSGIs has wide fluctuations in the amount of grants from year to year. This erratic behaviour is largely explained by the absence of any well conceived grant-in-aid policy by the State government. Arrears are often allowed to accumulate under different heads which are paid out in a lump sum periodically.

Inter-Panchayat Variations in Own Resource Mobilisation

A regression analysis by Lekha (1997) had revealed that the local tax income is highly correlated to changes in SDP and price. This is primarily because of the sensitivity of local property tax to changes in income and price. The estimated nominal income elasticity of local tax revenue and local property tax revenue was also found to be more than unity.

Table 3.9: Inter-Panchayat Variation in the Per Capita Revenue from Important Own Revenue Sources

	1994	
	Mean	*Coefficient of Variation*
Own Tax	17.15	68.15
Building Tax	5.67	144.46
Profession Tax	8.97	62.95
Entertainment Tax	4.92	103.01
Non-Tax	1.45	236.53
Licence Fee	0.62	202.47
Income from Property	3.53	173.42
Miscellaneous	1.36	306.64

Here we shall attempt a cross-section analysis of the inter-panchayat variations in own resource mobilisation effort. Table 3.9 gives the inter-panchayat difference in the per capita revenue from important own revenue sources. As is evident there exists a high degree of variation between the per capita revenue from various sources between Panchayats. What factors could account for these differences.

Tax or revenue mobilisation is determined by the tax capacity of a Panchayat and the tax effort made in utilising the capacity. Regression analysis attempts to examine the influence of various indicators of resource capacity on resource mobilisation. But a regression analysis will not measure the tax effort fully. The residual is usually assumed to be the tax effort. The resource capacity includes the various indicators of economic development, infrastructure development etc. The level of literacy and participation in Gram Sabha could be important determinants of resources that could be mobilised from the people. In addition we also use regional dummy variables to capture inter-regional variation in resource mobilisation. Table 3.10 describes the variables used in the analysis.

Table 3.10 : Definition of Independent Variables

Sl. No	*Variable*	*Description of Variables*
1 (Economic)	Index of Agricultural Development	Yd=WiYid Where Yid=XidMinXid/MaxXid-Min Where Xid = Productivity of crops at block level Wi = Proportion of area under crop in the gross cropped area sown under crop
	MPSOH	Organised Sector Employment
2	Index of Road Development	Length of metalled road/square kilometre
4	Housing	Number of concrete houses
3 (Social)	Literacy Rate	Proportion of literates in total population
4	Backwardness	Total Agricultural Population
4	Dummies for each region except Malabar	Concerned district =1 and rest=0
	Population	Total population of the Panchayat
G	Own Fund	The non-Plan own fund for the year 1994-95

Ordinary Least Square Semi-Log regression was used to examine the inter-Panchayat variation in own revenue mobilisation. Table 3.11 summarises the results. It could be noted that the adjusted Assigned tax is only 22. Economic development indicators like the proportion of organised secior employment and type of building have a positive influence on resource mobilisation. However, the index of agricultural development has an inverse relationship to the revenue mobilisation. This might be due to the fact that the presence of a tax based on directly on agricultural income is meagre in the resource structure of local bodies. The significant dummy variable points to the better performance of all regions in Kerala over the north Malabar region. The same pattern of influence is reflected in the case of Tax revenue determination. However, non-tax shows a different pattern of influence. Most of the economic variables are found to be non-significant in the case of non-tax resources. This points to the lower resource effort for non-tax resources. This in turn points to the fact that economically developed Panchayats are mobilising relatively higher own revenue. Generally grants are expected to have a dampening effect on the revenue mobilisation. District level analysis of the Panchayats has indicated the possible existence of such a relationship (Rajaraman, 2000). However, our analysis of the early 1990s has not proved this hypothesis. The coefficients of grants are not significant. A regression of grants on various independent variables does not bear any relation to the economic development variables which points to the absence of a well defined grants-in aid policy.

Table 3.11 : Results of the Ordinary Least Square Regression Analysis

Dependent Variables	*Own revenue*	*Own Tax*	*Non-Tax*
Explanatory Variables			
Constant	2.5692*	–296388	9.057
Population	0.00002*	25.26*	8.9036*
Area	0.0006*	2993.96*	0.00003*
MPSOH	0.0001*	42.8596.7*	0.0002**
Agricultural Labourers	–0.0005*	55.418*	0.4773

Contd...

Table 3.11 : *Contd.*

Dependent Variables	*Own revenue*	*Own Tax*	*Non-Tax*
Index of Agricultural Development	0.0001	–57.47*	0.0001
Grants	0.0001*	59.31*	0.0000
Share of Concrete Buildings	0.0001*	59.31*	0.0000
Literacy	–0.0015	–1477.28*	0.00017*
Dummy	–0.477*	–215685.3*	0.0101
Dummy	0.21*	102674.2*	–0.0213
Dummy	0.191*	75475.32*	0.365*
Adjusted R2	0.22	0.4099	0.1872

Dependent Variables	*Building Tax*	*Profession*	*Entertainment*
Explanatory Variables			
Constant	–11347	10.65*	73129.01
Population	7.514*	0.0003*	3.70*
Area	480.06*	0.0015*	–70.39169
MPSOH	34.828*	0.000152*	–8.500
Agricultural Labourers	–12.92*	–37.74*	–4.205
Index of Agricultural Development	12329.8*	0/006*	19012
Grants	0.049	–0.026	–.0232223
Share of Concrete Buildings	4.66*	.0005*	8.61*
Literacy	288.6	–0.0020	–1185.39*
Dummy	–119976.*	11362*	12367.09*
Dummy	49958.05*	39339*	46529.01*
Dummy	19319.14	18329*	32838*
Adjusted R2	0.423	0.312	0.133

Regressing on individual taxes like building, profession presents a similar picture. Building Tax is imposed on the rental value of buildings. Rental value depends on the nature of buildings. One can normally expect higher rental value for concrete houses. Building Tax is found to be positively related to organized sector employment. Contrary to the expectations Building Tax shows a positive relation to grants. Here again agricultural development is showing a negative relationship. Economic variables show absolutely no influences on Entertainment Tax. This may be due to low tax effort and that the tax is determined by the seating capacity of the cinema theatres and the spillover effect generated by the flow of resources to the neighbouring Panchayats or municipalities.

SECTION II

RECOMMENDATIONS OF THE STATE FINANCE COMMISSION

The Background

We have presented a brief overview of the traditional fiscal system of the LSGIs during the early 1990s. It must be stated that even before the SFC was appointed, a number of new developments had begun to change the traditional contours of local finance. The most important of these was the introduction of district councils in 1991. Their introduction was accompanied by a number of new fiscal arrangements: (a) introduction of untied fund grants to the Gram Panchayats; (b) introduction of non-statutory non-plan departmental grants for the district councils; (c) introduction of plan schemes for the district councils; and (d) transfer of many of the centrally sponsored schemes to the district councils. Even after the district councils were dismantled, the untied funds transfer continued and the other elements after disappearing from the sea reappeared again in the budget of 1996-97. By then conformity legislation under 73rd and 74th Constitutional Amendment was legislated and newly elected LSGIs under the new Acts assumed office in October 1995.

The SFC was appointed even before the passage of the conformity legislation in April 1994 with the following terms of reference:

"The Finance Commission shall review the financial position of the Panchayats and make recommendations as to:

(a) the principles which should govern

(i) the distribution between the State and the Panchayats of the net proceeds of the taxes, duties, tolls and fees leviable by the State which may be divided between them under the Constitution and the allocation between the Panchayats at all levels of their respective shares of such proceeds;

(ii) the determination of the taxes, duties, tolls and fees which may be assigned to or appropriated by the Panchayats;

(iii) the grant-in-aid to the Panchayats from the Consolidated Funds of the State;

(b) the measures needed to improve the financial positions of the Panchayats."

The same Terms of Reference *mutatis mutandis* was applicable to Finance Commission's exercise for the municipalities also.

The SFC submitted an interim report in October 1995 and its final report in February 1996. We shall first examine the recommendations of the SFC which have implications for transfer of resources from the State government to the LSGIs either through improving the yields from existing assigned taxes and enhancing the share of the LSGIs in the shared taxes or through assigning additional taxes and duties from the government. The non-plan-non-statutory grants constitutes yet another major source of resource transfer. The recommendations of the SFC with respect to the grants are taken up next. Finally, we shall take up the recommendations of the SFC for additional tax and non-tax revenues for the LSGIs and for improving the yields from the existing sources.

Assigned and Shared Taxes

In Table 3.12 we have summarised the recommendations of the SFC regarding the assigned and shared taxes and the anticipated additional yield on the basis of the SFC recommendations. In the Table 3.12 we have also noted the action taken by the government.

The most important recommendation was with reference to Motor Vehicle Tax. As per the calculations of the SFC, the Vehicle

Tax compensation and VRM dispersed to LSGIs and the arrears of VRM due to LSGIs came to 20.84 per cent and 16.69 per cent of the net collection of Vehicle Tax in 1993-94 and 1994-95 respectively. At 25 per cent of the net collection of the Motor Vehicle

Table 3.12 : SFC recommendations on Assigned and Shared Taxes

Name of Tax	*Recommendation*	*Anticipated increase during 1996-97 as per recommendation of SFC (rupees crores)*	*Action taken by State government*
Improving the Yield from the existing Assigned/Shared Taxes			
Duty on Transfer of Property	No increase in rate. But a new system of notifying prices of land taking into consideration the views and comments of LSGIs to be introduced in order to prevent under evaluation	—	Accepted
Basic Tax	Doubling of rate and introduction of minimum amount irrespective of holding size	12.5	Implemented in July 1998
Motor Vehicle Tax	Merger of VRM grant with MVT and increase in the share to 25%	22.6	Implemented with modification on April 1998. The share was limited to 20%
New Assigned Taxes			
Building Tax	One time on new buildings	7.0	Accepted
Stamp sale	50% of net collection	3.5	Accepted
Building Exemption fee	50% share	1.3	Accepted, however the practice of giving exemptions have been abolished

tax the LSGIs would have received an additional amount of Rs. 5.38 crores in 1993-94 and Rs.13.34 crores in 1994-95. The calculation of the SFC is that its recommendation would have fetched an additional income of Rs. 22.6 crores for the LSGIs in 1996-97.

The actual receipts of the LSGIs from the Assigned Taxes and Shared Taxes in 1996-97 was Rs. 100.85 crores. As per the calculation of the SFC implementation of its recommendations would have resulted in a total additional income of Rs. 46.9 crores.

75 per cent of the surcharge on duty of transfer of property collected from Panchayats was distributed among Gram Panchayats in proportion to the population while the distribution of the remaining 25 per cent was left to the discretion of the State government. The SFC recommended that the 25 per cent of the surcharge collection from rural areas and urban areas should be put into separate common pools to be distributed to promote horizontal equities among the LSGIs. The enhanced Basic Tax was to be shared with the broken District Panchayats.

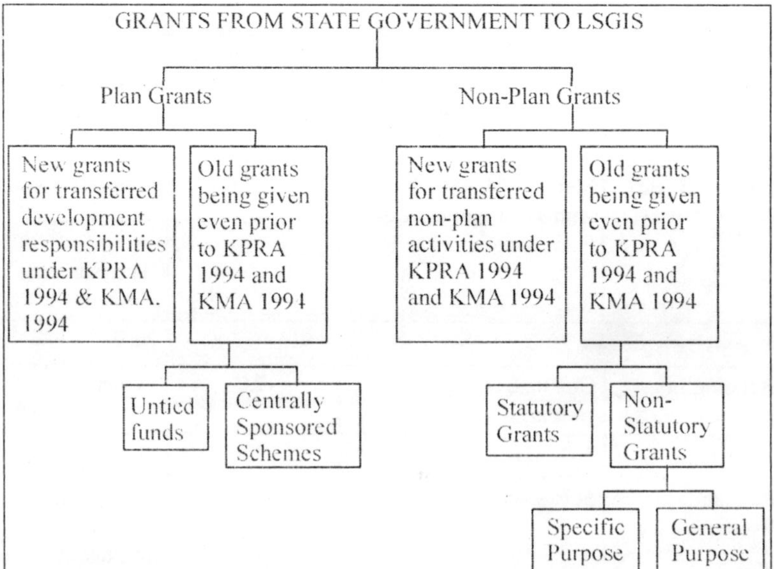

Note: KPRA 1994: Kerala Panchayati Raj Act, 1994 and KMA 1994 : Kerala Municipal Act 1994.

Even before the enactment of the new Acts, as we have already noted, under the Plan account a limited untied fund and centrally sponsored schemes were devolved to the LSGIs. In 1996-97 budget the untied funds were substantially enhanced to Rs. 212 crores. Besides, a number of plan schemes with an outlay of Rs. 117 crores were also earmarked to the LSGIs. The SFC confined its recommendations to the principles to be followed in distributing future plan funds between different tiers of LSGIs and also for intra-tier distribution. The SFC ratified the criteria for inter-tier distribution given in the budget document, viz. 55.82 per cent for Gram Panchayat, 14.33 per cent to Block Panchayat, 14.93 per cent to District Panchayat and 5.64 per cent to municipalities and 2.17 per cent to corporations. As for the future pattern of *inter se* distribution within different groups of LSGIs, it recommended the following criteria for devolution.

Table 3.13 : Criteria for Devolution of Plan Grants

Indicator	*For Urban LSGIs*	*For Rural LSGIs*
(i) Population in 1991 Census	75	70
(ii) Population of SC/ST in 1991 Census	10	10
(iii) Total workers excluding workers in manufacturing, processing, servicing and repairs outside household industry	15	10
(iv) Proportion of agricultural workers among workers	Nil	10
Total	100	100

The SFC, however, skirted the responsibility of examining the proportion of Plan funds that might be devolved to the LSGIs. It did collect information from the State Planning Board on the expenditure incurred by the government during 1991 to 1994-95 for functions which since then was assigned to LSGIs under the new Acts. The share of State plan outlay which were functional related to the LSGIs was estimated to range between 16.7 per cent of the total plan outlay in 1992-93 to 18.7 per cent in 1994-95. Yet, the SFC preferred to leave the determination of the future share of Plan grants to the LSGIs to the judgement of the planning authorities.

With respect to non-Plan grants, the enactment of the new acts had resulted in the transfer of large number of institutions and functionaries to the LSGIs and consequently substantial devolution of funds from different departments related to the upkeep and maintenance of the institutions and some of the mandatory functions. We shall be presenting more details of this new genus of non-Plan grants in the next section. However, the SFC decided to confine its recommendations to the traditional non-Plan grants about which we have already discussed in the previous section.

Table 3.14 : SFC Recommendations regarding Own Tax Revenues of LSGIs

Name of Tax	*Recommendation*	*Anticipated increase during 1996-97 as per recommendation of SFC (rupees crores)*	*Action taken by State government*
Improving the Yield from the existing Assigned/Shared Taxes			
Property Tax	Instead of Rental value, plinth area to be adopted as the basis for levying building tax for residential houses. Additional surcharge of 25 per cent to be hosted on rented out buildings. A minimum property tax of Rs. 15 in panchayats, Rs. 20 in municipalities and Rs. 25 in Corporations. Penal interest rate of 2 per cent per annum to be introduced on arrears payable to LSGIs	1.25	Accepted and provisions in the Act modified. All buildings to be assessed on the basis of plinth area, taking also into account the importance of locality, type of building and usage. Minimum amount have also been provided for in the Act.
Profession Tax	Persons other than salary and wage earners may be levied in flat rates and rates of	0.8	Accepted

Contd. ...

Table 3.14 : *Contd.*

Name of Tax	*Recommendation*	*Anticipated increase during 1996-97 as per recommendation of SFC (rupees crores)*	*Action taken by State government*
	professional tax in urban and rural LSGIs to be made uniform		
Entertainment Tax	Option for levying tax on the basis of setting capacity to be given to LSGIs. Entertainment Tax and additional Entertainment tax to be merged.	0.33	Accepted
Advertisement Tax	Government to fix minimum amount		Accepted
Tax on Sale of Land	Instead of land cess, a tax on sale of land from land owners at the time of sale of property to be introduced	8	Accepted
Licence Tax	Rates of fees to be revised taking into account the inflation. Only minimum rate to be specified and fixing of rates to be left to the LSGIs		Revised in 1996
Additional Tax and Non-Tax Revenue			
Tax on Cable TV Operation	Licence Fee and Entertainment Tax	0.1	Accepted
Tax on Immovable Property	District Panchayat may levy tax on the sale price of all immovable properties above Rs. 25000 @ 1 per cent.		Rejected

The non-statutory non-Plan grants that were actually disbursed constituted 0.33 per cent of State revenues during 1993-94 and 1994-95 after excluding the statutory transfers. The SFC noted that the specific purpose grants were often used for purposes other than prescribed and also there could be no effective mechanism to ensure compliance. There were as many as 23 different grants many of which were redundant. Therefore, the SFC recommended that the non-statutory non-Plan grants given for traditional functions may be fixed at 1 per cent of the State revenue and may be distributed between urban and rural LSGIs in proportion to their population. In calculating the State revenue the tax transfer and statutory grants to the LSGIs were to be excluded.

The above general purpose grant of 1 per cent of the revenue were to constitute the core of the rural and urban pools. In the rural pool 25 per cent of the basic tax and surcharge or stamp duty from the rural areas were to be included. 100 per cent of the basic tax and 25 per cent surcharge on stamp duty were to be included in the urban pool. It was estimated that in 1996 the rural pool would amount to Rs. 37.81 crores and urban pool 5.93 crores. The SFC also recommended the criteria for the distribution of rural and urban pools among Village Panchayat and municipalities. Weightage of 75 per cent and 85 per cent were given for population for devolution from rural and urban pools respectively. SC/ST population and tax effort of LSGIs received a weightage of 5 per cent each. The financial need of the LSGIs were also to be given consideration. The recommendation for general purpose grant of 1 per cent was not acceptable to the government.

As we have already seen in the previous section there is substantial scope for improving the yield from the existing own revenue sources of the LSGIs in Kerala. The SFC paid detailed attention to this aspect and came out with a number of proposals for increasing the yield from the existing sources, which are summarised in Table 3.14. The additional income for the LSGIs expected from the implementation of the above recommendations for changes in the rates or norms were estimated to yield more than Rs. 10 crores in 1996-97.

Maintenance Grant

An important area that received considerable attention from the SFC was the maintenance grants for buildings and roads transferred to LSGIs. The existing norms for buildings has been fixed in 1977 and the buildings were categorised into those built before and after 1996 with the former receiving a slightly higher rate on capital cost for maintenance. For ordinary buildings the former received 3 per cent of the capital cost and the latter 2 per cent of the capital cost measured in historical term. The SFC was able to really prove that the maintenance norms for buildings and the grants devolved for this purpose felt short of requirements. It prescribed that the maintenance grant should be fixed as a percentage to current cost of construction which would have resulted in substantial step-up of funds for maintenance of the buildings. Government rejected the recommendation. The Commission also recommended that since its norms were at 1992-93 price levels, a suitable price escalation needs to be applied to the norms periodically. It was also rejected by the government.

The SFC also undertook detailed calculation of the role maintenance requirements of the LSGIs. It identified a gap of Rs. 72 crores for maintenance of roads at normative levels after taking into consideration VTC and VRM grants and expenditure from the own funds of the LSGIs. The Commission recommended that 50 per cent of the gap was to be met by fund from centrally sponsored schemes and the remaining from the Government of Kerala. The recommendation was accepted.

SECTION III

THE POST-STATE FINANCE COMMISSION SCENARIO

Within a few months of submission of the final report of the SFC the basic parameters of the decentralisation process in the State underwent dramatic changes in a manner nobody could have foreseen. A new government led by the Left Democratic Front assumed power in May 1996. One of the first major decisions of the new government was to earmark 35-40 per cent of the outlay of the Ninth Five Year Plan (which was to start from 1997-98) for financing the local Plans drawn up by the Local Bodies. In the budget of 1996-97, a total of Rs. 329 crores had been earmarked for the local bodies, Rs. 212 crores in the nature of untied funds and Rs. 117 crores in the form of State sponsored schemes. In 1997-98, the first year of the Ninth Plan, the plan devolution for the Local Bodies increased to Rs. 1025.4 crores of which Rs. 749 crores was in the form of untied grants and the rest as State sponsored schemes. The progress of the funds from the State plan during the subsequent years may be seen in Table 3.15.

Table 3.15 : Devolution of Funds from the State Plan to the Local Bodies

Year	*Annual Plan Outlay*	*Untied Fund*	*Plan Grant-in-Aid*	*State Sponsored Schemes*	*Total*	*% (6 to 2)*
(1)	(2)	(3)	(4)	(5)	(6)	(7)
1990-91	635	18	—	—	18	2.83
1991-92*	807	19	—	91.64	110.34	13.67
1992-93	913	20	—	—	20.00	2.19
1993-94	1003	21	—	—	21.00	2.10
1994-95	1260	29	—	—	29.00	2.30
1995-96	1550	30	—	—	30.00	1.99
1996-97	2200	212	—	117.41	329.41	14.98
1997-98	2855	—	749	276.37	1024.37	35.91
1998-99	3100	—	950	166.50	1116.50	36.01
1999-2000	3250	—	1020	134.40	1154.40	35.52
2000-2001	3535	—	1045	224.21	1269.21	35.91

*Budget passed by LDF Government

Some of the salient features of the Plan devolution scheme adopted in Kerala may be noted. First is the magnitude of devolution. As can be seen from the Table the devolution from the Plan during 1990-91 to 1996-97 was limited to meagre untied funds that averaged Rs. 22.83 crores per annum. The provision of Rs. 91.6 crores as State sponsored schemes for the LSGIs provided in the budget of 1991-92 by the Left Democratic Front was discontinued by the new government that assumed power soon after the start of the financial year. Even in relation to the total resources available to the local bodies including their own resources and the non-Plan transfers from the State government, the additional Plan resources made available made a dramatic impact. As a result of the Plan devolution the ratio of expenditure of the Local Bodies to the total expenditure of the State government increased to 16 per cent in

1998-99. It is also to be noted that the entire salaries and allowances of the staff transferred to the Local Self Governments continued to be shouldered by the State government. No salary could be paid from the Plan funds. Therefore, the financial capability of the Local Self Governments for undertaking new development activities is much higher than is apparent from the formal increase in total resources.

A second feature of the Plan devolution has been the autonomy that it ensured for the Local Self Governments in drawing up projects and programmes. As can be seen from Table 3.15, 73 per cent of the funds devolved was in the form of untied grants in 1997 -98. The ratio rose to around 85-88 per cent in the subsequent years. In other States which have taken steps to decentralise the planning process, the devolution was schematic which seriously constraints the freedom of the local bodies. The major condition stipulated in Kerala has been that the LSGIs should prepare a comprehensive area plan for the plan grant-in-aid they are entitled to and then have it approved by the District Planning Committee before they can stake claim to their entitlement. Procedures were laid down to ensure that the planning process was participatory and transparent. The LSGIs could prepare any project or programme within the broad domain of their functions and in tune with their capability. Certain guidelines were also issued on sectoral allocation and the maximum amount of subsidy that could be given. The sectoral guidelines infringed, very little on the local autonomy as they were kept to a bare minimum to ensure certain overall coordination with the State plan targets. The LSGIs had to spent at least 40 per cent of their grant-in-aid on the material production sectors and could not spend more than 30 per cent on roads. Even with regard to these restrictions, relaxations were made for urban areas and for Special Component Plan and Tribal Sub-Plan.

A third point is that the arbitrariness that used to characterise the grant-in-aid system in Kerala was done away within the Plan devolution scheme. Transparent and objective criteria were adopted. First, the Plan funds were allotted to the urban and rural Local Bodies in the ratio of the population. Next, the grant-in-aid for the rural Local Bodies was allocated among the different tiers, for which different norms were adopted for TSP, SCP and General Sector Plan. The General Sector allocation was distributed to the Gram Panchayats, Block Panchayats and District Panchayats in the ratio 70 : 15 : 15. For the SCP, a higher allocation of 20 per cent of each was made to the Block and District Panchayats. For the TSP it was decided that given the present social reality in the tribal areas—weakness of the tribal movements, organised trend of the settlers, and past experience—the major share of the TSP should be with the District Panchayats. The allocation for the district was 60 per cent, and 20 per cent each for the Gram and Block Panchayats.

Reliance on population criteria alone for devolution of funds does not satisfy equity norms. The importance of a composite criterion taking into account the backwardness and the geographical area of the locality was officially accepted. The major stumbling Block lay in the absence of sufficient data at the Gram Panchayat level for an objective assessment of the degree of backwardness. Despite its limitations, an important reason for adopting an objective criterion such as population was that allegations of political favouritism could be avoided. A controversy over favouritism would have destabilised the fragile unity that has been built up during the campaign.

The details of the funds earmarked to Panchayati Raj and municipal institutions are provided as a separate volume (Appendix 4 of the budget documents). This annexure clearly spelt out the provisions of schemes (both Plan and non-Plan) that had been transferred to the local bodies and the share of different tiers of Local Bodies in the schemes. More importantly, it clearly stated the General Sector, SCP and TSP grant-in-aid provided to each individual Local Body in the State.

On the experience of the previous year's Plan formulation certain modifications were made with regard to the criteria for devolution. As in the past year, 15 per cent of the Plan grant under general sector was earmarked for the municipalities and corporations. The provision for the rural areas again apportioned in the ratio of 70 : 15 : 15 between Gram Panchayats, Block Panchayats and District Panchayats respectively. In the previous year the intra-tier distribution was entirely based upon the population criterion. But for the year 1998-99 the intra-tier distribution was made on the basis of formulae that took into acccunt not only population but also the relative backwardness of the locality and some of the other relevant factors. The criteria and their corresponding weights in the distribution formula for different local bodies are given in Table 3.16.

In the distribution of Plan grant under SCP and TSP, higher weight was given to rural population. The Plan grant was apportioned to the three tiers of panchayats and municipalities/corporations in the ratio of 1 : 25 : 1; the share for the three tiers of Panchayats, was again divided in the ratio of 60 : 20 : 20 to Gram Panchayats, Block Panchayats and District Panchayats respectively. In the case of TSP, the intra-tier distribution formula was modified. The share for three tiers of panchayats was divided in the ratio of 40 : 20 : 20 to Gram Panchayats, Block Panchayats and District Panchayats, respectively. Allocation of Plan grant under SCP and TSP among the Gram Panchayats, Block Panchayats, District Panchayats and municipalities/corporations was purely based on the population of Scheduled Castes and Scheduled Tribes of the respective Local Bodies.

Table 3.16 : Criteria for intra-tier distribution of Plan grant-in-aid

Indicators	*Weightage*			
	Gram Panchayat	Block Panchayat	District Panchayat	Municipalities/ Corporations
Population (excluding SC/ST)	65	65	55	75
Geographical area excluding	—	—	—	—
Area under forests	5	10	15	6
Area under paddy	5	—	—	—
Own income of Gram Panchayat	10	—	—	—
Composite index of agricultural labourers, persons engaged in livestock, fisheries etc., and marginal workers	15	25	20	—
Composite index of back-wardness houses without latrine and houses without electricity	—	—	10	20

Finally, the Plan devolution scheme in a sense was a sharp departure from the approach of the SFC. The approach of the SFC, which was inevitable, given the terms of reference, consisted of first determining the functions, institutions and personnel that had been devolved and then working out the financial requirements given the level of decentralisation. It distinguished between (a) traditional function and responsibilities of Local Bodies and (b) additional developmental responsibilities after the passage of 73rd and 74th Amendments. Its view has been that while the traditional functions may be financed through modifications of the traditional grants, tax share and own resources of Local Bodies, new responsibilities require additional Plan and non-Plan devolution from the State government. The SFC has confined itself to the traditional own resources and transferred resources of the local bodies. As regards to the new functions, its recommendations have been confined to maintenance of old assets transferred to the local bodies and new assets created by them. Determination of financial requirement of new responsibilities would depend very much upon the subjective interpretation, given the broad terms in which subject matters have been defined in the law. Therefore, it restricted its recommendations to the financial requirements of maintenance of assets which could be objectively identified. Finance was to follow functional and administrative decentralisation. However, in the Plan devolution scheme adopted by the new State government, finance was leading the process of decentralisation.

Financial devolution in Kerala is being used as an instrument to bring about a functional division of labour between the State government and the LSGIs. The formal functional distribution of power between the State government and the Local Bodies, in the Panchayati Raj and Municipal Acts, is according to subject areas rather than in terms of definite activities. This can lead to considerable overlap and duplication in a devolution scheme that gives full autonomy to LSGIs. Negotiation of schematic or activity-wise demarcation of functions would see the rational course of action in such a situation. But it would be very difficult and time consuming due to resistance from the line departments. Instead of going through the above route, the LSGIs were given the autonomy to formulate any project they could take up within their capabilities even at the risk of some duplication in the initial years. Sooner or later, given the resource crunch consequent to large-scale devolution, the State government departments would give up schemes and programmes that the LSGIs take up. A new equilibrium would thus be reached.

Preparation of the local Plans was central to the devolution scheme. Planning is a technical process that involves assessment of needs and resources, fixing of priorities, preparation of projects and formulation of Plans. But in the case of the decentralisation experiment in Kerala, the process of planning has been much more than a technical exercise. It was used as an instrument for social mobilisation in support of decentralisation. The mass mobilisation was intended to ensure that correct decisions were made at the local level, to bring about certain attitudinal changes among participants and to build up mass pressure from below for democratic reforms. The above experiment in democratic decentralisation popularly known as People's Planning Campaign has attracted world-wide attention for its innovativeness and fairly successful outcome in terms of physical achievements, generation of new development culture and successful institutionalisation.

Devolution of Departmental Schemes

We have been so far largely discussing the devolution of untied Plan grant-in-aid to the Local Bodies. We had also noted that part of the Plan devolution was in the form of schemes drawn up by the departments, but implemented through the Local Self Governments. These are known as State Sponsored Schemes. Similarly, the Centrally Sponsored Schemes are also been devolved to the local bodies. It may be noted that only the State contribution to the Centrally Sponsored Schemes are formally included in the State Plan outlay. Therefore, the Central Government contribution is an additionality to the Plan funds received by the Local Self Governments.

The SFC had considered the issue of Centrally Sponsored Programmes and decided against going into the details of this component because "its quantum and purposes for which it can be used are heterogeneously determined". Yet it recommended that 25 per cent of the funds for various Centrally Sponsored Programmes for poverty alleviation should be at the disposal of the Local Bodies to be spend on poverty alleviation programmes formulated by Local Bodies and approved by the District Planning Committee (DPC). Under People's Planning Campaign the entire Centrally Sponsored Programmes have to be integrated with the local plan and approved by the DPC. DRDA has been merged with the District Panchayat to ensure that there are no parallel structure working at cross purpose.

Yet another important development of the post-SFC period has been the emergence of non-Plan grants which are different from the traditional non-Plan grants received by the Local Bodies. These are assistance to Local Bodies for specific purposes provided by the departments for transferred schemes and institutions. The norms for specific schemes are to be worked out and the entitlement of each individual Local Body determined by the concerned departments. The concerned heads of department either directly or through district officers transfer these funds to the local bodies. Table 3.17 gives the trend in these non-Plan transfers from 1967-68 onwards.

Table 3.17 : Departmental Non-Plan Grants to Local Bodies

Year	*Gram Panchayat*	*Block Panchayat*	*District Panchayat*	*Municipalities*	*Corporations*	*Total*
1996-97	50.51	8.31	47.57	37.85	6.95	151.22
1997-98	53.77	15.09	55.44	47.05	6.58	177.94
1998-99	71.85	15.83	69.76	62.53	9.02	229.23
1999-2000	72.21	15.92	73.18	72.00	10.07	243.39
2000-2001	173.25	16.15	34.96	22.16	7.11	253.63

To sum up, the immediate post-SFC period witnessed substantial additions to the resources of the LSGIs from sources that had not been taken up by the SFC such as Plan funds, non-Plan departmental schemes, Centrally and State Sponsored Schemes and also institutional loans. The additional resources have far exceeded the anticipated additional yield from SFC recommendations. The anticipated yield during 1996-97 on the basis of the recommendations of the State Finance Commission given in Tables 3.12 and 3.14 was estimated to be Rs. 76.61 crores. On the other hand the additional resources from the non-Plan departmental schemes alone works out to be Rs. 151.22 crores for the year 1996-97. The non-Plan grants from the departments has steadily increased to Rs. 253 crores in 2000-2001. A substantial part of it was for maintenance and repair of physical assets which substantially compensates the loss of non-Plan revenue by the Local Self Governments consequent upon the refusal of the State government to accept the recommendation for using current construction cost instead of the historical cost for determining maintenance charges. It may also be noted that upto 10 per cent of the plan funds could be utilised for major one time repairs of assets by preparing appropriate projects.

The enormous additional resources made available to the Local Self Governments from outside the SFC sources would explain to a large extent the surprisingly niggardly approach adopted by the State government with respect to SFC recommendations. The share of MVT was reduced from the recommended 25 to 20 per cent. The recommendation of non-statutory non-Plan grant of 1 per cent of the total revenue was not accepted and the suggestion for maintenance as a percentage of current cost of construction was rejected. The scale of devolution as part of People's Planning Campaign lad been carried out "even at the risk of leaving the State government impoverished of funds to attend to its own functions" (Memorandum submitted to the Eleventh Finance Commission by Government of Kerala).

What we would like to emphasise is that it is important to look beyond the recommendation of SFC and the action taken thereon in order to get a comprehensive picture of the nature of financial devolution and the process of decentralisation. However, the Eleventh Finance Commission has proved to be particularly myopic with its insistence that "any devolution made by a State for the Panchayats and municipalities over and above the recommendations of the State Finance Commission is outside the purview of our consideration". Therefore the Commission did not find "adequate justification in the demand that a certain percentage of the funds transferred by the States to the Panchayats and municipalities be provided by the Finance Commission".

The lopsided Central-State fiscal relation is proving to be a major stumbling block for a genuine decentralisation process. The fiscal crisis of the State government is already having its adverse impact on the decentralization programme in the State. The Constitution casts a duty on Government of India as much as it does on State governments to meet its share of resource needs of Local Bodies.

Concluding Remarks

We have analysed the recommendations of the First Finance Commission of Kerala State. Its recommendations address some of the major issues of local finance that we had identified in our opening section. We saw that Kerala traditionally enjoyed high level of fiscal autonomy and, therefore, there was very little that the Finance Commission could do by way of enhancing the revenue raising powers of the Local Self Governments. However, taking into account the untapped local resource potential, the SFC made a number of recommendations to enhance the yield from the existing sources. It attempted to remove the arbitrariness in the pattern of fiscal transfers from the State government to the local bodies by laying down criteria for horizontal of the transfer of funds. Its recommendations included proposals for improvement of yields from the existing assigned taxes and assignment of additional taxes and duties. The SFC also argued for rationalisation and enhancement of the non-Plan non-statutory grants and maintenance grants. However, even full implementation of the SFC recommendations would not have a fundamental change with regard to the fiscal status of the Local Self Governments. The new functions and responsibilities assigned to the Local Self Governments by the 73rd and 74th Constitutional amendments required Additional resources in lieu of the State government's non-traditional sources. Such a decision-making process would necessarily have to be political.

The devolution of additional resources commensurate with the developmental planning responsibilities and maintenance of transferred institutions and schemes came from the side of the arena of SFC. We discussed in fair detail the financial devolution aspect of People's Campaign, their significance and implications. However, such a recourse through channels outside SFC concentrating on Plan devolution have given rise to a number of issues which would have to be tackled in future. We shall conclude this article listing some of these issues.

How can the Plan devolution statutory backing? We have seen how the Plan devolution introduced in 1991-92 was scrapped with a change in the State government. It can be achieved only through making the devolution a part of the statutory devolution scheme drawn up by the SFC.

Transfer of large number of assets and creation of new assets through local plans creating a tremendous pressure on the Local bodies for maintenance and repairing expenditure. Thus for example during the first three years of the People's Planning Campaign 3,51,699.17 sq. metres of public buildings and 17,188 kms of roads have been built. The non-Plan grants for transferred institutions and schemes even by the departments proved to be grossly inadequate to meet the recurring expenditures and maintenance assets. There is a severe mismatch between the Plan and non-Plan devolution. This is issue that calls for urgent rectification.

The impact of large-scale devolution of united funds on local resource mobilisation is an issue that is much debated within the People's Planning Campaign. On the one hand has been remarkable local resource mobilisation by way of voluntary labour, donations and beneficiary contributions while implementing projects and programmes through people's committees. However, the buoyancy of traditional tax and non-tax revenues is suspected to have come down. This is partly due to the heavy workload on limited staff who have to shoulder the responsibilities of Plan implementation as the employment of staff from other departments has not yet been completed. A heavy load has adverse impact on the tax collection. An important issue in this context is to link the plan fund devolution through an incentive criteria for additional own resource mobilisation.

The people's participation in Plan formulation and implementation has proved to be effective. How can people be involved in the resource mobilization process? Can the Gram Sabhas and the neighbourhood groups be linked to the process of identification of assessment and monitoring of the tax collection?

4

INTERNAL RESOURCE MOBILISATION BY PANCHAYATS: THE CASE OF MADHYA PRADESH

S.K. SINGH

This article seeks to examine and review various aspects of internal resources of Panchayati Raj Institutions (PRIs). In the present context, it is difficult to comprehend a situation in which Panchayats are assured of meaningful match between their resources and responsibilities assigned in the post-73rd Constitution Amendment era. What is desirable and achievable is that the Panchayats have the financial resources and functional freedom to cater to the locally felt needs and aspirations of the people. To realise and enjoy the level of financial self-sufficiency, the Panchayats cannot depend entirely on hand-outs from the higher levels of Government; they have to generate their own resources in order to achieve local felt needs of the people. Therefore, internal resource mobilisation is an important area of in depth study to determine the financial base and requirement to provide services to the people.

Keeping this in view, a case study was conducted in the State of Madhya Pradesh to analyse data obtained from state level as well as sample District, Janpad and Village Panchayat levels from primary and secondary sources. The data was obtained from Raigarh Zilla Panchayat, two Janpad Panchayats, namely, Dharamjaygarh and Sarangarh, and four Gram Panchayats, two within one JP, namely, Kedkela, Sirisinga, Kedar and Kanakabira. This was followed by discussion with the officials and elected representatives as well as with the cross-section of the Society to ascertain their perception on critical issues of Panchayat resources. The state was taken up for in depth examination in view of the fact that this state is a relatively forward looking so far Panchayats are concerned. An attempt has been made to analyse the provisions of the State Panchayat Act and reforms taken place after the amendment.

The avenues of resources mobilisation have been examined at length by the Local Finance Commission (1951), the Taxation Review Commission (1954), the Santhanam Committee (1963) and the Ashok Mehta Committee (1978). Several recommendations have been made to improve financial situation but largely remained unheeded. Moreover, there is growing literature on the subject (Mukherjee, 2001; Rajaraman, 1996; Oomen, 1998 etc.). These studies have observed that panchayats have failed to generate sufficient resources to meet their obligations. It also suggests that financial self-sufficiency of panchayats is shrinking and there is lack of an effective political will to solve this problem.

Notwithstanding the fact that panchayats are suffering from inadequacy of resources but also they are not in a position to generate sufficient income to reach to the level of self-sufficiency. Generally, the finances of panchayats are classified into three major sources: (i) own resources, which include tax and non-tax revenue, (ii) assigned revenues, and (iii) grants-in-aid. We have examined the expenditure of panchayats to have an overview of the financial composition of panchayats. In own resource, two important components are included; they are tax and non-tax revenues. Besides, the overall trends and patterns of expenditure of panchayats have been examined so as to ascertain their fiscal needs in light of functional devolution.

Tax-Revenues

The revenue raising power is important in view of self-sufficiency and fiscal autonomy. Generally, panchayats at each level are assigned number of taxes but majority of them is not buoyant and elastic source. Besides, panchayats have several problems in tax administration. The MP Panchayat Adhiniyam, 1993 empowers panchayats to levy and collect several taxes. There is no difference between the earlier Panchayat Acts of 1981 and 1990 with the existing Act of 1993 so far the taxation powers concerned. In other words, taxes assigned to panchayats in the Pre- and Post-73rd Amendment period has not changed. By and large, the principles or consideration for taxation powers also remained the same.

Gram Panchayat

In the Act of 1993, Section 77 (along with the Schedule I, II & III) provides taxation powers to Gram Panchayat and Janpad Panchayat. These bodies are empowered with two types of taxation powers — (i) obligatory taxes and (ii) optional taxes and fees.

Statement 1.1 provides the list of taxes that Gram Panchayat can levy, it also includes both categories of tax items. Among the important obligatory taxes, Gram Panchayats are empowered to levy property tax, lighting tax and profession tax. In the optional tax items, important is vehicle tax and water tax. They are also empowered to levy other tax items for which the state legislature is empowered under the Constitution. It is clear from the list that Gram Panchayats are vested with such taxation powers and items, which are usually given to these bodies. Though it contains a long list but only few items are in operation. And even some of the compulsory taxes are not being levied due to various reasons. Moreover, some of the tax items do not have much scope and potential to raise revenue, if imposed even. The services rendered by panchayats are usually unsatisfactory, hence people are not willing to pay taxes. More so, the available infrastructure is inadequate to the extent that better delivery of services cannot be provided.

Statement 1.2 contains the rates of each tax items of gram panchayat prevailing before and after the 73rd Amendment. It can be seen that the existing rates have been enhanced from the earlier rates for all items. Thus, the scope for raising revenue has been enlarged. As the government is empowered to prescribe rates of taxable items, a pertinent issue needs consideration whether these units should be allowed to fix rates themselves or the government should prescribe minimum and maximum rates. The rates are since prescribed for all items; therefore, the autonomy of panchayats to fix rates is taken away. Among the taxes, the rates of profession tax have remarkably increased which could augment more revenues. But, in fact, very few units levy this tax and revenue mobilisation is not to the expectation.

Janpad Panchayat

Janpad Panchayat has only one compulsory tax under their domain, that is, entertainment tax. Among the optional taxes, Janpad Panchayat can levy development tax on agriculture land and additional stamp duty. The rates of entertainment tax have been prescribed under rules notified by the government. It can be seen in the Statement 1.3 that the existing rates have been doubled than the earlier, even then, it is quite low as compared to other states. This revision has taken place after thirty years. In case of development tax on agriculture land, it is rarely utilised by them although it could be a good source of income in view of modernisation taking place in the agriculture sector.

Zilla Panchayat

Zilla Panchayat in the state is not vested with any taxation power. According to the amendment of 1997 in the present Panchayat Act of 1993, Zilla Panchayat has been empowered to increase the rate of cess on land revenue to the extent of Rs.10 on every rupee of land revenue. This additional cess income will be distributed among Zilla Panchayat, Janpad Panchayat and Gram Panchayat in the ratio of 25:25:50 respectively. Surprisingly, no Zilla Panchayat has exercised this power so far and hence no income is generated. This source is still untapped.

Procedure for Levying Tax or Fee

The following procedure is to be maintained before imposing tax by Gram Panchayat.

(i) A resolution has to be passed for the rate at which the tax or fee is to be imposed.
(ii) The rates so fixed have to be notified to the public by drumbeats or affixing notice at conspicuous place.
(iii) After considering objections/suggestions, rates finally decided will have to be again notified.

As seen above, the taxation powers of these bodies have not changed for a long time. Despite the revision of rates prescribed with minimum and maximum, the tax net has not increased, and in absolute terms it is not giving high revenue. The reasons are that the size of Gram Panchayats is small (average population 1736), for Janpad Panchayats the population size varies from 34972 to 293668. Secondly, about 43 per cent people in rural area are below poverty line hence a large portion of rural population is out of the tax net. Thirdly, the tax administration is not up to mark. Fourthly, initiative of local leaders, particularly of reserve categories, to raise revenue is discouraging and their perception in this matter is different.

Non-Tax Revenues

Gram Panchayat

The Non-Tax sources of revenues for Gram Panchayat are given in Statement 1.1. In this sphere, Gram Panchayats have been assigned two types of sources, that is, obligatory and optional sources. In the obligatory non-tax sources, Gram Panchayats are empowered to levy market fees and fees on registration of cattle. Among the optional category, a good number of items have been listed for levying. These items have not changed from the old Act and continue to be the same.

Statement 1.2 provides the comparative rates of non-tax sources that are prevailing before and after the amendment. As seen in the Statement 1.2, rates have undergone changes and it has been increased. The new rates have been modified as per the notification of the government on February 29, 1996. Under the provisions of the Act of 1993, a Gram Panchayat is required to place the proposal for imposing any tax/fee in the meeting of Gram Sabha. After resolving to impose any tax or fee, it shall have to proclaim the resolution for information of the public by beat of drum or written notice affixed at Gram Panchayat office or any conspicuous place in the area or both. After considering the objections, if any, and getting the clearance from the Janpad Panchayat, the gram panchayat adopts the taxes/fees to be imposed. It is required that the schedules of rates fixed are to be notified in usual procedure as stated earlier. The Janpad Panchayat while approving the proposal specifies the date from which the tax or fee mentioned therein should come into force.

Janpad Panchayat

In the non-tax sources of revenue, Janpad Panchayats are empowered to levy fees for any licence for use and occupation of land or other property (Statement 1.3). In addition to this, they are empowered to auction/lease ferry services and impose fines on defaulters of payment of tax. A comparative prescribed rate is given in the Statement 1.3. The powers are the same as compared to earlier powers and changes in rates has been notified. Regarding ferry services, they are empowered to auction it.

Zilla Panchayat

Among non-tax sources, Zilla Panchayats have been vested with power to raise resources from water bodies (tanks) within their jurisdiction. Statement 1.3 provides the classification according to the size of water bodies for which each tier is vested with powers. Generally, Zilla Panchayat sources of revenue from non-tax are fishery rental (leasing of tanks), rent or fee form property. Therefore, Zilla Panchayat has limited sources of non-tax revenue.

Trends in Local Revenue Mobilisation

After discussing about the tax and non-tax sources and their prevailing rates in the state, we will now examine the trends in local resource mobilisation by these bodies. In fact, lots of variations exist across the states in the overall magnitude of resources mobilised by panchayats from taxes and non-tax sources. The wide variation in magnitude of incomes of panchayats from one state to another and even among the panchayats within one state is due to size of panchayats in terms of population coverage. Discussions presented below will broadly give an idea about the trends in the internal resources mobilisation by these bodies.

Tax Revenues

Table 4.1 provides six years data of total receipts from all sources itemwise for all Gram Panchayats in the state. Evidently, the per capita income from any taxable item is either slightly higher than one rupee or less than one rupee. Increase in per capita income from property tax, profession tax, water rate and lighting rate is noticed over a period of time, but it is not much significant. Other two taxable items (Drainage tax and Building rent) does not show increase, rather it is fluctuating. It is expected that property tax and profession tax could have given more income to panchayats, as these items have scope and potential, but it is not. Among the taxes, contribution of water tax is highest and more than other sources and it is showing steady increase. Even, the per capita income from all taxable items put together, it is not significant and it ranges between Rupees 1.30 to Rupees 2.88. Nevertheless, it is showing increasing trend steadily and it has become more than double in six years.

Table 4.2 shows that the percentage of tax revenue to the total receipt for gram panchayat is minimum 1.5 per cent in 1992-93 and maximum 2.99 per cent in 1994-95. Thus, the contribution of tax revenue is not much significant and obviously gram panchayats are depending much on other sources. The percentage increase in tax revenue has gone up maximum to 59 per cent in 1994-95 and minimum to 7 per cent in 1995-96. Nevertheless, it is always increasing and it has become more than doubles in absolute terms in five year period. Such wide variation reflects on the mechanism of tax collection and it may be due to the collection of more arrears

Table 4.1 : Receipts of Gram Panchayats of Madhya Pradesh

S.No.	Items	1992-93		1993-94		1994-95		1995-96		1996-97		1997-98	
		AMOUNT	PC	AMOUNT	PC	AMOUNT	PC	AMOUNT	PC	AMOUNT	PC	AMOUNT	PC
A	TAX REVENUE												
(i)	Property	11156	0.32	14368	0.41	26325	0.75	19125	0.55	26008	0.76	26528	0.76
(ii)	Profession	2173	0.06	890	0.03	2037	0.06	2547	0.07	2255	0.06	2300	0.07
(iii)	Water Rate	15901	0.46	25072	0.72	35082	1.01	46068	1.32	45828	1.31	46745	1.34
(iv)	Lighting Rate	6375	0.18	6492	0.19	12283	0.35	12202	0.35	13556	0.39	13827	0.4
(v)	Drainage Tax	436	0.01	72	0	89	0	95	0	336	0.01	343	0.01
(vi)	Building Rent	9528	0.27	5648	0.16	8028	0.23	9814	0.28	10255	0.29	10460	0.3
	TOTAL TAX REVENUE	45569	1.3	52542	1.51	83844	2.4	89851	2.57	98238	2.82	100203	2.88
B	NON-TAX REVENUE												
(i)	Fairs, Market and Festivals	14350	0.41	17651	0.51	33582	0.96	28816	0.83	24387	0.7	24875	0.71
(ii)	Fishery Rental	3286	0.09	6135	0.18	9480	0.27	9319	0.27	18591	0.53	18963	0.54
(iii)	Bus Stand Fees	729	0.02	318	0.01	770	0.02	652	0.02	1200	0.03	1224	0.04
(iv)	Cart Stand	155	0	195	0.01	315	0.01	387	0.01	341	0.01	348	0.01
(v)	Ferry Service	17585	0.5	18563	0.53	35456	1.02	33807	0.97	35822	1.03	36538	1.05
(vi)	Fines and Penalties	51	0	40	0	879	0.03	794	0.02	806	0.02	822	0.02
(vii)	Fees for ZP Shelters (Kanji House)	14396	0.41	15046	0.43	21055	0.6	23593	0.68	23902	0.69	24380	0.7
(viii)	Any other fees (Market & Other)	45138	1.29	31017	0.89	42645	1.22	53785	1.54	54211	1.55	55295	1.59
(ix)	Animal Registration Fee	2617	0.08	2435	0.07	4051	0.12	5180	0.15	6586	0.19	6718	0.19
(x)	Interest	2170	0.06	2097	0.06	2255	0.06	2458	0.07	2458	0.07	2458	0.07
	TOTAL NON-TAX REVENUE	100477	2.86	93497	2.69	150488	4.31	158791	4.56	168304	4.82	171621	4.92
	TOTAL LOCAL REVENUE (A+B)	146046	4.16	146039	4.2	234332	6.71	248642	7.13	266542	7.64	271824	7.8
C	ASSIGNED REVENUES												
(i)	Surcharge on Commercial Tax												
(ii)	Local Cess	2280	0.07	2280	0.07	2280	0.07	2280	0.07	2280	0.07	3800	0.11

Contd....

Table 4.1 : *Contd. ...*

S.No	Items	1992-93		1993-94		1994-95		1995-96		1996-97		1997-98	
		AMOUNT	PC	AMOUNT	PC	AMOUNT	PC	AMOUNT	PC	AMOUNT	PC	AMOUNT	PC
(iii)	Mines and Minerals									4141	0.12	4224	0.12
(iv)	Land Revenue	22500	0.65	22500	0.65	22500	0.65	22500	0.65	22500	0.65	75000	2.15
	TOTAL ASSIGNED REVENUES	24780	0.72	24780	0.72	24780	0.72	24780	0.72	28921	0.84	83024	2.38
D	**GRANTS-IN-AID (STATE)**												
(i)	General Purpose Grant from State Government	292422	8.39	382877	10.98	377008	10.81	527039	15.11	720484	20.66	742377	21.29
(ii)	Specific Purpose Grant (Basic F. of G.P.)											1673050	47.98
(iii)	Grant for Development Purpose									771700	22.13	771700	22.13
E	**TFC GRANTS**												
(i)	Centrally spons. Sch. State	569531	16.33	490070	14.05	488021	14	655758	18.81	313238	8.98	619758	17.77
(ii)	Centrally spons. Sch. Central	2007170	57.56	1960279	56.22	1675978	48.06	2554949	73.27	2347416	67.32	2662534	76.36
	Sub-Total (D+E)	2869123	82.28	2833226	81.25	2541007	72.87	3737746	107.19	4152838	119.09	6469419	185.53
	GRAND TOTAL	3039949	87.16	3004045	86.17	2800119	80.3	4011168	115.04	4448301	127.57	6824267	195.71

AMOUNT (Rs. Thousand)

PC = Per Capital (Rupees)

Source: Commissioner of Panchayats, Government of Madhya Pradesh.

Table 4.2 : Abstract of Receipts and Expenditure of Gram Panchayat

(Rs. Thousand)

S. No.	*Items*	*1992-93*	*1993-94*	*% of increase*	*1994-95*	*% of increase*	*1995-96*	*% of increase*	*1996-97*	*% of increase*	*1997-98*
1	Tax Revenue	45569	52542	15.3	83844	59.6	89851	7.2	98238	9.3	100203
	% of Total	1.50	1.75	–	2.99	–	2.24	–	2.21	–	1.47
2	Non-Tax Revenue	100477	93497	-6.9	150488	61.0	158791	5.5	168304	6.0	171621
	% of Total	3.31	3.11	–	5.37	–	3.96	–	3.78	–	2.51
3	Assigned Revenue	24780	24780	0.0	24780	0.0	24780	0.0	28921	16.7	83024
	% of Total	0.82	0.82	–	0.88	–	0.62	–	0.65	–	1.22
4	Grants-in-Aid	292422	382877	30.93	377008	-1.53	527039	39.80	720484	36.7	2415427
	% of Total	9.62	12.75	–	13.46	–	13.14	–	16.20	–	35.39
5	TFC & Centrally Sponsored	2576701	2450349	-4.90	2163999	-11.69	3210707	48.37	3432354	6.90	4053992
	Schemes	–	–	–	–	–	–	–	–	–	–
	% of Total	84.76	81.57	–	77.28	–	80.04	–	77.16	–	59.41
	TOTAL	3039949	3004045	34.38	2800119	107.31	4011168	100.85	4448301	75.64	6824267
	TOTAL EXPENDITURE	3098807	3061131	-1.22	2842724	-7.13	4141523	45.69	4660366	12.53	7076786

Source : Commissioner of Panchayats, Government of Madhya Pradesh.

in a particular year and increase in rates. Also, the sharp variation in the increase justifies the scope and potential of available tax sources, if the tax administration improves.

In its report, the MP State Finance Commission (1996), based on data collected from sample gram panchayats, observed that only 36 per cent of sample gram panchayats have imposed property tax, 26 per cent have imposed lighting tax and utilisation of sanitation tax is negligible as it is 3 per cent only. The Commission further observed that hardly about one-third gram panchayats collect property tax, however, after the 73rd Amendment there has been some increase in the imposition of property tax. In case of lighting tax, though about 93 per cent villages are reported to be electrified and about 34 per cent households have access to electricity but realisation is not to that extent. The imposition of sanitation tax is about 3 per cent which is quite obvious in view of the number of households (about 4 per cent) having toilet facilities in rural areas of the state. More so, in case of profession tax, there was an increase in utilising this tax after the 73rd Amendment as compared to earlier, but thereafter in 1994-95 it shows declining trend. There could be possibility of decline due to increase in the minimum annual income level from Rs. 500 to Rs. 1,1000 in 1996; the number of persons coming into the tax net would have decreased. But even then, the coverage is not to the full extent. The less coverage of profession tax in rural areas can be substantiated by the explanation given by the sample gram panchayats of this study that they are quite hesitant in exercising this power. Regarding realisation of water tax, the Commission further found that since it is to be collected only if potable water is supplied through water supply system, so it has limitations. Moreover, due to non-functional water supply systems in many cases, gram panchayats may not have wide coverage. Hence this source has limitations to raise revenue.

Table 4.3 provides composition of resources of sample gram panchayats. Out of four sample gram panchayats, one gram panchayat (Kedar) do not have any income from tax revenue since it has predominantly tribal population. The annual average of income from tax sources ranges between Rupees 15 thousand (Kedkela) to nil (Kedar), two others have less than one thousand. This shows

Table 4.3 : Composition of Resources of Sample Gram Panchayats

Year	Internal Tax	Resource Non-Tax	Total (2+3)	Assigned Revenues	JRY	Grant-in-aid others	Total (6+7)	Total of (5+8)	Grand Total of Receipts	Total Expen-diture	Col. 4 as of Col.10	Col. 4 as% of Col.4	Col. 2 as% of Col.4	Col. 5 as of Col.10	Col. 9 as% of Col.10	Col. 5 as% of Col.11	Col. 9 as% of Col.11
1	2	3	4	5	6	7	8	9	10	11	12	13	14	15	16	17	18
1.KEDKELA (Population: 2418)																	
1996-97	3731	15435	19166	2179	96287	86240	182527	184706	203872	206839	9.4	9.27	19.47	1.07	90.6	1.05	89.3
1997-98	19205	17381	36586	0.00	112360	147957	260317	260317	296903	278943	12.32	13.12	52.49	0.00	87.68	0.00	93.32
1998-99 (upto 11/98)	23435	7501	30936	3193	33253	164953	198206	201399	232335	233254	13.32	13.26	75.75	1.37	86.68	1.37	86.34
Annual Avg.	15457	13439	28896	1790.67	80633.33	133050	213683.3	215474	244370	239678.67	11.68	11.88	49.24	0.81	88.32	0.81	89.65
2.SISRINGA (Population:3000)																	
1994-95	104	6628	6732	0	100734	18030	118764	118764	125496	123886	5.36	5.43	1.54	0.00	94.64	0.00	95.87
1995-96	2411	9700	12111	1430	97692	30601	128293	129723	141834	107911	8.54	11.22	19.91	1.01	91.46	1.33	120.21
1996-97	510	15457	15967	2641	97935	91100	189035	191676	207643	207665	7.69	7.69	3.19	1.27	92.31	1.27	92.3
1997-98	0	6980	6980	1074	99000	145400	244400	245474	252454	254218	2.76	2.75	0.00	0.43	97.24	0.42	96.56
Annual Avg.	756.25	9691.25	10447.5	1286.25	98840.25	71282.75	170123	171409.3	181856.75	173420	6.09	6.77	6.16	0.68	93.91	0.76	101.24

Contd. ...

Table 4.3 : *Contd. ...*

Year	*Internal Tax*	*Resource Non-Tax*	*Total (2+3)*	*Assigned Revenues*	*JRY*	*Grant-in-aid others*	*Total (6+7)*	*Total of (5+8)*	*Grand Total of Receipts*	*Total Expen-diture*	*Col. 4 as of Col.10*	*Col. 4 as% of Col.4*	*Col. 2 as% of Col.4*	*Col. 5 as of Col.10*	*Col. 9 as% of Col.10*	*Col. 5 as% of Col.11*	*Col. 9 as% of Col.11*
1	2	3	4	5	6	7	8	9	10	11	12	13`	14	15	16	17	18
3.KEDAR (Population:1743)																	
1995-96	0	23382	23382	816	14025	127219	141244	142060	165442	163973	14.13	14.26	0	0.49	85.87	0.5	86.64
1996-97	0	23390	23390	1526	30085	243819	273904	275430	298820	307211	7.83	7.61	0	0.51	92.17	0.5	89.65
1997-98	0	28191	28191	1047	29115	129346	158461	159508	187699	199087	15.02	14.16	0	0.56	84.98	0.53	80.12
Annual Avg.	0	24987.67	24987.7	1129.67	24408.33	166794.67	191203	192332.7	217320.33	223423.67	12.33	12.01	0	0.52	87.67	0.51	85.47
4.KANAKBIRA (Population:1551)																	
1995-96	300	14312	14612	2171	39788	35815	75603	77774	92386	72931	15.82	20.04	2.05	2.35	84.18	2.98	106.64
1996-97	2040	14550	16590	1403	44274	78982	123256	124659	141249	139601	11.75	11.88	12.3	0.99	88.25	1.01	89.3
1997-98	575	15772	16347	1351	44111	410725	454836	456187	472534	493911	3.46	3.31	3.52	0.29	96.54	0.27	92.36
Annual Avg.	971.67	14878	15849.7	1641.67	42724.33	175174	217898.3	219540	235389.67	235481	10.34	11.74	5.96	1.21	89.66	1.42	96.10

Source : Respective Village Panchayats.

that performance of tax revenue fluctuates sharply. The column 14 of Table 4.3 provides the percentage of tax revenue to the total internal resources including non-tax revenue. It can be seen that one gram panchayat (Kedkela) has sizeable income from tax revenue to the total internal resources (maximum 75%) and it shows increasing trend and the annual average income from tax revenue comes to 49 per cent which is encouraging. But, in case of other sample gram panchayats, it is only 5 to 6 per cent. The per capita income from tax revenue in the sample GPs (Table 4.4) varies from minimum of 3 paisa to maximum of Rs. 7.94 (Kedkela, 1997-98). It can, therefore, be said that there is a scope for mobilising resources through tax income. It depends more on local leadership to take initiative to raise revenue from the taxable items assigned to

Table 4.4 : Per Capita Income and Expenditure of Sample Gram Panchayats

Village Panchayat Year	*Tax*	*Internal Resources*	*Assigned Revenue*	*Grants*	*Receipts*	*Expenditure*
1. KEDKELA						
1994-95	–	–	–	–	–	–
1995-96	–	–	–	–	–	–
1996-97	1.54	7.92	0.90	75.49	84.31	85.54
1997-98	7.94	15.13	0.00	81.97	122.78	115.36
2 SISRINGA						
1994-95	0.03	2.24	0.00	39.59	41.83	41.29
1995-96	0.08	4.03	0.48	42.76	47.27	35.97
1996-97	0.17	5.32	0.88	63.01	69.21	69.22
1997-98	0.00	2.32	0.36	81.47	84.15	84.73
3 KEDAR						
1994-95	–	–	–	–	–	–
1995-96	0	01.34	0.47	81.03	94.91	94.07
1996-97	0	13.41	0.88	157.15	171.44	176.25
1997-98	0	16.17	0.60	90.91	107.68	114.22
4 KANAKBIRA						
1994-95	–	–	–	–	–	–
1995-96	0.19	09.42	1.40	48.74	59.56	47.02
1996-97	1.31	10.69	0.90	79.47	91.06	90.00
1997-98	0.37	10.53	0.87	264.81	304.66	318.44

Source : Commissioner of Panchayats, Government of Madhya Pradesh.

gram panchayats. It was reported by one sample gram panchayat (Sirisinga) that they have imposed profession tax, as there are several shops under its jurisdiction. They expressed inability in collection of tax amount because those shopkeepers are not ready to pay profession tax on the plea that they are already paying sales tax to the government so why should they pay the profession tax; and how many taxes they will pay. The local leaders are not in a position to convince the prospective taxpayers that sales tax is entirely different than profession tax. Moreover, they do not have any enforcement machinery to realise the tax amount. The plausible way to tackle this situation would be: since the gram panchayat imposed the profession tax by passing a resolution from the general body of the GP, instead, had it been discussed in the gram sabha prior to passing the resolution, people would have arrived at the consensus on this issue. As all villagers would have been a party to this decision, hence it would have facilitated the gram panchayat to realise its move.

It was also reported by the sample gram panchayats that they have increased the rate of house tax from Rs. 2 to Rs. 5, only few persons have deposited the enhanced amount, now they have to pursue people to pay it. Usually, people pay taxes at the time of election when the contesting candidate for each ward is persuaded to collect taxes within his jurisdiction. Though gram panchayats do maintain record of taxpayers and arrears amount due with each taxpayer, but due to inadequate staff position in the gram panchayat, tax amount is not completely realised.

The reason for the higher tax collection of one sample gram panchayat (Kedkela) was the personal efforts of the Sarpanch. The Sarpanch of this gram panchayat pointed out that he has taken initiative and interest in mobilising tax revenue. The efforts in this direction were to increase the tax amount of house tax, collection of arrears of street light, collection from Kanzi house and imposition of profession tax. It is a pointer for other gram panchayats that if local leaders take special effort and initiative then they could realise the goal.

Janpad Panchayat

The tax revenue of Janpad Panchayat is mainly from entertainment tax. The other tax source is the development tax on agriculture land, which is not realised by any Janpad Panchayat. Table 4.5 provides data pertaining to total receipts of Janpad Panchayats of the state for six-year period. It shows that collection of revenue from taxes is only from entertainment tax. The per capita income from this source is less than Rupee one, which is not significant, and it has fluctuating trend. Despite the increase in the rates in 1996, increase in revenue collection from this source has not increased much, as expected. In rural areas in the state, such entertainment performance is static, it is occasional in nature, and hence income from this source is not assured. Table 4.6 shows that the percentage increase in income for this source is fluctuating and contribution of tax revenue to total receipt of Janpad Panchayats is between 1 to 6 per cent. In sample Janpad Panchayats, the income from this source is not encouraging. Table 4.7 shows that annual average tax income of sample Janpad varies from three to six thousand, which is not significant. The annual average percentage of tax income to the total internal resources of sample Janpads is 1 per cent to 5 per cent. The per capita tax revenue for sample Janpad Panchayats (Table 4.8) is quite low and negligible. Thus, these bodies do not have assured and significant income from tax sources rather it is quite low.

Zilla Panchayat

As stated above, Zilla Panchayats do not have any tax revenue sources. Hence, data pertaining to ZPs in Tables 4.9, 4.10 and 4.11 do not show any figure with respect to tax revenue.

Non-Tax Revenues

The non-tax revenues are another important source of internal resources of these bodies. The items under non-tax sources are already mentioned above.

Table 4.5 : Receipts of Janpad Panchayats of Madhya Pradesh

S.No.	Items	1992-93		1993-94		1994-95		1995-96		1996-97		1997-98	
		AMOUNT	PC	AMOUNT	PC	AMOUNT	PC	AMOUNT	PC	AMOUNT	PC	AMOUNT	PC
A	TAXES												
(i)	Entertainment	2227	–	11016	–	9311	–	16802	–	16346	–	16507	
	Sub-Total (A)	2227	0.06	11016	0.32	9311	0.27	16802	0.48	16346	0.47	16507	0.47
B	NON-TAX REVENUE/USER CHARGES												
(i)	Fairs and Festivals	1349	–	4631	–	5439	–	7207	–	8292	–	8374	–
(ii)	Fishery	–	–	473	–	773	–	2159	–	2202	–	2246	–
(iii)	Ferry Service	2445	–	4467	–	6955	–	18594	–	15004	–	15754	–
(iv)	Obligatory Services (Education)	–	–	–	–	–	–	–	–	452019	–	1839204	–
(v)	Interest on Deposit money	13203	–	18202	–	17975	–	18887	–	19075	–	19265	–
	Sub-Total (B)	16997	–	27773	–	31142	–	46847	–	496592	–	1884843	–
C	ASSIGNED REVENUE												
(i)	Surcharge on Stamp Duty	90073	–	118703	–	126262	–	126262	–	144426	–	181097	–
(ii)	Local Cess on land revenue	1520	–	1520	–	1520	–	1520	–	–	–	–	–
(iii)	Mines and Minerals	–	–	–	–	–	–	641	–	705	–	775	–
(iv)	Land Revenue	7500	–	7500	–	7500	–	7500	–	–	–	–	–
	Sub-Total (C)	99093	–	127723	–	135282	–	135923	–	145131	–	181872	–
D	**GRANTS-IN-AID (STATE)**												
(i)	General Purpose Grant	–	–	–	–	–	–	–	–	–	–	–	–
(ii)	Specific Purpose Grant (Honorarium)	–	–	–	–	–	–	51381	–	54380	–	55575	–

Contd....

Table 4.5 : *Contd. ...*

S.No.	*Items*	*1992-93*		*1993-94*		*1994-95*		*1995-96*		*1996-97*		*1997-98*	
		AMOUNT	*PC*	*AMOUNT*	*PC*	*AMOUNT*	*PC*	*AMOUNT*	*PC*	*AMOUNT*	*PC*	*AMOUNT*	*PC*
(iii)	Grant for Development Purpose	–	–	–	–	–	–	–	–	–	–	242507	–
	Sub-Total (D)	–	–	–	–	–	–	51381	–	54380	–	298082	–
E	TFC GRANTS	–	–	–	–	–	–	–	–	70000	–	70000	–
F	CENTRALLY SPONSORED SCHEMES	–	–	–	–	–	–	–	–	–	–	955263	–
	(15% of JRY)	–	–	–	–	–	–	–	–	–	–	–	–
G	OTHERS (Adm.Exp.Transferred from Zilla Panchayat)	–	–	–	–	–	–	485	–	297	–	392	–
	Sub-Total (E+F+G)	–	–	–	–	–	–	485	–	70297	–	1025655	–
	GRAND TOTAL	1118317	–	166512	–	175735	–	251438	–	782746	–	3406959	–

AMOUNT (Rs. Thousands)

PC = PER CAPITA (Rupees)

Source: Commissioner of Panchayats, Government of Madhya Pradesh.

Table 4.6 : Abstract of Receipts and Expenditure of Janpad Panchayats

(Rs. Thousands)

S. No.	*Items*	*1992-93*	*1993-94*	*% of increase*	*1994-95*	*% of increase*	*1995-96*	*% of increase*	*1996-97*	*% of increase*	*1997-98*
1	Tax Revenue	2227	11016	394.7	9311	-15.5	16802	80.5	16346	-2.7	16507
	% of Total	1.88	6.62	–	5.30	–	6.68	–	2.09	–	0.48
2	Non-Tax revenue	16997	27773	63.4	31142	12.1	46847	50.4	496592	960.0	1884843
	% of Total	14.37	16.68	–	17.72	–	18.63	–	63.44	–	55.32
3	Assigned Revenue	99093	127723	28.9	135282	5.9	135923	0.5	145131	6.8	181872
	% of Total	83.75	76.70	–	76.98	–	54.06	–	18.54	–	5.34
4	Grants-in-Aid	–	–	–	–	–	51381	–	54380	5.8	298082
	% of Total	–	–	–	–	–	20.43	–	6.95	–	8.75
5	TFC & Centrally Sponsored	–	–	–	–	–	485	–	70297	14394.2	1025655
	Schemes	–	–	–	–	–					
	% of Total						0.19	–	8.98	93.69	30.10
	TOTAL	118317	166512	486.95	175735	2.57	251438	131.36	782746	15364.14	3406959
	TOTAL EXPENDITURE	100652	129629	28.79	136101	4.99	202184	48.55	806377	298.83	3409192

Source : Commissioner of Panchayats, Government of Madhya Pradesh.

Table 4.7 : Composition of Resources of Sample Gram Panchayats

Year	*Internal Tax*	*Resource Non-Tax*	*Total (2+3)*	*Assigned Revenues*	*Grant-in-aid others*	*Investment Loans*	*Total (5+6)*	*Total of (4+8)*	*Grand Total of Receipts*
1	2	3	4	5	6	7	8	9	10
1.DHARMJAYGARH (Population 142652)									
1994-95	3610	56889	60499	333760	873817	1930	1207577	1268076	1270006
1995-96	445	76747	77192	385565	1024092	930	1409657	1486849	1487779
1996-97	1520	254496	256016	360415	1270600	360	1631015	1887031	1887391
1997-98(BE)	5000	1770500	1775500	415000	2592800	2000	3007800	4783300	4785300
1998-99(BE)	5000	1370500	1375500	500000	4096800	2000	4596800	5972300	5974300
Annual Avg.	3115	705826.4	708941	398948	1971621.8	1444	2370570	3079511	3080955.2
2.SARANGARH (Population: 153382)									
1994-95	2130	35270	37400	334790	563720	300000	898510	935910	1235910
1995-96	700	64060	64760	408520	1788150	270000	2196670	2261430	2531430
1996-97	22000	57750	79750	386350	7383090	832000	7769440	7849190	8681190
1997-98	0	38570	38570	0	17636929	0	17636929	17675499	17675499
1998-99	8000	90000	98000	425000	5727466	440000	6152466	6250466	6690466
Annual Avg.	6566	57130	63696	310932	6619871	368400	6930803	6994499	7362899

Contd. ...

Total Expenditure	*Col. 4 as of Col.10*	*Col. 4 as% of Col.11*	*Col. 2 as of Col.4*	*Col. 5 as of Col.10*	*Col. 6 as% of Col.10*	*Col. 8 as% of Col.10*	*Col. 5 as% of Col.11*	*Col. 6 as% of Col.11*	*Col. 8 as% of Col.11*	*Col. 9 as% of Col.11*
11	12	13	14	15	16	17	18	19	20	21
1. DHARMJAYGARH (Population 142652)										
822681	4.76	7.35	5.97	26.28	68.8	95.08	40.57	106.22	146.79	154.14
1323092	5.19	5.83	0.58	25.92	68.83	94.75	29.14	77.4	106.54	112.38
2249964	13.56	11.38	0.59	19.1	67.32	86.42	16.02	56.47	72.49	83.87
4407780	37.1	40.28	0.28	8.67	54.18	62.85	9.42	58.82	68.24	108.52
5753595	23.02	23.91	0.36	8.37	68.57	76.94	8.69	71.2	79.89	103.8
2911422.4	16.726	17.75	1.556	17.668	65.54	83.208	20.768	74.02	94.79	112.54
2. SARANGARH (Population: 153382)										
1774630	3.03	2.11	5.7	27.09	45.61	72.7	18.87	31.77	50.63	52.74
2382890	2.56	2.72	1.08	16.14	70.64	86.78	17.14	75.04	92.19	94.9
7835130	0.92	1.02	27.59	4.45	85.05	89.5	4.93	94.23	99.16	100.18
7868017	0.22	0.49	0	0	99.78	99.78	0	224.16	224.16	224.65
4296479	1.46	2.28	8.16	6.35	85.61	91.96	9.89	133.31	143.2	145.48
4831429.2	1.638	1.724	8.506	10.806	77.338	88.144	10.166	111.7	121.87	123.59

Source : Respective Janpad Panchayats.

Table 4.8 : Per Capita Income and Expenditure of Sample Janpad Panchayats

Year	*Tax*	*Internal Resources*	*Assigned Revenue*	*Grants*	*Receipts*	*Expenditure*
DHARMJAYGARH						
1994-95	0.02	0.42	2.33	6.12	8.09	5.76
1995-96	0.003	0.54	2.7	7.17	10.42	9.27
1996-97	0.01	1.79	2.52	8.09	13.23	15.77
1997-98	0.03	12.44	2.9	18.17	33.54	30.89
1998-99	0.03	9.64	3.5	28.71	41.88	40.33
SARANGARH						
1994-95	0.01	0.24	2.18	3.67	8.05	11.57
1995-96	0.004	0.42	2.66	11.65	16.05	15.53
1996-97	0.14	0.51	2.51	48.13	56.59	51.08
1997-98	0.00	0.26	0.00	114.98	115.23	51.29
1998-99	0.05	0.63	2.77	37.34	43.61	28.01

Source : Commissioner of Panchayats, Government of Madhya Pradesh.

Table 4.9 : Receipts of Zila Panchayats of Madhya Pradesh

S.No.	Items	1992-93		1993-94		1994-95		1995-96		1996-97		1997-98	
		AMOUNT	PC	AMOUNT	PC	AMOUNT	PC	AMOUNT	PC	AMOUNT	PC	AMOUNT	PC
A	NON-TAX REVENUE												
(i)	Fishery Rental	–	–	538	0.01	834	0.01	2320	0.04	2366	0.04	2413	0.04
(ii)	Any other fees Property Rent Other	1223	0.02	537	0.01	478	0.01	1282	0.02	3131	0.05	3265	0.06
(iii)	Administrative Service Charges (DRDA)	–	–	–	–	–	–	14506	0.26	20867	0.36	145977	2.47
(iv)	Interest on Deposit money	2448	0.05	4178	0.08	3760	0.07	4934	0.09	7652	0.13	7729	0.13
	Sub-Total (A)	3671	0.07	5253		5072	0.09	23042	0.41	34016	0.59	159384	2.69
B	ASSINGED REVENUE	–	–	–	–	–	–	–	–	–	–	–	–
(i)	Mines and Minerals	–	–	–	–	–	–	–	–	–	–	–	–
(ii)	Land Revenue	7500	0.14	7500	0.14	7500	0.13	7500	0.13	59213	1.02	59213	1
	Sub-Total (B)	7500	0.14	7500	0.14	7500	0.13	7500	0.13	59213	1.02	59213	1
C	GRANTS-IN-AID FROM STATE												
(i)	General Purpose Grant	–	–	–	–	–	–	–	–	13567	0.23	15000	0.25
(ii)	Specific Purpose Grant Honorarium Training etc.	2477	0.05	3343	0.06	4956	0.09	32914	0.58	32722	0.56	31247	0.53
(iii)	Grant for Development Purpose	30000	0.56	30000	0.55	30000	0.54	212267	3.73	1114777	19.22	1809583	30.58

Contd....

Table 4.9 : *Contd.* ...

S.No.	*Items*	*1992-93*		*1993-94*		*1994-95*		*1995-96*		*1996-97*		*1997-98*	
		AMOUNT	*PC*	*AMOUNT*	*PC*	*AMOUNT*	*PC*	*AMOUNT*	*PC*	*AMOUNT*	*PC*	*AMOUNT*	*PC*
D	TFC GRANTS	–	–	–	–	–	–	–	–	30000	0.52	30000	0.51
E	CENTRALLY SPONSERED SCHEMES	–	–	–	–	–	–	–	–	–	–	–	–
(i)	Central	–	–	–	–	–	–	–	–	–	–	3630824	61.35
(ii)	State	–	–	–	–	–	–	–	–	–	–	1295618	21.89
(iii)	National Old Age Pension	–	–	–	–	–	–	261608	4.6	504243	8.69	450604	7.61
(iv)	National Maternity benefit schemes	–	–	–	–	–	–	34804	0.61	29722	0.51	39193	0.66
F	OTHERS (health worker)												
	Central	–	–	–	–	–	–	–	–	–	–	14740	0.25
	State	–	–	–	–	–	–	–	–	–	–	23515	0.4
	Total (C+D+E+F)	32477	0.61	33343	0.61	34956	0.63	541593	9.53	1725031	29.74	7340324	124.03
	GRAND TOTAL	43648	0.82	46096	0.84	47528	0.85	572135	10.07	1818260	31.35	7558921	127.72

AMOUNT (Rs. Thousand)

PC = Per Capital (Rupees)

Source : Commissioner of Panchayats, Government of Madhya Pradesh.

Table 4.10 : Composition of Resources of Zilla Panchayat: Raigarh

(Population : 1559232) *(In Rs.)*

RECEIPTS										
Year	*General Purpose*	*Specific Purpose*	*Tenth Finance Commission*	*JRY*	*Family Benefit*	*Maternity Benefit*	*Old age Pension*	*Balika Samruddhi*	*Health*	*Total*
1	2	3	4	5	6	7	8	9	10	11
1994-95	–	–	–	121309000	–	–	–	–	–	121309000
1995-96	–	–	–	148723000	2120000	1193000	3465000	–	–	155501000
1996-97	–	–	–	68666000	2734000	–	9464000	–	4337000	85201000
1997-98	555550	–	25560000	74020000	11380000	988000	18708000	200000	679900	132091450
1998-99	497777	204794	25190000	70607000	6396000	2287000	11933000	1686500	448000	119250071
Annual Average	526663.5	204794	25375000	96665000	5657500	1489333.3	10892500	943250	1821633.3	122670504

EXPENDITURE										
Year	*Tenth Finance Commission*	*Salary Panchayat Staff*	*Salary Teachers*	*Salary of Health Staff*	*Family Benefit*	*Maternity Benefit*	*Old age Pension*	*Balika Samruddhi*	*EAS*	*Total*
1	2	3	4	5	6	7	8	9	10	11
1994-95	–	220800	–	–	–	–	–	–	130251200	130472000
1995-96	–	211700	490000	–	335500	–	–	–	151100000	152137200
1996-97	–	214000	650000	264800	4357000	1129000	8750000	–	132644800	148009600
1997-98	24360000	230000	2280000	605000	9683000	960000	14493000	180000	148191400	200982400
1998-99	25105000	268700	28441000	598600	9909000	2378600	12885000	1702500	131517100	212805500
Annual Average	24732500	229040	7965250	489466.6667	6071125	1489200	12042667	941250	138740900	168881340

Source: Raigarh Zilla Panchayat.

Table 4.11 : Abstract of Receipts and Expenditure of Janpad Panchayats

(Rs. Thousands)

S. No.	*Functions*	*1992-93*	*1993-94*	*% of increase*	*1994-95*	*% of increase*	*1995-96*	*% of increase*	*1996-97*	*% of increase*	*1997-98*
1	Non-Tax Revenue	3671	5253	43.1	5072	-3.4	23042	354.3	34016	47.6	159384
	% of Total	8.41	11.40	–	10.67	–	4.03	–	1.87	–	2.11
2	Assigned Revenue	7500	7500	0.0	7500	0.0	7500	0.0	59213	689.5	59213
	% of Total	17.18	16.27	–	15.78	–	1.31	–	3.26	77 –	0.78
3	Grants-in-aid	32477	33343	2.7	34956	4.8	245181	601.4	1161066	373.6	1855830
	% of Total	74.41	72.33	–	73.55	–	42.85	–	63.86	–	24.55
4	TFC & Centrally Sponsored Schemes	–	–	–	–	–	296412	–	563965	90.3	5484494
	% of Total	–	–	–	–	–	51.81	–	31.02	–	72.56
	TOTAL RECEIPTS	43648	46096	45.76	47528	1.4	572135	955.7	1818260	1201.0	7558921
	TOTAL EXPENDITURE	43829	46984	7.20	47740	1.61	565544	1084.63	1749180	209.29	7366897

Source : Commissioner of Panchayats, Government of Madhya Pradesh.

In respect of non-tax revenues of gram panchayats, it has good number of items to mobilize resources and has better scope as compared to tax sources. It can be seen in Table 4.11 that there are ten items listed and data (six year) reveals that the per capita income is increasing and it has reached to about Rupees five in 1997-98. The per capita income from this source is about double than tax revenue. Among the items of non-tax sources available with gram panchayats, the contribution is more from fees, market rate, ferry services and kanji house. Table 4.2 shows that the share of non-tax revenue to the total receipts of the gram panchayats varies between 3 to 6 per cent which is more than the tax income. The percentage increase in the revenue from this source is showing increasing trend. In the sample gram panchayats (Table 4.3), the annual average income from this source ranges from ten to twenty-five thousand rupees, which is reasonable as compared to tax revenue.

While analysing the data on non-tax revenues of sample gram panchayats, the State Finance Commission found that 11 per cent gram panchayats mobilize resources from market fee and 15 per cent from registration of cattle. Moreover, there has been increase in the number of Gram Panchayats collecting fees from items assigned to them and resources are mobilised from non-tax sources particularly after the 73rd Amendment period. Another important area for raising income is from water bodies. In the state, invariably all districts have water bodies through which they earn ferry rent or leasing tanks for fisheries activities. As Gram Panchayats are vested with the powers to lease out tanks below 10 hectare, this has good scope to raise revenues. In leasing out fisheries ponds, sample gram panchayats reported that recovery of lease amount is difficult. According to the latest government notification, they have to lease out for ten years period and it cannot be cancelled within the lease period even in case of non-payment of lease amount. Earlier GPs were leasing out for three years but now it has to be leased out for enhanced period of ten years. Thus, it has restricted their autonomy, loss in income and they have to suffer.

Janpad Panchayat

The revenues augmented by Janpad Panchayats are generally from ferry services, leasing out fisheries ponds, fairs and festivals and interest from deposits. The state level data (Table 4.5) shows that non-tax revenue of JPs is substantial and more than tax revenue. It shows increasing trend and it has gone up by 760 per cent in 1996-97 (Table 4.6). The trend is highly encouraging. The per cent share of non-tax revenue to total receipts of Janpad has gone up to 63 per cent which is substantial.

Among the non-tax revenue sources, the contribution from interest on deposits is highest than any other item. In the sample Janpad panchayats also, Dharamjaygarh was receiving very high income from interest on deposits and from auction of ferry ghat. Table 4.7 shows that sample Janpads have higher income from non-tax revenues than tax. As also, the non-tax income in sample Janpads shows increasing trend. In one sample Janpad (Sarangarh), realisation of non-tax revenues is not regular because it is predominantly tribal area. They are not imposing any fine or penalty on encroachment. This power is unutilised. Remarkably, the annual average income from this source is more than 7 lakh in Dharamjaygarh whereas in Sarangarh it is only 57 thousand.

Evidently, income from fairs and festivals has limited scope and it cannot be a regular income source. The new dispensation has been empowered to lease out fisheries ponds having an average area of 10-100 hectares. If it is properly harnessed and exploited, it can give better income. Also, the ferry services have better scope to increase income provided it is auctioned objectively, without any motive.

One sample Janpad reported that they are planning to construct house out of their available own resources and it will be given to the staff members on rental basis. This will serve two purposes; staff will get accommodation, and in turn, JP will have regular income from rent.

Zilla Panchayat

Generally, Zilla Panchayat has income from non-tax sources. Among them, the items, which are very common, are rent from fisheries, rent from properties and interest from deposits. The data pertaining to non-tax revenue for all Zilla Panchayats of state shows

(Table 4.10) that the per capita income from this source has increased from 0.07 paisa to Rs. 2.69 during 1992-93 to 1997-98.

The new dispensation of Zilla Panchayats has been empowered to lease out fisheries tank with average water spread of more than 100 to 2000 hectares. This is new source of income with good scope provided it is properly utilised. Now, ZPs are also getting administrative service charges from DRDA from 1995-96.

Table 4.11 shows that percentage increase in non-tax revenue is fluctuating and it shows negative growth in 1994-95 whereas in subsequent year it has steep increase by 354 per cent. The contribution of non-tax revenue to the total receipts of ZPs varies from 2 per cent to 11 per cent. It is also evident that they are heavily dependent upon grants hence per cent contribution from non-tax income is quite low. The sample Zilla Panchayat does not have any income from non-tax sources (Table 4.9). The ZP has no water tank under them so they do not get any income and they have no such properties vested with them to earn income.

So far the mobilisation of internal resources are concerned, the performance of these bodies are not up to the expectations. For Gram Panchayats, it constitutes about five to seven per cent of their total receipts. In sample GPs, the annual average per cent of internal resources to total receipt is 6 per cent to 12 per cent (Table 4.3, Col. 12), which is higher than the state level. It also shows that the contributions of own income to total receipt is 30 per cent to 15 per cent for sample GPs. Table 4.4 shows that the per capita internal resources of sample GPs fluctuate between Rs. 15 to Rs. 2. For Janpad Panchayats, the internal resources constitute minimum 16 per cent to maximum 65 per cent. In sample JPs, the annual average of internal resources is 16 per cent and the per capita varies from 24 paisa to Rs. 12, which is insignificant. For ZPs, the highest share of own revenue to the total receipt is 11 per cent but it has subsequently decreased to 2 per cent because of higher allocation of grants to these bodies in recent years. In fine, the above discussions on available data and field observations, it is indicative that Gram Panchayats are not properly utilising either obligatory or optional sources of tax and non-tax revenues. The reasons are inadequacy of staff and their proficiency, non-availability of requisite infrastructure and lack of initiative by local leaders and their will to do so. Besides, Gram Sabha is not activated to use it as a forum for building up awareness among villagers regarding crucial issues of finances so that full support of people can be enlisted in these matters. As also, there is no effort by the government to assess the resources of low tax yield and suggest suitable measures to these bodies.

The State Finance Commission has also observed that Gram Panchayats have not been able to exploit to optimum level even obligatory taxes entrusted to them. The helplessness is due to various reasons. It is mainly because of inadequacy of staff for collection of revenue, lack of sufficient support of people, non-availability of rules published by the government with regard to imposition and collection of specific taxes, etc. It is also because of indifference, ignorance, fear of adverse public relation and unpopularity of local leaders.

Measures Required for Better Local Revenue Mobilisation

The plausible measures needed to improve the financial situation of panchayats on the basis of identified problems are given below. These measures will have direct bearing upon the mobilisation performance, if is considered for future action. Local leaders of panchayats as well as functionaries responsible for finances should have better understanding of financial powers and fully acquainted with rules/regulations to raise resources within their purview. Undoubtedly, finance is becoming increasingly complicated technical subject and particularly the elected representatives would find it difficult to appreciate the implications on the financial structure of Panchayats. Therefore, a specific sensitisation programme focusing financial matters should be introduced for all functionaries.

Another important aspect is to activate Gram Sabha and use it as a forum to build awareness among people, especially in the matters relating to taxes, payment of taxes, etc. Once awareness is built towards appreciation for value of money and imperatives of development, then, people will cooperate and proverbial attitude not to pay taxes will definitely reduce. This will facilitate in the revenue mobilisation endeavour. Finance being so central to policy-making process, the Standing Committees established at each level has to play a pivotal role, which is not coming forth now. A serious effort is required to make these bodies effective to meet the expected task in all financial matters. The newly appointed 'Panchayat Karmi' at the gram panchayat level should be made responsible for collection of taxes and non-tax revenues. Alternatively, it may be privatised and task may be assigned to a local person on commission basis, as experienced elsewhere.

Levying of new tax items from obligatory and optional items much depends upon the quality of services rendered by these bodies. People may be ready to pay taxes if services are prompt and of good quality. Therefore, upgradation of infrastructure facilities and quality service is needed. Among the new tax avenues to augment resources, Mandi tax has better prospects. It may be considered for levying.

For improving better infrastructure facilities, various grants like Tenth Finance Commission (TFC), State Finance Commission (SFC) grants should be properly utilised to develop rural areas. And, these grants may be given as untied funds so that they enjoy freedom in utilising on the basis of local needs and requirements. Revision of rates of tax and non-tax items should be done objectively, without any motive. These bodies may be given autonomy in these matters. Periodic assessment of taxes should be adhered to.

To streamline and tone up the tax administration, Electronic Data Processing (EDP) would be the appropriate answer. Some states like Andhra Pradesh have started on these lines. It is essential to open a cell exclusively to deal with this matter at Janpad or Zilla Panchayat level with computer facilities. This unit will monitor and review all aspects of taxation and accordingly instructions could be given to lower units for timely action and thereby achievements. The Eleventh Finance Commission has recommended for developing data bank for units of Panchayats and for that they have devolved funds.

Enforcement powers should be vested with the Zilla Panchayat to tackle tax evaders. This will facilitate quick action against evaders. Tax evaders should be exposed in the Gram Sabha meetings. A scheme of incentive may be introduced for such panchayats who collects cent per cent revenue. These measures may help revenue raising capacity of panchayats, and thus, financial position may improve.

As stated above, we have restricted our discussions to own sources of revenues of Panchayats and efforts on internal resource mobilisation. However, this travel and pattern of expenditure of Panchayats also have hearing upon mobilising internal resources. Therefore, it is essential to discuss briefly overall trends of expenditure of panchayats so as to examine their fiscal needs and the nature and extent of the services they provide.

Trends and Patterns of Expenditure

When the financial composition of Panchayats is analysed, it is essentially required to examine the trends and patterns of expenditure to make it meaningful. Of course, there is limitation of the available data. Hence, the overall financial composition, and conclusions drawn thereon, on the basis of available data may be treated at best only as approximate and tentative. As the data is not available on classified manner on income and expenditure on revenue account, capital account and public account, we have classified according to the available data.

Broadly, we will classify Panchayats expenditure into the categories of: (a) General Administration; (b) Expenditure on services; (c) Expenditure on Development Grants; and, (d) Other Expenditures. The per capita expenditure has been calculated on the basis of projected population of the respective year.

Gram Panchayat

Table 4.12 provides broad function-wise expenditure data for Gram Panchayats for six year period, that is, from 1992-93 to 1997-98. Clearly, the expenditure on general administration has registered an increase in absolute terms as also the per capita. The expenditure on this account is more than expenditure on services. In fact, gram panchayats are supposed to provide these basic services since it is obligatory on their part. Although, expenditure on services has also increased over a period of time, but not in the same proportion as

Table 4.12 : Expenditure of Gram Panchayats of Madhya Pradesh

S.No.	Items	1992-93		1993-94		1994-95		1995-96		1996-97		1997-98	
		AMOUNT	PC	AMOUNT	PC	AMOUNT	PC	AMOUNT	PC	AMOUNT	PC	AMOUNT	PC
A	GENERAL ADMINISTRATION												
(i)	Salary of Panchayat Staff												
	(a) Village Assistant	216322	6.2	328277	9.41	305808	8.77	394139	11.3	525324	15.07	550717	15.79
	(b) Panchayat Staff	26881	0.77	26950	0.77	47336	1.36	66886	1.92	107765	3.09	113153	3.25
	(c) Panchayat Karmi							52900	1.52	123417	3.54	129133	3.7
(ii)	Terminal Benefits	7440	0.21	9920	0.28	12400	0.36	14880	0.43	18619	0.53	22358	0.64
(iii)	Maintenance	22549	0.65	23193	0.67	37317	1.07	42351	1.21	50656	1.45	53189	1.53
	Sub-Total (A)	273192	7.83	388340	11.13	402861	11.56	571156	16.38	825781	23.68	868550	24.91
B	EXPENDITURE ON SERVICES												
(i)	Water Supply	22844	0.66	24400	0.7	25299	0.73	81299	2.33	98568	2.83	103496	2.97
(ii)	Street Lighting	16661	0.48	15029	0.43	34755	1	41732	1.2	49504	1.42	51979	1.49
(iii)	Education	6639	0.19	15536	0.45	12500	0.36	15755	0.45	24132	0.69	25339	0.73
(iv)	Public Health	725	0.02	2560	0.07	2064	0.06	3622	0.1	6838	0.2	7180	0.21
(v)	Sanitation	5384	0.15	5012	0.14	7266	0.21	6803	0.2	10130	0.29	10637	0.31
(vi)	Roads	75317	2.16	57456	1.65	65544	1.88	53754	1.54	85963	2.47	90261	2.59
(vii)	Others	23817	0.68	27480	0.79	41879	1.2	49541	1.42	89329	2.56	93795	2.69
(viii)	Parks and Play grounds	6369	0.18	8004	0.23	4387	0.13	7094	0.2	7846	0.23	8238	0.24
(ix)	Library and Reading Room	7334	0.21	6748	0.19	642	0.02	1047	0.03	7947	0.23	8344	0.24
(x)	Markets	3428	0.1	2192	0.06	4448	0.13	11610	0.33	3397	0.1	3567	0.1
(xi)	Bus Stands	4296	0.12	3425	0.1	5880	0.17	7403	0.21	15077	0.43	15831	0.45
	Sub-Total (B)	172814	4.95	167842	4.81	204664	5.89	279660	8.01	398731	11.45	418667	12.02

Contd....

Table 4.12 : *Contd. ...*

S.No.	*Items*	*1992-93*		*1993-94*		*1994-95*		*1995-96*		*1996-97*		*1997-98*	
		AMOUNT	*PC*	*AMOUNT*	*PC*	*AMOUNT*	*PC*	*AMOUNT*	*PC*	*AMOUNT*	*PC*	*AMOUNT*	*PC*
C	EXPENDITURE ON DEVELOPMENT GRANTS												
(i)	Grant from State Government	76100	2.18	54600	1.57	71200	2.04	80000	2.29	3500	0.1	62527	1.79
(ii)	Specific purpose Grant (G.P.)											1673050	47.98
(iii)	TFC Grants									771700	22.13	771700	22.13
(iv)	Centrally spons.sch.state	569531	16.33	490070	14.05	488021	14	655758	18.81	313238	8.98	619758	17.77
(v)	Centraıly spons.sch.central	2007170	57.56	1960279	56.22	1675978	48.06	2554949	73.27	2347416	67.32	2662534	76.36
	Sub-Total (C)	2652801	76.07	2504949	71.84	2235199	64.1	3290707	94.37	3435854	98.53	5789569	166.03
	GRAND TOTAL	3098807	88.85	3061131	87.78	2842724	81.55	4141523	118.76	4660366	133.66	7076786	202.96

AMOUNT (Rs. Thousands)

PC = PER CAPITA (Rupees)

Source: Commissioner of Panchayats, Government of Madhya Pradesh.

for the general administration. The per capita expenditure on administration has increased more than three fold during 1992-93 to 1997-98. It is because of deployment of additional staff at the gram panchayat level, as prescribed by the government; and with the increase in the salary of Village Assistant who is permanent staff. The per cent expenditure itemwise is given Table in the below.

Table 4.13 : Percentage Expenditure of Gram Panchayats

Items	*1992-93*	*1993-94*	*1994-95*	*1995-96*	*1996-97*	*1997-98*
1. General Administration	8.8	12.7	14.2	13.8	17.7	12.3
2. Expenditure on Services	5.6	5.5	7.2	6.7	8.6	5.9
3. Expenditure on Development Grants	85.6	81.8	78.6	79.5	73.7	81.8
Total	100.00	100.00	100.00	100.00	100.00	100.00

It shows that expenditure on development grants constitutes the highest percentage, but it is fluctuating. It is due to variation in allocation of grants in a particular year; spill over of the expenditure and unspent amount. The per capita expenditure on this account has increased more than two folds during this period (Table 4.12).

Though the expenditure on essential services like water supply, street lighting, sanitation, education and health has increase steady but it is still less than the establishment expenditure. A quantum jump in allocation of funds for these services is due to fact that the SFC has recommended devolving funds to gram panchayats for basic services from 1995 onwards.

Table 4.2 shows that per cent increase in the total expenditure of gram panchayats was negative for two consecutive years but from 1995-96 it has increased by 45 per cent. Clearly, it demonstrates a demarcated trend in the expenditure before 1995-96 and after. As mentioned earlier, it is due to more devolution of funds to panchayats from a large number of developmental activities under various schemes.

In the sample gram panchayats, total expenditure of four gram panchayats show increasing trend (Table 4.3). The annual average of receipts and expenditures show gram panchayats is in surplus except one sample panchayat having deficit. This is because of the grants received are not spent in a particular year and it spilled over to another year and therefore, the total expenditure is accounted for more than the total receipt. The expenditure from assigned revenues constitutes a very low percent of total expenditure for sample gram panchayats (Table 4.3, Col. 17). The maximum per cent of expenditure is from grants and assigned revenues (Col. 18, Table 4.3). The expenditure from own sources of revenue also show increasing trend (Col. 13) and annual average varies from 6 to 12 per cent. This is due to regional variation within the district.

Table 4.12 provides per capita expenditure itemwise for six year period for GPs. The maximum per capita expenditure on establishment comes to Rupees 24 in 1997-98 whereas in the same year the expenditure on services is Rupees 12 and on development it is Rs. 166, which is highest. The per capita total expenditure shows increasing trend and it has registered maximum in 1997-98 for Rupees 202, which is quite high as compared to other years. It seems that panchayats are showing scanty attention towards services. More developmental expenditure will result in infrastructure development and capital overheads. With proper initiative, they may be able to develop the area and it may improve conditions of living and levels of income of rural people.

Janpad Panchayats

The expenditure data of Janpad Panchayats is presented in the Table 4.14. It is evident that there is a steep rise in the expenditure on administration over a period of time. Nevertheless, it always indicates surplus. The expenditure on services has also increased but not as of administration. The salary of staff has gone up due to merger of erstwhile block administration with Janpad. Naturally, the salary and other related component have gone up tremendously. Besides, the payment of salary of Siksha Karmi has been given to Janpad from 1996-97. So far the expenditure on development grants

Table 4.14 : Expenditure of Janpad Panchayats of Madhya Pradesh

S.No.	Items	1992-93		1993-94		1994-95		1995-96		1996-97		1997-98	
		AMOUNT	PC	AMOUNT	PC	AMOUNT	PC	AMOUNT	PC	AMOUNT	PC	AMOUNT	PC
A	GENERAL ADMINISTRATION												
(i)	(a) Salary of Panchayat Staff and other Expenditure	88397		111361		112687		114991		188768		207644	
	(b) Salary of Shiksha Karmi									452019		1839204	
(ii)	Terminal Benefits												
(iii)	Maintenance of Assets	1248		1273		1299		1325		1460		1646	
	Others (Administration)	6904		8682		11761		16899		22726		18455	
	Sub-Total (A)	96549	2.77	121316	3.48	125747	3.61	133215	3.82	664973	19.07	2066949	59.28
B	EXPENDITURE ON SERVICES												
(i)	Ferry Services	1223		2234		3478		9297		7502		7877	
(ii)	Fair and Festival	1079		3705		4351		5766		6634		6699	
(iii)	Markets, Mela, Exhibition	1801		2374		2525		2525		2888		3622	
	Sub-Total (B)	4103	0.07	8313	0.17	10354	0.22	17588	0.43	17024	0.41	18198	0.42
C	EXPENDITURE ON DEVELOPMENT												
(i)	GRANTS												
(ii)	Grant from State Government											242507	
(iii)	Centrally Sponsored Schemes (JRY)											955963	
(iv)	TFC Grants									70000		70000	
	Other Expenditure (Honorarium)							51381		54380		55575	
	Sub-Total (C)		0.05		0.07		0.07	51381	1.55	124380	3.65	1324045	38.08
	GRAND TOTAL	100652	2.89	129629	3.72	136101	3.9	202184	5.8	806377	23.13	3409192	97.78

AMOUNT (Rs. Thousands) PC = PER CAPITA (Rupees)

Source: Commissioner of Panchayats, Government of Madhya Pradesh.

is concerned, Janpads were not involved initially in developmental work but from 1996-97 they are receiving grants under TFC and other state schemes. This component also constitutes the expenditure on honorarium given to office bearers of the Janpad. The total expenditure shows increasing trend (Table 4.6) and it has gone up by 298 per cent in 1996-97, which is quite high as compared to other years, especially in 1994-95 (4.99%).

The per capita expenditure (Table 4.14) also shows increasing trend and the per capita total expenditure in 1997-98 has reached to Rupees 97. The per capita expenditure on establishment has reached maximum to Rs. 59 in 1997-98 which is quite high as compared to service expenditure (less than Re. 1) and development expenditure (Rs. 35). Thus, the Janpads are spending more on establishment than other component of expenditure in terms of per capita expenditure.

In sample Janpad Panchayats, the annual average expenditure is less than the total annual receipts. As seen for the state level performance on expenditure, the expenditure in both samples Janpads is increasing. The per cent expenditure to the total receipts (Table 4.7) is less that is they have surplus. But, this situation is misleading so far the financial requirement is concerned. The per cent of total income from assigned revenue and grants to the total expenditure (Table 4.7, Col. 20) has fluctuations. In case of Dharmjaygarh, it is declining whereas in the other sample Janpad it is increasing. It appears that one sample Janpad is not fully utilising grants for the development purposes, as expected.

Zilla Panchayat

Table 4.15 shows that Zilla Panchayats were not getting development funds earlier and they were only providing water supply services to people. The expenditure on establishment has tremendously increased in absolute terms. The salary of staff has gone up in 1997-98 by two fold as compared to 1992-93. As Zilla Panchayats are now disbursing salary of Shiksha Karmi and health workers, the expenditure on establishment from 1996-97 onwards has gone up.

Table 4.15 : Expenditure of Zilla Panchayats of Madhya Pradesh

S.No.	Items	1992-93		1993-94		1994-95		1995-96		1996-97		1997-98	
		AMOUNT	PC	AMOUNT	PC	AMOUNT	PC	AMOUNT	PC	AMOUNT	PC	AMOUNT	PC
A	GENERAL ADMINISTRATION												
(i)	Salary of Panchayat Staff	6081		6715		6772		8124		8758		12304	
(ii)	Salary of Shiksha Karmi									120158		488902	
(iii)	Salary of Health Workers: Central											23515	
	State											14740	
(iv)	Maintenance of Assets	365		403		406		487		525		738	
(v)	Others	4906		6523		5606		8087		18000		18738	
	Sub-Total (A)	11352	0.33	13641	0.39	12784	0.37	16698	0.048	147441	4.23	558937	16.03
B	EXPENDITURE ON OBLIGATORY STUDIES												
(i)	Water Supply (Reserve Fund)	30000		30000		30000		212267		264830		307660	
(ii)	Forest									1425		1425	
(iii)	Public Health									3248		7560	
(iv)	Others (Development Dept.)									725116		1004036	
	Sub-Total (B)	30000		30000		30000		212267		994619		1320681	

Contd. ...

Table 4.15 : *Contd. ...*

S.No.	Items	1992-93		1993-94		1994-95		1995-96		1996-97		1997-98	
		AMOUNT	PC	AMOUNT	PC	AMOUNT	PC	AMOUNT	PC	AMOUNT	PC	AMOUNT	PC
C	EXPENDITURE ON DEVELOPMENT GRANTS												
(i)	Grant from State Government (Honorarium Trg.)	2477		3343		4956	0.1	32914	0.65	32722	0.64	31247	
	Centrally Sponsored Schemes												
(ii)	JRY 20% & 15%, IRDP,												
	EAS - State Share											1295618	
	Central Share											3630824	
	National Old Age Pension/NFB							267891	5.27	514082	10.11	459613	
(iii)	National maternity benefit schemes							35774		30316		39977	
	TFC Grants									30000	0.59	30000	
	Sub-Total (C)	2477	0.07	3343	0.1	4956	0.14	336579	9.65	607120	17.41	5487279	157.37
	GRAND TOTAL	43829	0.4	46984	0.49	47740	0.51	565544	9.698	1749180	21.64	7366897	173.4

AMOUNT (Rs. Thousands)
PC = PER CAPITA (Rupees)
Source: Commissioner of Panchayats, Govt. of Madhya Pradesh.

In the area of delivery of services, they were earlier responsible for only water supply, but from 1996-97, they were entrusted with additional responsibility of health and forest work. In the sphere of water supply, the expenditure has gone up very high in 1997-98. This is because of more grants coming for this service. The expenditure on development grants has also increased tremendously because from 1995-96 they are getting various grants for development purposes. Table 4.11 shows the per cent increase in total expenditure. Evidently, it has increased and recorded maximum by 1084 per cent in 1995-96, the year from when the allocation of funds is more.

The per capita expenditure on establishment has increased from less than a rupee for 1992-93 to Rupees 16 in 1997-98. The per capita expenditure (Table 4.15) on development grants has also gone up to the maximum by Rs. 15. Similarly, the per capita total expenditure has gone up from less than one rupee to Rs.173 in 1997-98. A clear shift in expenditure trend is visible from 1995-96 onwards because of devolution of funds and functions to Zilla Panchayats in the state.

In the sample district Raigarh, the trend is similar in terms of expenditure (Table 4.9). With the increase in the functional responsibilities and devolution of funds, trend is quite obvious. The pattern of expenditure indicates that they are spending more on development works than the delivery of civic services. They are spending more on maternity benefit, old age pension, employment schemes and family benefit schemes. The sample ZP does not have own income so there is no expenditure out of this source.

The foregoing analysis shows that expenditure trend is increasing and the pattern of expenditure has variations in respect of establishment, service delivery and developmental work. It is due to the fact that devolution of functions and funds to the new dispensation of Panchayats in the state has taken place remarkably.

Conclusion

The analysis of financial structure of panchayats in the state comes out with similar rhetoric of dependency syndrome and grant-culture.

It is extremely fragile and a matter of concern. The complexity of financial situation is due to poor efficiency in tax efforts, low taxable capacity in rural areas and effort to use revenue raising powers to optimal level. In the democratic decentralise frame; augmentation of internal resources is crucial. Therefore, the possible way to augment resources depends upon better exploitation of the fiscal domain given under present legislation, expansion of their fiscal domain and granting flexibility to Panchayats in respect of tax rate adjustment. Moreover, as pointed out earlier, it largely depends upon political will to make them unit of self-governance. There are various measures to improve own revenue collection capabilities that have been suggested. The Eleventh Finance Commission has also recommended several measures in this regard, which requires serious consideration by State Government and Panchayats.

ANNEXURE - I

STATEMENT 1.1

Tax and Non-Tax Assigned to Gram Panchayat

Obligatory Taxes	*Optional Taxes, Fees, etc.*
1. A property tax on the lands or buildings or both, the capital value of which including the value of the land is more than six thousand rupees other than (a) the buildings and lands owned or vested in the Union or State Government, Gram Panchayat, Janpad Panchayat or Zilla Panchayat. (b) The buildings and lands or positions thereof used exclusively for religious or educational purpose. 2. A tax on private latrines payable by the occupier or owner of the buildings to which such latrines are attached when cleaned by Gram Panchayat agency. 3. A light tax, if the Gram Panchayat has made light arrangements. 4. A tax on person, exercising any profession or carrying on any trade or calling within the limits of Gram Panchayat area. *Non-Tax Sources* 1. Market fees on persons exposing goods for sale in any market or at any place or any building or structure therein belonging to or under the control of the Gram Panchayat. 2. Fees on the registration of cattle sold in any market or in any place belonging to or under the control of the Gram Panchayat.	1. A tax on building not covered under item (1) of Schedule-1. 2. A tax on animals used for riding, driving, drought or burden or on dogs or pigs payable by the owners thereof. 3. A tax on the bullock-carts, bicycles, rickshaws used for hire within the limits of Gram Panchayat area. 4. Water rate where the Gram Panchayat makes arrangements for regular supply of water. 5. Any other taxes, which the State Legislature has, power to impose under the Constitution of India. *Non-Tax Sources* 1. Fees for the use of dharamshalas, rest houses, slaughterhouses and encamping grounds. 2. Fees for drainage where the Gram Panchayat has introduced system of drainage. 3. A tax on persons carrying on the profession of purchaser, agent, commission agent, weigh man, or a measure within the meaning of Madhya Pradesh, Krishi Upaj Mandi Adhiniyam, 1972 (No. 24 of 1973). In the area of Gram Panchayat excluding the area of a mandi. 4. A fees payable by the owners of the vehicles other than motor vehicle, where such vehicles enter the Gram Panchayat area. 5. A temporary tax for special works of public utility.

Contd. ...

STATEMENT 1.1*: Contd.*

Obligatory Taxes	*Optional Taxes, Fees, etc.*
	6. A tax for the construction or maintenance of public latrines and a general scavenging tax for removal and disposal of refuse. 7. Fees for bullock cart stand and tonga stand. 8. Fees for temporary structure or any projection over any public place or temporary occupation thereof. 9. Fees for grazing cattle over the grazing grounds vested in the Gram Panchayat.

[The powers to impose obligatory and optional taxes by Gram Panchayat under the old MPPA, 1981 and 1990 in schedule I, of section 67(1) are same in the new Act of 1993 in Schedule I of Section 77(1). Therefore, there is no change in taxation powers in pre- and post-73rd Amendment.]

STATEMENT 1.2

Rate of Taxes of Gram Panchayat

Rate of Building Tax

Rate Prevailing before 73rd Amendment [Sub-section (1) of section 81 of MPPA, 1962 as per rules of April, 1966]			*Existing Rate [Sub-section (2) of Section 77 of MPPA, 1993 and as per rules of February 29, 1966]*		
Particulars	*Minimum*	*Maximum*	*Particulars*	*Minimum*	*Maximum*
1. On Building of capital value exceeding Rs. 1,000 but not exceeding Rs.2,000	1. 20 Paise per Rs.100 of the capital value or fraction thereof.	1. 30 Paise per Rs. 100 of the capital value or fraction thereof.	1. On building of capital value exceeding Rs. 6,000 but not exceeding Rs. 12,000	1. 20 Paise per Rs. 100 of the capital value or fraction thereof.	1. 30 Paise per Rs. 100 of the capital value or fraction thereof.
2. On building of capital value exceeding Rs.2,000	2. Rupee 1 per 500 Rupees of the capital value or fraction thereof but not more than Rs.100	2. Rupees 1.50 per 500 Rupees of the capital value or fraction thereof but not more than Rs. 150	2. On building of capital value exceeding Rs. 12,000	2. Rupee 1 per 500 Rupees of the capital or fraction thereof but not more than Rs. 100	2. Rupees 1.50 per 500 Rupees of the capital value or fraction thereof but not more than Rs.150

Rate of Profession Tax

Rates Prevailing Before 73rd Amendment [As per rules of April 1966 and under section 81(1) of 1966 Act.]			*Existing Rate [As per rules of February 29, 1996 and under section 77(2) of MPPA, 1993]*		
Annual Income (Rs.)	*Minimum (Rs.)*	*Maximum (Rs.)*	*Annual Income (Rs.)*	*Minimum (Rs.)*	*Maximum (Rs.)*
500 to 1000	1.00	2.00	11000 to 15000	100.00	200.00
1001 to 2000	2.00	4.00	15001 to 20000	150.00	300.00
2001 to 4000	4.00	8.00	20001 to 30000	200.00	400.00
4001 to 6000	8.00	12.00	30001 to 40000	300.00	600.00
6001 to 8000	12.00	16.00	40001 to 50000	450.00	900.00
8001 to 10000	16.00	20.00	—	—	—
More than 10,000	20.00	30.00	More than 50,001	650.00	1400.00

Rate of Vehicle Tax

Rate Prevailing Before 73rd Amendment [As per rules of October 12, 1962 and under section 82(2) of 1962 Act]		*Existing Rate [As per Sub-section (2) of Rules February 29, 1996 and under item 3 of Schedule-II of MPPA, 1993]*	
Particulars	*Rate*	*Particulars*	*Rate*
1. Rate of tax payable by owner of vehicle under section 82(2)	1. Rs. 2 per vehicle per annum.	1. Rate of tax payable by owner of vehicle under item (3), Schedule-11 of the Act.	1. Rs.10 per vehicle per annum.
2. A fee payable by owners of vehicle other than motor vehicle are kept within Gram Sabha area under section (82) (h)	2. Re. 1 per vehicle per annum	2. A fee payable by owners of vehicle other than motor vehicle where such vehicles enter the Gram Panchayat	2. Per vehicle Rs. 5 per day.

Rate of Optional Taxes

Rate of fees on persons exposing Goods for sale in any market or place belonging to or under the control of the Gram Panchayat or for the use of any building or structure thereon.

Particulars	*Minimum*	*Maximum*
1. For every plot measuring not more than one square metre	1. 20 Paise per day or Rs. 2 per month.	1. 20 Paise per day or Rs. 4 per month.
2. For every additional space of one square metre or part thereof	2. 5 Paise per day or Re. 1 per month.	2. 10 Paise per day or Rs. 2 per month.
3. For goods brought to the market for sale	3. 3 Paise per basket or head load (not being a bag) or 10 Paise per bag or 40 Paise per cart load.	3. 5 Paise per basket or head load (not being a bag) or 20 Paise per bag or 75 Paise per cart load.

Rate of Other Fees

Rate Prevailing Before 73rd Amendment [As per rules of October 12, 1962 and under section 82(2) of 1962 Act]		*Existing Rate [As per rules of February 29, 1996 and under item 3 of Schedule-II of MPPA, 1993]*	
Particulars	*Rate*	*Particulars*	*Rate*
1. Rate of fees for use of sarai, dhram-shalas, etc. under section 82(G)		1. Rate of fees for use of sarai, dharmshalas, etc. under item (4) of Schedule-II of the Act	
(i) Varandah	Re. 0.12	(i) Varandah	Re. 0.50
(ii) Small Room 3x3 metres or less	Re. 0.25	(ii) Small Room 3x3 metres or less	Rs. 2.00
(iii) Big room (more than 3x3 metres)	Re. 0.50	(iii) Big room (more than 3x3 metres)	Rs. 4.00
(iv) Rooms furnished with furniture	Re. 1.00	(iv) Rooms furnished with furniture	
(v) Encamping ground up to 3x3 metres	Nil	(v) Encamping ground up to 3x3 metres	Rs. 8.00

Contd. ...

Rate Prevailing Before 73rd Amendment [As per rules of October 12, 1962 and under section 82(2) of 1962 Act]		*Existing Rate [As per rules of February 29, 1996 and under item 3 of Schedule-II of MPPA, 1993]*	
Particulars	*Rate*	*Particulars*	*Rate*
(vi) Encamping ground above 3x3 metres	Re. 0.06	(vi) Encamping ground above 3×3 metres	Nil
2. Slaughter House	Re. 0.50 per animal	2. Slaughter House	Re. 0.30
3. Water rate piped water system per tap	Re. 1.00 per month	3. Water rate piped water system per tap	Rs. 2.00 per animal
4. Drainage fee value of building above Rs. 10,000	Rs. 6.00 per month	4. Drainage fee	Rs.20.00 per month
5. Fees for buyer, broker, commission agent.	Rs. 4.00 per annum	5. Fees for buyer, broker, commission agent.	1% of capital value of building per annum Rs.25.00 per annum
6. Fee on cart stands/ tonga stand.	Rs. 4.00 per vehicle/annum	6. Fee on cart stands/ tonga stand.	Rs.20.00 per vehicle/annum
7. Fee for grazing cattle on grazing land	Rs. 4.00 per cattle/annum	7. Fee for grazing cattle on grazing land	Rs.20.00 per cattle/annum

STATEMENT 1.3

Tax and Non-Tax Assigned to Janpad Panchayat

Obligatory Taxes

1. A Tax on theatre or theatrical performances and other performances of public entertainment.

Optional Taxes

1. Development tax on agriculture land.
2. Additional Stamp duty.

Non-Tax Sources

1. Fees for any licence or permission for use and occupation of lands or other properties vested with it.

Contd.

[Before 73rd Amendment, obligatory taxes, optional taxes and non-tax revenue sources under sub-sections (1) & (2) of Section 67 of MPPA, 1981 and sub-section (1) of Section 75 of MPPA, 1990 is the same after the 73rd Amendment under sub-section (1) of Section 77 of MPPA, 1993 for Janpad Panchayats].

Rates of Taxes of Janpad Panchayats

1. Entertainment Tax:

	Before 73rd Amendment [Under sub-section (2) of Section 15 of 1962 Act and as per rules of December 11,1963]		*After 73rd Amendment [Under section (2) of section 77 of MPPA, 1993 and as per rules of February 29, 1996]*	
	Minimum (Per show)	*Maximum (Per show)*	*Minimum (Per show)*	*Maximum (Per show)*
1. Cinema	Rs. 5/-	Rs. 10/-	Rs. 10/-	Rs. 20/-
2. Drama/Circus	Rs. 5/-	Rs. 10/-	Rs. 7/-	Rs. 15/-
3. Carnival fee Tamasha, Wrestling Performance	Rs. 3/-	Rs. 5/-	Rs. 5/-	Rs. 10/-
4. Any other performance or amusement	Re. 0.50/-	Re. 1/-	Rs. 5/-	Rs. 5/-

The rules on entertainment tax lay down the condition that any amusement that is not open to the general public on payment will be exempted. The tax is payable by the manager organising the show. In the event of any breach of any rule the offender shall be punishable with fine which may extend to five hundred rupees.

2. Fines and Penalties:

(i) Encroachment fine Rs. 1000/-
(ii) Removal from posts if such person does not give charges. Penalty worth Rs. 1000/-
(iii) In case the fees on market fair is not paid fine of Rs. 50 is imposed on the defaulter and if the fine is also not paid penalty of Rs. 5 per day is imposed till the amount is not in full.

3. Ferry:

Janpad Panchayat auctions it.

Other Revenue Sources

Apart from the powers vested under the Act for raising own resources, the PRIs have been delegated powers to mobilize resources by leasing water bodies (Tanks) within their jurisdiction for fisheries development as follows:

Up to 10 hectares	:	Gram Panchayat
Up to 10 to 100 hectares	:	Janpad Panchayat
Up to 100 to 2000 hectares	:	Zilla Panchayat

5

RURAL, PERI-URBAN CONTRAST IN FINANCIAL MANAGEMENT : A STUDY WITH SPECIAL REFERENCE TO GRAM PANCHAYATS IN KERALA

C. PRATHEEP AND B. MOHANAN

Introduction

Though Gram Panchayats have existed in India from time immemorial, their performance was far from satisfactory because of several factors including insufficient financial resources. However, the 73rd Constitutional Amendment and Conformity Acts in States empowered the Local Self Governments to mobilize more own resources and to secure more funds from the Central and State Governments for their smooth functioning and to carry out developmental activities. As per the Constitutional amendments and enactment of subsequent rules and regulations, the various sources of revenue of Panchayat Raj institutions are own taxes, own non-taxes, Grants-in-aid, devolution of funds from the State Government, financial devolution through Central and State Finance Commissions, loans from the financial institutions. Though the constitutional provisions are the same, resource structure varies not only in various States of India but also in different Gram Panchayats in the same State. Per cent of own revenue collection of the high income States was 4.50 while Middle income States was 2.40 , in the lower income States was 2.24 and in the smaller States it was 4.84. All India average was 3.66 per cent of the NSDP. This shows that 3.48 per cent of the income was received from the own tax, 2.9 per cent from the Own non-tax, 28.4 per cent from the assignment and devolution, 58.3 from the grants, and 7 per cent from the other incomes.

Compared to other States in India, the financial position of Gram Panchayats in Kerala is far better. Various sources of revenue of the Gram Panchayats are income from different taxes, realisation from special acts, income from properties, Panchayat fees, Government grants, plan funds and devolution as per the recommendations of Central and State Finance Commissions. But Gram Panchayats in Kerala have a difference in revenue, expenditure and in management due to a number of reasons and urban-rural dichotomy is one of the areas of differences. In Kerala, peri-urban Panchayats differ from rural Panchayats in many respects. In this study the researchers tried to analyse the revenue, expenditure and management of selected peri-urban and rural Gram Panchayats to identify the current financial position, similarities, differences, influential factors in peri-urban and rural Gram Panchayats of Kerala. The researchers selected ten Gram Panchayats, i.e., five rural and five peri-urban Gram Panchayats by using stratified random sampling method on the basis of revenue, population and region. Selected Gram Panchayats are Beypore, Cheruvannur-Nallalam, Kakkodi, Koorachundu, Peruvayal from Kozhikode District and Kudappanakunnu, Pallickal, Venganoor, Kanjiramkulam, and Vizhinjam Gram Panchayats from Thiruvananthapuram District of Kerala. Both primary and secondary data have been used. Financial data for the period from 1998-99 to 2002-03 have been processed and analysed.

Sources of Revenue

The mean total revenue of the sample Panchayats is Rs. 96,64,548 per year. Source-wise classification shows that 21 per cent of the income is from the taxes, 2 per cent from realisation under special acts, 5 per cent from properties, 3 per cent from panchayat fees,

6 per cent from government grants, 60 per cent from plan fund and 3 per cent from other sources. This shows that the major source of revenue of Gram Panchayats in Kerala is income from plan fund. Income from the own tax is only one-fifth of the total. Regression equation was fitted with total revenue as dependent variable and taxes, Realisation from special acts, Panchayat fees, Government grants, plan funds and miscellaneous as dependent variables. Only variable which was found to be significantly influencing the total revenue is plan fund. Compared to plan fund all other variables are found to be negligible. Fitted equation is Total revenue = 42,27,434.2 + 0.941 Plan fund t-value of regression coefficient is 5.025 which is significant at 5 per cent level. R^2 of the above fitted equation is 0.894. This indicates that 89 per cent of the variation in the total revenue is due to Plan funds.

Decentralised planning was introduced in Kerala in the year 1997 and about forty per cent of the State Plan amount was given to the Local Self Governments. This helped the Gram Panchayats to get more financial help to implement various development projects. Two-third of the revenue of the selected Gram Panchayats is form the Government by way of grants and Plan funds. This shows that Panchayats by and large depend on Government grants. However, tax collection is increasing but Plan devolution is not steady. The correlation between tax collection and Plan devolution is minus 0.1677 and R^2 value is 0.2812. This indicates that there is no correlation between the tax collection and Plan fund devolution from State Government. Before the introduction of decentralised planning, all government grants were given to the Panchayats through the tied and untied funds. The left democratic front radically changed financial allocation methods and approaches. The approach of the ruling political party is very important in the Plan fund devolution and it may be not wise to depend upon the Plan fund for the revenue of the Panchayats.

We have tried to analyse the revenue of the Panchayats without the Plan fund. It is found that the total revenue of the Panchayats without the Plan fund is only Rs. 38,83,697. Of this more than fifty per cent of the revenue is generated from taxes. Government grants contribute only 15 per cent. Other sources are 12.5 per cent from properties, 6.1 per cent from Panchayat fees and 8 per cent from other sources. This reveals that if Plan fund is not available, income from tax is the major share of the revenue of the Panchayats. Total revenue = 838886.8 + 12.772 Panchayat fees t-value of regression coefficient is 12.108 which is significant at 5 per cent level. R^2 of the above fitted equation is 0.948. This indicates that 95 per cent of the variation in the total revenue excluding plan fund is due to Panchayat fees.

Per capita income with plan fund is highest in one of the financially poor Panchayats. Per capita income without Plan fund may be considered as one of the yardsticks of financial efficiency of the Panchayats also. The influence of Plan fund in the per capita income is remarkable and there were much difference in the per capita income with Plan fund and without Plan fund.

Existing rules and regulations authorize Panchayats to get loans from financial institutions for development projects. But none of the sample Panchayats availed loans for development projects. This means that the loan sources are not utilized fully by the Panchayats.

In 1999-2000 the growth rate was 14 per cent and in 2002-03 growth per cent was more than 22 per cent. But in 2000-01 and 2001-02 the growth per cent was as low as even one per cent. The collection of these taxes increases every year but this was due to the interest of the Panchayat employees and members. The percentage of tax collection is high whenever the employees and members show interest.

The efforts in the collection of tax in the Panchayats are not similar. This is despite the fact that the rate of tax in all the Panchayats are similar, tax collecting procedure is same, rules and regulations are similar. This percentage difference in the collection of tax is mainly due to the efficiency in financial management in the Panchayats. Analysis shows that tax collection trends in the Panchayats are not similar and higher in the financially well-managed Panchayats and low in the financially ill managed Panchayats.

Except in the year 2001-02 there was increase in the Panchayat fees. The highest change is in the year 1999-2000 and the lowest increase is in the year 2002-03. The analysis shows that the income from the Panchayat fee is increasing but at a decreasing rate in the sample Panchayats except in one year. From 1998-99 to 2002-03 revenue from Panchayat fees increased in all the sample Panchayats except one. It shows that though there was increase in the collection of Panchayat fees in the Panchayats, the rate of change varied widely in various Panchayats.

Government grants to the Panchayats are decreasing over the years. During 1999-2000 the rate of decrease was 30 per cent, in 2000-01 the rate of decrease was 22 per cent and in 2001-02 75 per cent; but in 2002-03 the amount from the grant was increased by 318 per cent. This does not mean that government financial support was reducing, but the increased financial help was being shifted from the head of grants to the head of Plan fund. Previously all the funds which were provided by the government was through the government grants but now all these were routed through the Plan fund. This shows that government grants are decreasing in the sample Panchayats.

Revenue through Plan fund decreased over the years except in one year. In the year 1999-2000 the decrease was 30 per cent, while in 2000-01 it was 22 per cent. The highest decrease, 76 per cent was recorded in the year of 2001-02. This was attributed to Kerala Government's cut the plan expenses by 25 per cent owing to the financial constraints and this adversely affected the Gram Panchayats.

Peri-Urban, Rural Contrast in Revenue

Total revenue of peri-urban Panchayats is Rs.1,32,72,048.00 but revenue of rural Panchayats is only Rs. 64,26,318.00. Except the revenue from Plan sources, peri-urban panchayats are getting more revenue than the rural Panchayats. This shows that revenue differences do exist between peri-urban Panchayats and rural Panchayats. In all sources of revenue except government grants, rural Panchayats are getting lower revenue than the peri-urban Gram Panchayats. Difference is very large in taxes, income from properties and in Plan funds. But in Plan funds allocation, rural Panchayats are getting more revenue than the peri-urban Panchayats.

In the case of peri -urban Panchayats no variable was found to influence the total revenue. In the case of rural Panchayats, Plan fund was found to be influencing the total revenue. The suitable equation is Total revenue = 1061250.1 + 1.188 Plan fund where, t-value of regression coefficient is 7.302 which is significant at 5 per cent level R^2 of the above fitted equation is 0.947. This indicated that 95 per cent of the variation in the total expenditure is due to plan funds.

The analysis on the percentage share of peri-urban and rural Panchayats from 1998-99 to 2002-03 shows that Tax revenue of the peri-urban Panchayats is 22.86 per cent and whereas it is 15.2 per cent in rural Panchayats. Regarding income from the Panchayat properties also peri-urban Panchayats get more income than the rural Panchayats. But in government grants and in Plan funds, rural Panchayats get a higher share than peri-urban Panchayats. This shows that in own sources of revenue, peri-urban Panchayats are getting more percentage and in government grants and plan funds, rural Panchayats receive more.

The correlation between the tax revenue and plan fund is estimated to find out the relation between the Plan fund and tax revenue. Correlation between revenue and Plan fund in peri-urban Panchayats is insignificant (–0.36). But in rural Panchayats, the correlation between the revenue and Plan is positively firm and significant (0.66). This shows that there are differences in peri-urban Panchayats and rural Panchayats in the case of tax and Plan fund. In peri-urban Panchayats, total revenue excluding Plan fund is influenced by revenue from realization from special acts. The Apt equation is Total revenue = 4230271.3 + 4.607. Realisation t-value of regression coefficient is 14.128 which is significant at 5 per cent level. R^2 of the above fitted equation is 0.985. This indicates that 98 per cent of the variation in the total expenditure Plan fund is due to realization from special acts.

In rural Panchayats total revenue excluding Plan fund is influenced by Panchayat fees. The most suitable equation is total revenue=1236860.6 + 6.43 Panchayat fees. t-value of regression coefficient is 5.763 which is significant at 5 per cent level. R^2 of the above fitted equation is 0.917. This indicates that 92 per cent of the variation in the total revenue excluding Plan fund is due to Panchayat fees.

In peri-urban Panchayats per capita availability including Plan fund is Rs. 276.00 and without plan fund is Rs. 122.00, i.e. Rs. 156.00 is got from the Planning Board. In rural Panchayats, per capita income availability with plan fund is Rs. 287.00 and without Plan fund is Rs. 89.00, i.e. Rs. 198.00 is received from the Planning Board. This shows that per capita revenue availability from planning source is higher in rural Panchayats than in peri-urban Panchayats.

Expenditure of the Gram Panchayats

The consolidated statement of expenditure from 1998-99 to 2002-03 shows that management expenses of the Panchayats constitute 18 per cent of the total and these have been increasing all these years except in one year. Public works expense was not uniform in these years. Plan expenses of the Panchayats declined over the years from 1999-2000. Mean Plan expense of the Panchayats is more than fifty lakhs per year which was a major share of the expenses of the Panchayats. Expenses on public works, water supply, education, social welfare, lighting, animal husbandry, and Panchayat properties expenses are less when compared with the Plan and managerial expenses. Analysis shows that mean expenses of the Panchayats is Rs. 84,27,626 and the major expenses of the Panchayat are Plan and managerial expenses. Plan expenditure of the Panchayats declined except in one year but managerial expenses increased steadily.

Fitted equation is year-wise expenditure including plan fund = 3795699.3 + 3.927 management-value of regression coefficient is 3.335 which is significant at 5 per cent level. R^2 of the above fitted equation is 0.788. This indicates that 79 per cent of the variation in the expenditure is due to management.

Consolidated statement of the income and expenditure of the sample Panchayats shows that 60 per cent of the sample Panchayats were spending more than 90 per cent of the revenue to the expenditure from 1998-99 to 2002-03. Average annual per cent of the expenditure was 90 per cent of the income.

Year-wise analysis of the total expenditure excluding the Plan fund shows that expenditure is not steady in the Panchayats. 1999-2000 and 2000-01 expenditure showed an increase while there was a decrease in expenditure in the year of 2001-02. Average annual percentage of expenditure was 83 per cent over the revenue of the Panchayats.

The per capita expenditure in 1998-99 was Rs. 217. The per capita expenditure increased to 254 in 1999-2000 and to 260 in 2000-01. But in 2001-02 expenditure fell to Rs. 215. It showed that per capita expenditure is changed from year to year. Only the variable which influences the year-wise expenditure excluding Plan fund is expenditure on street lighting. Fitted equation is : Year-wise expenditure excluding Plan fund = 588125.01 + 9.923. Regression coefficient is 6.753 which is significant at 5 per cent level. R^2 of the above fitted equation is 0.938. This indicates that about 74 per cent of the variation in the expenditure is due to street lighting expenditure.

Peri-Urban, Rural Contrast in Expenditure

Average mean expenditure of a peri-urban Panchayat is Rs. 1,11,63,922 and average expenditure of a rural Panchayat is Rs. 56,91,341. This shows that there are remarkable differences between peri-urban Panchayats and rural Panchayats in expenditure profile.

Mean total revenue of the peri-urban Panchayats is Rs. 1,33,38,101 and expenditure, Rs. 1,11,63,922. During this period, mean expenditure of Rural Panchayats was Rs. 56,91,340.00. Revenue over expenditure in peri-urban Panchayat is Rs. 21,74,179 and in rural Panchayat is Rs. 2,99,659. This shows that there is a remarkable difference between peri-urban Panchayats and rural Panchayats in revenue and expenditure.

Analysis shows that peri-urban Panchayats have more funds to spend on various items of work. The mean difference between revenue and expenditure of peri-urban Panchayats is Rs. 21,74,179.00. But the difference between revenue and expenditure of rural Panchayats is only Rs. 2,99,659.00

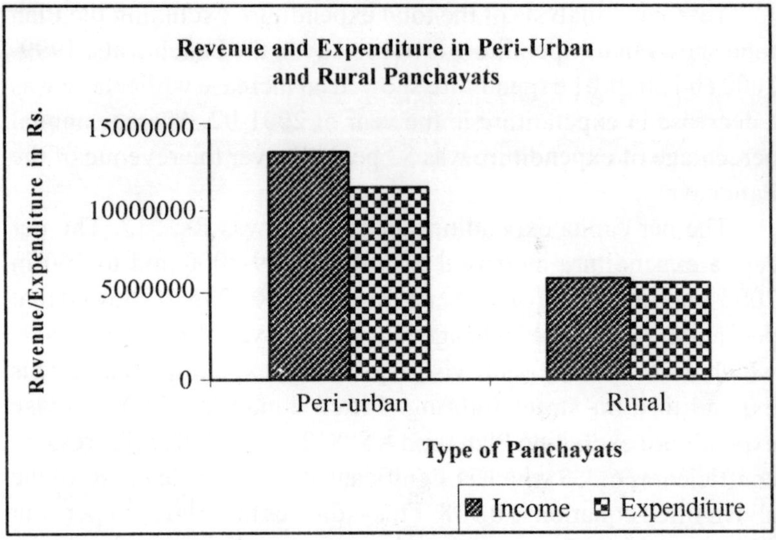

Management expenditure in peri-urban Panchayats is 41 per cent while in rural Panchayat it is 62 per cent. In water supply, public health, lighting and in Panchayat properties, peri-urban Panchayats spend more than the rural Panchayats. Analysis of the consolidated revenue and expenditure statement of the Panchayats from 1998-99 to 2002-03 shows that 60 per cent of the Panchayats spend more than 90 per cent of the revenue. Average annual difference between revenue and expenditure is Rs.12,36,919 and annual average percentage of expenditure is 87 per cent of the revenue. This shows that higher income panchayats spend less than those of the low income panchayats.

Analysis also shows that rural Panchayats depend on Plan fund to meet expenditures. Without the Plan fund the rural Panchayats may not be able to meet their expenditures. During the study period, rural Panchayats showed a deficit of Rs. 34,854.00. But peri-urban Panchayats' difference of income over expenditure is Rs. 13,47,679.00. This showed that rural Panchayats depend more on Plan fund than the peri-urban Panchayats. In peri-urban Panchayats per capita availability of fund is Rs. 276.00 and per capita expenditure is Rs. 230.00, i.e. Rs. 46.00 is the per capita surplus. But in rural Panchayats per capita availability of funds is

Rs. 287.00 and expenditure is Rs. 272.00, i.e. the surplus of Rs. 15.00. This shows that per capita surplus is higher in peri- urban Panchayats than in rural Panchayats.

Revenue and Expenditure : Influencing Factors

There are various factors that influence the revenue and expenditure of the Panchayats. It is very important to identify these factors. Tax collection efforts and expenditure of the Panchayats are dependent on various factors like population, number of wards, land area, density of population etc. An attempt was made to identify the dependent factors affecting tax collection and expenditure of the Panchayats. Pearson correlation value is 0.854 and correlation is significant at the 0.01 level.

Factors like tax collection and population were analysed to find out the influence of population and revenue of the Gram Panchayats. More populated Panchayats were able to collect more income than the less populated Panchayats. In order to understand the relationship between the population and tax collection, Pearson correlation method was used. Pearson Correlation value of tax collection and population is 0.854 and correlation is significant at the 0.01 level. This means that tax collection is higher in the more populated Panchayats while it is less in the less populated Panchayats.

In order to know the relationship between the tax collection and number of wards, Pearson correlation method was used. The value of the relationship between the tax collection and number of wards is positive 0.863 and correlation is significant at the 0.01 level. This mean tax collection is higher in the Panchayats where number of wards are more. One of the main sources of tax is the house tax or the property tax. Property tax will be higher in the Panchayats where number of houses will be more. In order to understand the relationship between the tax collection and number of houses, Pearson correlation method was used. The result of the correlation between the tax collection and number of houses is positive 0.774 and correlation is significant at the 0.05 levels. This table and correlation analysis confirm the fact that tax collection and number of houses are closely related.

Highest government grants was received by Kanjiramkulam Panchayat and lowest amount was received by Kudappanakunnu Panchayat. The value of the correlation between the tax collection and Government Grants shows that there is negative correlation to the value of – 0.146. This means that the grants are higher in the Panchayats where tax collection is low and government grants is low in the Panchayats where the tax collection is higher.

In the selected Panchayats, Peruvayal Panchayat is the biggest Panchayat in terms of land area and Kudappanakunnu is the smallest Panchayat. The correlation analysis says that there is no relationship between the tax collection and land area. Pearson Correlation value is 0.373 and correlation is insignificant. This table and correlation analysis says that there is negative correlation between the tax collection and land area in the Panchayats.

Total income and total expenditure is correlated in the Panchayats. The correlation value is calculated as positive 0.984 and relation is significant at the level of 0.01.

The correlation between population and own tax collection in peri-urban Panchayats is 0.057. In rural Panchayats the correlation between population and own revenue collection is 0.802. This shows that correlation is higher in rural Panchayats compared to the peri-urban Panchayats. Correlation between the number of houses and tax collection in peri-urban Panchayats is non-significant. But in rural Panchayats, the correlation is 0.687. This shows that in the revenue generation in rural Panchayats the number of houses is a significant factor.

Both in peri-urban Panchayats and in rural Panchayats, the influence of land area on the own revenue collection is not significant. Correlation between land area and tax collection in peri-urban Panchayats is –0.889 and the correlation in rural Panchayats is 0.010.

Combined effort of various factors were analysed and given in following table. From the various factors, Index of institutions is the most significant factor, while population is the second significant factor and the number of houses is the third significant factor in the determination of revenue of the Gram Panchayats in Kerala.

Combined effect of various influencing factors

Variable	*Correlation*	*Partial Correlation*
Population	0.768	0.3925
Index of Institutions	0.821	0.6253
No. of houses	0.583	–0.6359
Land area	–0.198	0.0655

Financial Management Practices in the Gram Panchayats

Financial management in Local Self Governments may be defined as the efforts of revenue estimation, mobilisation, budgeting, implementation of budgeting, allocation of revenue in the programmes, accounting, evaluation of programmes and keeping the financial data in a democratic way. In this definition there are various functions of financial management: (1) Revenue Estimation, (2) Mobilisation, (3) Budgeting, (4) Implementation of budgeting, (5) Allocation of revenue, (6) Evaluation of programmes, (7) Accounting and (8) Data keeping. Researcher analyses the existing financial management practice of the Gram Panchayats.

No scientific revenue estimation is done in the Gram Panchayats. What they are doing is fixing the property tax at the time of submission of application by the applicants in order to get house number. No local authority staff are doing any scientific method for the calculation. Proper tax assessment by doing mapping of revenue resources should be done in the Gram Panchayats. All the taxes are compulsorily collected by the concerned staff of the Gram Panchayats. Since Tax collection is one of the jobs of the collecting staff, if the employees are busy with other activities of the Panchayat, the tax collection will automatically be less. People's plan was introduced in Kerala in order to decentralize the planning process but the workload of the employees increased and this affected badly the tax collection efforts. Panchayat employees are not much interested in the collection of various taxes. Proper rewards and incentives and administrative steps to encourage the staff to take tax collection seriously might enhance revenue from tax in Panchayats.

There are various sources of revenue in the selected Gram Panchayats of Kerala. Sources are Panchayat taxes, realisation under special acts, revenue derived from the Panchayat properties, Panchayat fees, government grants and contributions and other miscellaneous revenues. Panchayat taxes include income from building/property tax, service taxes, tax on vessels, profession tax, show tax, land cess, duty on transfer of duty etc. Realisation under special acts includes receipts under PFA Act, receipts under ET Acts etc. Revenue under Panchayat properties includes rent of lands and buildings, income from auction, markets, bus stand receipts, receipts from slaughter house, ferry rents etc. Panchayat fees includes Licence fee from D&O trades, construction of building, private markets etc. Government grants include grants from Central Government, State Government, District Panchayat and Block Panchayats. Other incomes include library cess, lapsed deposits etc. (Constitutional provisions in the Panchayat Raj Acts were given in the Appendix). The income from the show tax was less because of many reasons. Theatre in the rural areas are facing crisis of less number of cinema viewers because of the popularity of various TV channels and the influence of Video cassettes. Second was the reducing of tax rates by the Government of Kerala applicable to the whole of local bodies. Other reasons for declining of income from show tax is a tacit understanding between the theatre owners and Gram Panchayat staff in many parts of Kerala. Surprise visits of the Finance Standing Committee members, regular and proper inspection by the Gram Panchayat staff were among the action taken by the selected Panchayats to tide over the alarming fall in revenue from this sector.

Regarding the property tax of the Gram Panchayat, the resource was not tapped fully because of many reasons in the selected Panchayats. The property tax assessment has to be done every five years. But this has not been done for the last so many years because of the lack of action of the State Government. This lead to loss of many crores of rupees to the local bodies. Many Gram Panchayats complained about the existing method of tax calculation of the Gram Panchayats. Gram Panchayat employees were visiting houses to collect tax from the houses.

Almost all the Gram Panchayats in Kerala have lands of their own which are being used as village markets. The income from these markets of Gram Panchayats are not fully collected in many cases. Existing practice of auctioning is the main reason for that. The auction money will always be low compared to the potentialities. If the Panchayat directly collects 'gate fee' it would definitely increase the revenue of the Panchayats.

Our study reveals that budget appropriation policy in the Gram Panchayat is not scientific. Present practice of Panchayat staff is that they just add some amount to the last year's figures and these are presented before the Panchayat Committee meeting. As per the existing rule every Gram Panchayat should have a minimum of 5 per cent surplus in the expenditure over revenue in the budget. The authorities may consider, in the larger interest, withdrawal of this requirement. There is no financial management methods in the budgeting of the Gram Panchayats. This system has to be changed. Application of good financial management requires training in the modern financial administration practices. Introduction of Zero base budgeting may enhance the financial position of the Panchayats.

Periodical training is very essential for the staff to impart new insights and to update their knowledge and this may help increase efficiency also. Kerala Institute of Local Administration (KILA) is authorized to provide training to the members and staff in the local administration department. Due to the shortage of staff, the KILA is not able to provide training to all the persons on time. Panchayat employees are not trained properly. Almost all the employees feel the need for more training in tax administration to increase the tax collection. New accounting procedure have been introduced in the Panchayats of Kerala. Proper training is required to improve the tax administration in the Panchayats.

In Gram Panchayats only age old method of manual preparing the accounts is done. No computerization of records of accounts has been introduced in Kerala. Auditing is not taking place in time in the Gram Panchayats by the local fund audit of the Government of Kerala. There are many reasons for delay in the auditing of accounts in the Gram Panchayats in Kerala. The Gram Panchayat secretaries are not preparing and submitting the annual financial statements of the Gram panchayats in time. This practice has to be discouraged. Accounting procedure and method of auditing should be improved.

Evaluation is very important to understand the real benefit of the schemes implemented at the Gram Panchayat level. This will help for the further planning and implementation of the programmes in an effective and efficient way. This will reduce the expenditure of the Gram Panchayats also. Evaluation is not done properly in Panchayats. Panchayats should have the evaluation wing if it is not possible at the Panchayat level, this work could be entrusted with any of the voluntary research institutes. Panchayat members and employees are not at all aware of the need for this evaluation. Proper awareness should be given in this matter.

At present there is no local finance data bank, which is very important for planning, evaluation and implementation of various projects and programmes. This includes all the information regarding resources availability, availability of funds and implementation of various schemes for the last ten years, audited statement of records, various sources of revenue, revenue potential, items of expenditure, Plan fund details, details regarding the grants from the States and Central governments, complete details of the population, employment details, geographical information etc. Gram Panchayat data is not collected and kept properly in the Gram Panchayats of Kerala. This is one of the important bottlenecks of the Gram Panchayats in Kerala.

Major findings of the study are the average revenue of a Gram Panchayat during 1998-99 to 2002-03 is Rs. 96,64,548. Three-fifth (60%) of the total revenue comes from Plan fund.

Own revenue collection is increasing. It increased from 17 to 25 per cent during the study period. The total revenue of Panchayats is influenced by Plan fund. (Total revenue =4227434.2+0.94 Plan fund) 89 per cent of the variation is due to Plan fund. In the peri-urban Panchayats, the independent variables analysed do not have significant influence in the total revenue. In rural Panchayats the total revenue is influenced by Plan fund (Total revenue =1061250.1+1.188 Plan fund) the total revenue of all Panchayats excluding Plan fund is influenced by Panchayat fees. In peri-urban Panchayats the total revenue excluding Plan fund is influenced by realization from special acts. In rural Panchayats the total revenue excluding Plan fund is influenced by Panchayat various fess collected by the Gram Panchayats. Own tax collection of Gram Panchayats is not uniform all through the five years. Percentage of change over the previous years is low in 2000-01 and 2001-02. In the year 2001-02 the change was just 1.5 per cent over the previous year. Average annual expenditure of a Gram Panchayats is Rs. 84,27,626. More than three-fourth (62 per cent) of the expenditure of a Gram Panchayat is on Plan items. Management expenditure constitutes about 18 per cent of the total expenditure of Panchayats. Both in amount and in relative share, management expenditure shows an increase year by year. In the case of management expenses in low revenue Panchayats, the relative share is high whereas in higher revenue Panchayats it is low. In Plan expenditure the relative share is low in the high income Panchayats and high in the low revenue Panchayats. Average annual per capita expenditure of the sample Panchayats is Rs. 242. Revenue over expenditure in peri-urban Panchayats is Rs. 21,74,179 and in rural Panchayats is Rs. 2,99,659. There are wide differences in fund availability in peri-urban and rural Panchayats. Without Plan fund, rural Panchayats show a deficit of Rs. 34,854 in revenue over expenditure. But in peri-urban Panchayats the difference in revenue over expenditure is Rs. 13,47,679. This shows that rural Panchayats depend more on Plan fund than the peri-urban Panchayats. In peri-urban Panchayats per capita availability of fund is Rs. 276 and expenditure is Rs. 230, i.e. the surplus is Rs. 46. In rural Panchayats per capita availability of fund is Rs. 287 and expenditure is Rs. 272, i.e. the surplus is Rs. 15. This shows that per capita surplus is higher in peri-urban Panchayats than in the rural Panchayats. In the peri-urban Panchayats Rs. 1,11,63,922 is spent on various items of expenditure, and in rural Panchayats, Rs. 56,91,341. This shows that expenditure with Plan fund is higher in peri-urban Panchayats than in the rural Panchayats. Management expenditure in peri-urban Panchayats is 41 per cent but in rural Panchayat it is 62 per cent. In water supply, public health, lighting and in Panchayat properties, peri-urban

Panchayats spend more than the rural Panchayats. The correlation between population and own tax collection in peri-urban Panchayats is 0.057 and in rural Panchayats it is 0.802. This shows that correlation is higher in rural Panchayats compared to the peri-urban Panchayats. Correlation between the number of houses and tax collection in peri-urban Panchayats is non-significant but in urban Panchayats the correlation is 0.687. This shows that the number of houses is very influential in rural Panchayats than the peri-urban Panchayats. Both in peri-urban Panchayats and rural Panchayats, the influence of land area on own revenue collection is not significant.

In order to improve the financial situation and management of the Gram Panchayats many measures have to be implemented and suggestive measures are the following: More scientific methods of resource assessment should be undertaken, resource mapping should be carried out, identify more alternative sources of revenue, expenditure should be productive, modify the accounting procedure, introduce computerization in the assessment and collection of revenue, more incentive should be given to the good performance in revenue collection, penalty should be introduced for default, introduce land tax on the basis of value calculated on the basis of plinth area, introduce entertainment tax on the basis of seating capacity, impose profession tax on all the employees working in all sectors, entrust Secretary to assess property tax, increase revenue from Panchayat properties, Government should fix only minimum rate of tax, prepare resource mapping in the Panchayats, introduce ICTs for Gram Panchayat management, tax collection efforts should be rewarded at the individual level and at the Panchayat level, prepare assessment register, demand register and arrear register on the basis of available records at the Panchayat level, strengthen local finance data base, introduce tax on cable TV operator's income, introduce parking fee for cars, autos and other vehicles and increase fine for unauthorized building construction.

Concluding Observations

The basic objective of the study has been to throw light on the rural and peri-urban contrast in financial administration of local governments in Kerala. One could see marked differences between peri-urban and rural local bodies in revenue mobilization and expenditure. Rural Panchayats depend more on the State governments for funds than the peri-urban Panchayats. In rural Panchayats, own revenue is just sufficient to meet the establishment or the management expenditures. Alternative sources of revenue have to be found out to strengthen the financial position of the rural Panchayats. Financial management of Gram Panchayats and transferred institutions are far from satisfactory. In order to strengthen Gram Panchayats and to make them Local Self Governments financial dependency to the State governments is required to be progressively reduced. Finally, policy measures have to be evolved to narrow down the differences between the peri-urban and rural Panchayats in the matter of financial administration.

REFERENCES

Amaresh Bagchi and Nicholas Stern (1994): *Tax Policy and Planning in Developing Countries,* Oxford University Press, New Delhi.

Chandrashekar, P.K. (Ed.) (2000): *Panchayat Raj in India—A Status Report 1999, Task Force on Panchayat Raj,* Rajiv Gandhi Foundation, New Delhi.

Dilip Ghosh and Santanu Ghosh (2003): "Do matching Grants ensure greater resource mobilisation? A micro-economic exercise" in Chaubey. P.K (Ed.), *Fiscal Federalism in India,* Deep & Deep Publications Pvt. Limited, New Delhi.

Dilip Ghosh and Santanu Ghosh (2003): "The dismal State of Panchayat Finance: A Case Study of West Bengal", in Chaubey. P.K (Ed.), *Fiscal Federalism in India,* Deep & Deep Publications Pvt. Limited, New Delhi.

Govinda Rao, M. (1998): "India: Inter Governmental Fiscal relations in a Planned Economy" in Richard M. Bird and Francois Vaillancourt (Ed.), *Fiscal Decentralisation in Developing Countries,* Cambridge University Press, Cambridge.

Govinda Rao, M. and Tapas, K. Sen (1996): *Fiscal Federalism in India: Theory and Practice,* Concept Publishing Company, New Delhi.

Gulati, I.S. (1987): *Central-State Budgetary Transfers,* Oxford University Press, Bombay.

Harold D. Smith (1945): *The Management of Your Governance,* McGraw-Hill Book Company, London.

Hemlata Rao (1994): *Federal State Financial Relations,* Ashish Publishing House, New Delhi.

Indira Rajaraman (2003): *A Fiscal Domain for Panchayats*, Oxford University Press, New Delhi.

Jha, S.N. and Mathur, P.C. (Ed.) (1999): *Decentralisation and Local Politics*, Saga Publications, New Delhi.

Joshi, R.P. and Narwani, G.S. (2002): *Panchayat Raj in India - Emerging Trends across the States*, Rawat Publications, New Delhi.

Karunakaran Pillai,G. (2003) : "Decentralized Public Finance : The role of the Eleventh Finance Commission" in Chaubey, P.K. (Ed.), *Fiscal Federalism in India*, Deep & Deep Publications Pvt. Limited, New Delhi.

Mahi Pal (2003): Panchayati Raj: The experiences of a decade and task ahead, *Public Governance and Decentralisation*, Mittal Publications, New Delhi.

Misra, S.N, Anil Dutta Misra and Sweta Misra (Ed.) (2003): *Public Governance and Decentralisation*, Mittal Publications, New Delhi

Oommen, John (1998): "Panchayati Raj Finances in Kerala: Tasks ahead" in *Local Finance in India*, Manohar Publishers, New Delhi.

Oommen, M.A in Jha, S.N. and Mathur, P.C. (Ed.) (1999): *Decentralisation and Local Politics*, Saga Publications, New Delhi.

Palanithurai, G. (Ed.) (1996): *New Panchayati Raj System: Status and Prospects*, Kanishka Publishers, New Delhi.

Parthasarathi, Shone (1995): *Fiscal Policy and Governance,Property Tax Policy and Local Governance*, Om Prakashan, Mathura.

Raimann Pattanayak (Ed.) (1994): *Financial Administration and Management*, Anmol Publications Pvt. Limited, New Delhi.

Raj Singh (Ed.) (2000): *New Panchayati Raj—A Functional Analysis*, Anmol Publications Pvt. Ltd., New Delhi.

Robert, W. Johnson (1962): *Financial Management*, Boston Allyn and Bacon, Inc., Bostan.

Singh, Udai Bhan (2003): *Fiscal Federalism in Indian Union*, Concept Publishing Company, New Delhi.

Surat Singh (2001): *Problems and Prospects of Panchayat Finances*, Mittal Publications, New Delhi.

Teresa Ter-Minassian (1997): *Fiscal Federalism in Theory and Practice*, International Monetary Fund, Washington.

Thimmaiah, G. (1998): Local Government Finance: Some Issues, Konrad Adenauer Foundation, Manohar Publishers and Distributors, New Delhi.

Thomas Issac with Richard W. Franke (2000): *Local Democracy and Development*, Left World, New Delhi.

6

PANCHAYAT FINANCE : THE CASE OF WEST BENGAL

DILIP KUMAR GHOSH

In India, the issues in fiscal federalism mostly pertain to the question of sharing of resources between the Centre and the States. On the contrary there has been not so much debate and discussions on the existing and the ideal nature of fiscal relation between the State Governments and the local governments. It is a stark reality that while the States constantly clamour for greater financial powers and larger share of the Central resources, they more or less remain silent on the same when it comes to the relation between the State and local bodies. Immediately after independence, the national government initiated a number of experimentations on the issues of local finance. It will be of relevance to have a glimpse on the observations of the different committees formed for this purpose.

The Local Finance Enquiry Committee was constituted by the Union Government in 1950 for making recommendations on the ways and means of improving the conditions of the financial resources of the local bodies. The committee suggested that the nation building activities demanded increasing sums of money, but 'the resources at the disposal of the local bodies are of a stationary character'. In course of probing the reason behind chronic paucity of funds, the Committee identified "the reluctance of local bodies generally to make use of their existing financial powers and resources to the fullest extent and to impose taxation even when the need for such a step was clearly admitted" as the prime reason for low resource base of the local bodies. The Team for the Study of Community Projects and National Extension Service (in November 1957) also made similar observations in their report. One such indication is quoted below:

> "The collection of Panchayat taxes is generally not satisfactory. Arrears accumulate until they are merely written off; and it is not always that the assessee fail to pay because of his inability to do so."

Thereafter, in 1962, the Government of India in Ministry of Community Development, Panchayati Raj and Cooperation constituted a Committee on Resources and Finances of Panchayati Raj Institutions under the Chairperson of K. Santhanam. This committee felt that the Panchayats should have substantial and growing resources for sustaining themselves. It is relevant here to produce an excerpt from its recommendations:

> "Financial resources have to be adequate for the functions allotted to each Panchayati Raj Institutions. Nowhere in the world can local bodies function without substantial assistance from Government. At the same time it will detract from the dignity and autonomy of a self-governing institutions if it is to be entirely dependent on assistance from above. It is essential for stability and growth of these institutions that they should have substantial and growing resources which are entirely within their power to exploit and to develop."

In spite of repeated persuasion, the painful observation of Santhanam Committee was that "the total income of a vast majority of the Panchayats is far from adequate to give them a firm foundation". The Committee on the Panchayati Raj Institutions (1978) under the Chairmanship of Asoka Mehta viewed that 'part of the inability of the Panchayati Raj Institutions to come up to the expectation lay in their weak financial resources'. For augmenting the resource base, Asoka Mehta Committee suggested that 'it is necessary to ensure adequate availability of funds for the discharge of the responsibilities that may be entrusted to the Panchayati Raj Institutions'. In opinion of the Committee, this could be done through opening of avenues for the Panchayats 'to have their own resources both by their effort as also in transferring some relevant State resources'.

After Asoka Mehta Committee, major directive in the field of financial resources of the Panchayats came with the Constitution (Seventy Third Amendment) Act, 1992 when Articles 243-H and 243-I were inserted into the Constitution. In giving power to impose taxes by the Panchayats, the Constitution makes following provision in the Article 243-H (all provisions are reproduced here):

> "The Legislature of a State may, by law:
> (a) authorize a Panchayat to levy, collect and appropriate such taxes, duties, tolls, and fees in accordance with such procedure and subject to such limits;
> (b) assign to a Panchayat such taxes, duties, tolls and fees levied and collect by the State Government for such purposes and subject to such conditions and limits;
> (c) provide for making such grants-in-aid to the Panchayats from the Consolidated Fund of the State; and
> (d) provide for constitution of such Funds for crediting all moneys received respectively, by or on behalf of the Panchayats and also for the withdrawal of such money therefrom, as may be specified in the law."

In Article 243-I, a provision has been made for the constitution of Finance Commission in each State. It has been delineated in this Article that the State Governments shall constitute State Finance Commission (SFC) for their respective State within one year from the commencement of the 73rd Amendment to the Constitution. In fact the provisions in Article 243-H and 243-I have 'afforded a fresh opportunity for the States to review the existing State-Local fiscal relations, and to explore all possibilities of strengthening the finances of the PRIs (NIRD, 2001).

In this backdrop, the present study has been taken up with focus on West Bengal. The underlying reason for considering West Bengal is that the Left Parties under the leadership of the Communist Party of India (Marxists) has been governing the State since 1977. The State Government has well intention also to empower the Panchayats at three tiers (village, block and district). Many provisions are incorporated in the West Bengal Panchayat Act (WBP Act) for resource mobilisation by the Panchayats. Additionality is that in this State regular elections to the Panchayat bodies at an interval of five years have been organised since 1978. Uninterrupted functioning of the Panchayats for a period of around twenty-eight years has resulted in institution building in the rural areas. Whether these institutions are able to secure the distinction of the institutions of Local Self Government, however, is an issue for further scrutiny.

The present study is undertaken with following three objectives:

(i) to present an overview of the resource mobilisation scenario in the Panchayats;
(ii) to examine the utilisation pattern of own resources mobilised; and
(iii) to explore the extent of untied funds provided to the Panchayats.

Accordingly, the present article is structured in the following manner:

Section I discusses the provisions of the West Bengal Panchayat Act regarding resource mobilisation by the Panchayats at different tiers. Only the village tier of the Panchayat structure has the authority to impose taxes. The intermediate tier and the district tier in the Panchayat structure have the power to impose non-tax items like tolls, fees and rates on a few services provided by them. Utilisation of the resources mobilised by the Panchayats at different tiers is a driving factor in augmentation of own resources. Santhanam Committee in this respect suggested that "efforts of a Panchayat to raise local resources by taxation and by other ways will be more successful if people know that the proceeds are to be used for the provision of civic amenities and not for mere administrative expenses". Section II makes the reflection on these issues. Provision of untied fund to the Panchayats at different tiers is an essential element to make decentralised planning process successful and giving autonomy to the Panchayats in decision-making. Section III of the paper presents the scenario in this respect. The people's involvement in the activities of the Panchayats is an essential force behind the mobilization of resources for the Panchayats. This aspect is discussed in Section IV on the basis of their attendance in different public meetings like Gram Sansads and Gram Sabhas.

The present study is developed on the basis of secondary data culling from different sources. The main data source is the Department of Panchayats and Rural Development (DPRD), Government of West Bengal. In West Bengal there are 3,354 Gram Panchayats, 333 Panchayat Samitis, 17 Zilla Parishads and one Mahakuma Parishad. There is no system for getting disaggregated data from a single source like the DPRD or the directorate of the Department. For getting any data relating to Gram Panchayats or Panchayat Samitis, researchers have to go down the line from the district. Here, the district disaggregated data are used.

SECTION I

In West Bengal, the Gram Panchayats are empowered to impose tax and non-tax respectively on the basis of the Sections 46 and 47 of the West Bengal Panchayat Act. According to Section 46, the Gram Panchayats can impose tax on yearly basis on lands and buildings within the local limits of its jurisdiction. The lands and buildings exclusively used for public purposes or for religious, educational or charitable purposes are excluded from this tax. The maximum rates of tax is calculated in the following manner :

(i) at the rate of one percentum of the annual value of such land and buildings when the annual value does not exceed rupees one thousand, and

(ii) at the rate of two percentum of the annual value of such land and buildings when the annual value exceeds rupees one thousand.

The annual value in relation to any land or buildings is equal to the amount of six percentum of the market value of such land or buildings at the time of assessment (Sub-section 6 of Section 46 of the West Bengal Panchayat Act). From the DPRD, data on tax collection by the Gram Panchayats are available for the period of 1997-98 to 2002-03. Thereafter tax and non-tax revenue collections are merged together to indicate the own resource mobilization. For the Gram Panchayats, tax is a major source of revenue. In Table 6.1, per capita collection of taxes by the Gram Panchayats in different years are given.

Table 6.1: Per capita collection of taxes by Gram Panchayats (in Rupees)

District	*1997-98*	*1998-99*	*1999-2000*	*2000-01*	*2001-02*	*2002-03*	*Growth Index*
Burdwan	1.84	1.85	2.87	3.18	3.63	3.61	1.962
Birbhum	1.41	1.66	1.48	1.48	1.40	2.22	1.574
Bankura	0.56	0.66	0.53	0.51	0.36	1.24	2.214
Midnapur	3.49	1.22	1.26	1.33	1.42	1.93	0.553
Howrah	1.46	1.81	2.25	2.73	3.17	6.31	4.321
Hooghly	1.90	2.36	2.58	2.96	3.27	4.22	2.221
North 24 Parganas	1.49	1.70	1.70	1.72	1.76	2.97	1.993
South 24 Parganas	0.98	1.04	1.08	1.17	1.27	1.73	1.765
Nadia	1.13	1.53	1.12	0.88	0.79	2.41	2.132
Murshidabad	0.61	0.58	0.69	0.78	0.84	0.97	1.590
Uttar Dinajpur	0.57	0.55	0.62	0.68	0.79	1.04	1.824
Dakshin Dinajpur	1.00	0.95	1.00	1.15	1.30	1.31	1.310
Malda	0.67	0.66	0.66	0.67	0.69	1.50	2.238
Jalpaiguri	1.08	1.41	0.95	0.93	0.81	2.45	2.268
Darjeeling	1.60	1.73	2.32	2.89	3.54	4.18	2.612
Cooch Behar	0.49	0.49	0.52	0.51	0.55	1.23	2.510
Purulia	0.07	0.07	0.06	0.06	0.07	0.10	1.428
West Bengal	1.45	1.22	1.23	1.28	1.35	2.26	1.558

Note: Growth Index = (Value in 2002-03 / Value in 1997-98).

Source: Department of Panchayats and Rural Development, Govt. of West Bengal.

From Table 6.1 it can be seen that there exists appreciable variation in collection of taxes by the Gram Panchayats. On an average it is as low as 7 Paise in Purulia district to as high as Rs. 2.95 in Howrah district. If a particular year, say 2002-03 is considered, then it can be noticed that per capita collection of taxes by the Gram Panchayats varies from the minimum of 10 Paise in Purulia district to the maximum of Rs. 6.31 in Howrah district. In the development ranking of the districts, Howrah is placed at a higher rank in comparison to Purulia district. Further, Howrah has some locational advantages also; it is situated very near the State capital Kolkata and its villages have better infrastructural facilities in comparison to those of backward districts like Purulia. To impress upon the hypothesis that in developed districts, the per capita collection of Gram Panchayat tax is more than that in less developed districts, in Table 6.1(a), the development ranks calculated by Chatterjee and Ghosh (2003) are used side by side the average per capita tax collection for the period.

Table 6.1(a): District rank vis-à-vis per capita collection of Gram Panchayat tax

District	*Average per capita collection (in Rupees)*	*Rank on the basis of collection (R_1)*	*Development rank (R_2)*	*Difference in Rank*
Burdwan	2.83	3	3	0
Birbhum	1.61	7	8	+1
Bankura	0.64	15	9	–6
Midnapur	1.77	6	7	+1
Howrah	2.95	1	6	+5
Hooghly	2.88	2	1	–1
North 24 Parganas	1.89	5	2	–3
South 24 Parganas	1.21	10	14	+4
Nadia	1.31	8	4	–4
Murshidabad	0.74	13	12	–1
Uttar Dinajpur	0.71	14	17	+3
Dakshin Dinajpur	1.12	11	16	+5
Malda	0.81	12	15	+3

Contd. ...

Table 6.1 (a) *Contd. ...*

District	*Average per capita collection (in Rupees)*	*Rank on the basis of collection (R_1)*	*Development rank (R_2)*	*Difference in Rank*
Jalpaiguri	1.27	9	10	+1
Darjeeling	2.71	4	5	+1
Cooch Behar	0.63	16	13	–3
Purulia	0.07	17	11	–6

Note: (a) Kolkata is not considered in the development rank column as it is totally urban. Ranks of other districts are adjusted accordingly.
(b) Difference in rank = R_2 - R_1.

Source: (i) Table 1 for average per capita tax collection.
(ii) Chatterjee and Ghosh (2003) for development rank.

The difference between two ranks in Table 6.1(a) shows that some districts having better ranking from the development perspective, have lower ranks in terms of the value of average per capita tax collection. The *vice versa* situation can also be noticed. For example, the cases of Birbhum, Midnapur, Howrah, South 24 Parganas, Uttar Dinajpur, Dakshin Dinajpur, Malda, Jalpaiguri and Darjeeling can be cited. For making a firm comment on the factors responsible for making positive difference in ranks, it is necessary to undertake investigation in the resource potentials of the Gram Panchayats of the districts. Obviously, the initiatives of the Panchayats are there to mobilize resources. Whatever be the factors, one thing is clear from Table 6.1(a) that development status of a district can influence resource mobilisation at local level. A frequency distribution of districts on the basis of average per capita collection of tax and NSSO regional classification will simply corroborate this assertion [Table 6.1(b].

From the frequency distribution it can be easily realised that in the districts with low development status, collection of tax is also low. Of the four regions in the State, central plain region has better development than the western plain or Himalayan region. According to the survey results of the DPRD (2002) for determining below poverty line families in the rural areas, most of the districts with high percentage of BPL families are concentrated in eastern and western plain regions of the State. For example, in Purulia and

Bankura, respectively 43.65 and 42.48 per cent families are living below poverty line. Whereas in Burdwan, Howrah and Hooghly, the proportion of BPL families are respectively 26.24 per cent, 32.18 per cent and 29.08 per cent.

Table 6.1(b): Frequency distribution of districts

Range of Per Capita collection of Gram Panchayat tax	*Himalayan region*	*Eastern region*	*Central plains region*	*Western plains region*	*Total No. of districts*
Upto Re. 0.50	X	X	X	Purulia	1
Re. 0.51 to Re. 1.00	Cooch Behar	Murshidabad, Uttar Dinajpur, Malda	X	Bankura	5
Rs. 1.01 to Rs. 1.50	Jalpaiguri	Nadia, Dakshin Dinajpur	South 24 Parganas	X	4
Rs. 1.51 to Rs. 2.00	X	Birbhum	North 24 Pargannas	Midnapur	3
Rs. 2.01 to Rs. 2.50	X	X	X	X	X
Rs. 2.51 and above	Darjeeling	X	Burdwan, Howrah, Hooghly	X	4
Total No. of Districts	3	6	5	3	17

Source: Table 6.1 (a).

From the frequency distribution it can be easily realised that in the districts with low development status, collection of tax is also low. Of the four regions in the State, central plain region has better development than the western plain or Himalayan region. According to the survey results of the DPRD (2002) for determining below poverty line families in the rural areas, most of the districts with high percentage of BPL families are concentrated in eastern and western plain regions of the State. For example, in Purulia and Bankura, respectively 43.65 and 42.48 per cent families are living below poverty line. Whereas in Burdwan, Howrah and Hooghly, the proportion of BPL families are respectively 26.24 per cent, 32.18 per cent and 29.08 per cent.

The trend of low collection of taxes can also be seen in case of mobilisation of non-tax revenue. In West Bengal Panchayat Act there are many provisions (Section 47) for imposition of non-tax items by the Gram Panchayats. The Gram Panchayats may levy fees, rates and tolls on many subjects on delivery of services or making provisions for services. The maximum rates are indicated by the State Government. For example, some of the widely accepted items for imposition of rates and fees by the Gram Panchayats are indicated in Box 6.1 along with the prescribed maximum rate by the State Government.

Box 6.1

Item for rates and fees, tolls	*Maximum Rate*
(1) Registration fee for rickshaw van, hand drawn cart, bullock cart or carriage drawn by buffalo or horse etc.	Per annum Rs. 12.00 (carriage fitted with rubber tyre) Per annum Rs. 24.00 (carriage not fitted with tyre)
(2) Water rate for irrigation	Rs. 350 per acre
(3) Registration of trades	Rs. 50 per annum (not paying professional tax) Rs. 100 to Rs. 250 per annum (paying professional tax)
(4) Registration of small scale unit	
where capital investment ranging from Rs. 25,000 to less than Rs. 5 lakhs	Rs. 100 to Rs. 250 per annum
where capital investment exceeds Rs. 5 lakhs	Rs. 300 to Rs. 500 per annum

The items mentioned in Box 6.1 are only illustrative and widely chosen non-tax revenue sources for the Gram Panchayats. There are many more items listed in the West Bengal Panchayat (Gram Panchayat Administration) Rules, 2004. The Gram Panchayats have many sources also to augment their own resource base; in reality they are rarely exploited. For example, fees for registration for shallow or deep tube-wells fitted with motor driven pump sets and installed for irrigation on commercial purposes are normally not realized by the Gram Panchayats. The grassroots reality is the absence of such database for preparing any assessment. Other areas from where the Gram Panchayats can raise resources are fees for showing any poster or advertisement or banner in any private or public place over any land, building, wall, hoarding or structure within their jurisdiction. Particularly the Gram Panchayats with urban character can utilize this source. Maximum fee that can be imposed should not exceed Rs. 250 in each case. The concept on user charges is rarely known to the Panchayat members. Besides their unwillingness, lack of awareness of the Panchayat members regarding the sources of non-tax revenue is a stumbling block in resource mobilization process. For putting emphasis on collection of tax and non-tax revenue by the Gram Panchayats, the State Government through an amendment of the West Bengal Panchayat Act made it mandatory for the Panchayats to prepare their own bye-laws. The progress in this respect is not so encouraging. According to the Annual Report 2004-05 of the Department of Panchayats and Rural Development, Government of West Bengal, out of 3,354 Gram Panchayats only 1,791 have adopted their final bye-law at the end of the year 2004-05 in percentage, only 53.40 per cent of total Gram Panchayats. At the end of the year 2003-04, it was only 36.10 per cent. The factors behind delay of the preparation of bye-laws are mainly emanated from the unwillingness of the Panchayats to raise resources through their own initiatives. The lack of proactive approach of the Gram Panchayats towards building their own resource base is also visible when there persists huge gap between assessment and realisation. In this connection, the relevant observation in the Report of the Examiner of Local Accounts on the Panchayat Raj Institutions (2003-04) is presented below:

> "…. In 1961 Gram Panchayats against a total cumulative demand of Rs. 36.51 crore, Rs. 24.46 crore could not be realised as at the end of 2002-03. The unrealized amount constituted 67 per cent of the total demand. This was

indicative of a lack of initiative and poor internal controls in Gram Panchayats, resulting in weakening of their own resource base."

For the Panchayat Samitis at Block level (intermediate tier) the West Bengal Panchayat Act makes provisions in Sections 116, 117 and 133 to impose fees, tolls etc. Section 116, gives power to the Panchayat Samitis to levy licence fee on certain offensive or dangerous trades. The licence is renewable annually with remittance of requisite fee in favour of the Panchayat Samiti. In Section 117, the WBP Act specifically laid down that 'a Panchayat Samiti may require the owner of the lessee of a *hat* or market or an owner or a lessee of land intending to establish a *hat* or market thereon, to obtain a licence in this behalf from the Panchayat Samiti on payment of a fee'. This source is an important source of revenue. Most often licence fees are not calculated objectively. By Section 133 of the West Bengal Panchayat Act, the Panchayat Samitis have been given authority to levy tolls, fees and rates for different services provided. For example, the Panchayat Samitis can set up toll-bars on any road other than *katcha* road or on any bridge constructed by it or vested on it. Setting up of toll bars have the employment generation potentialities also, as collection of tolls normally is leased out to individuals. The maximum rates for such toll, fees and rates are prescribed by the State Government and the scales for the imposition thereof follow the provision of the bye-laws framed by the Panchayat Samitis (Section 134 of the West Bengal Panchayat Act).

In case of Zilla Parishads, the West Bengal Panchayat Act makes provisions in Sections 180 and 181 for mobilisation of own resources. Like Panchayat Samitis, Zilla Parishads also can levy tolls on the road or any bridge constructed or vested in it or placed under its management. In case of fees and rates, Zilla Parishads have the power to impose them on certain services provided. For example, any Zilla Parishad can impose water rate or lighting rate if such arrangements are made by them. Section 162 extends power to the Zilla Parishads to grant licence in lieu of certain fees for holding fair or *mela* in their jurisdiction. There are so many provisions in the West Bengal Panchayat Act for mobilisation of resources by the Panchayats through their own efforts. The crux of the issue is to what extent these are used for augmenting resource base. The Department of Panchayats and Rural Development, Government of West Bengal expresses its concern in the following words:

> "... In the present system, Panchayats depend mostly on the flow of fund from State Exchequer. While fund for maintenance of establishment is provided by the State Government, fund for implementation of development programmes are released by both the Central and the State Governments.
>
> "... The Panchayats have been urged to augment resources through proper assessment of tax and realisation of it in full as well as to improve collection of non-tax revenue by fully utilising the revenue potential". (Annual Administrative Report of the DPRD, Government of West Bengal, 2004-05).

On the basis of the rural population in Census 2001, per capita collection of revenue (both tax and non-tax) for four consecutive years from 2002-03 are calculated. The revenue collection by all three tiers are put together. With the persuasion from the State Government, the situation is improving, but slowly. For example, according to the source of the DPRD, the own resource mobilisation by the Panchayats increased to Rs. 74.09 crore in the year 2005-06 from the previous year's collection of Rs. 64.43 crore. In Table 6.2, per capita collection of own revenue (tax plus non-tax) by the Panchayats in all three tiers is presented for the four years in a row from 2002-03.

From Table 6.2, it can be seen that in the districts where collection is already higher in comparison to the other districts, the value of growth index is found to be low. For example, the cases of Howrah and Hooghly districts can be seen. This may be due to the complacency within the Panchayat representatives for searching new areas of revenue sources. The Report of the Examiner of

Table 6.2: Per capita collection of tax and non-tax revenue by the Panchayats

District	*Per capita collection of revenue (in rupees)*				*Growth Index*
	2002-03	*2003-04*	*2004-05*	*2005-06*	
Burdwan	13.34	19.34	23.26	26.84	2.011
Birbhum	7.67	10.62	13.25	14.08	1.835
Bankura	3.17	8.76	11.06	14.12	4.454
Midnapur	7.96	8.01	9.35	14.10	1.771
Howrah	10.29	12.02	13.58	17.90	1.739
Hooghly	13.48	16.96	21.84	22.18	1.645
North 24 Parganas	7.23	6.59	9. 79	12.06	1.668
South 24 Parganas	4.71	5.03	8.28	8.16	1.732
Nadia	6.65	6.49	8.21	9.43	1.418
Murshidabad	5.20	4.67	6.52	8.11	1.559
Uttar Dinajpur	3.48	4.37	5.25	5.20	1.494
Dakshin Dinajpur	7.66	6.17	12.50	13.75	1.795
Malda	6.23	5.64	13.53	9.71	1.558
Jalpaiguri	6.20	9.12	8.78	11.93	1.924
Darjeeling	4.84	6.06	10.17	14.46	2.987
Coochbehar	4.74	6.09	8.44	11.13	2.348
Purulia	2.00	1.54	6.08	1.91	0.955
West Bengal	7.13	8.40	11.11	12.61	1.768

Note: (i) Rank indicates rank of district on the basis of value of growth index.

(ii) Growth index = $\frac{\text{Value in 2005-06}}{\text{Value in 2002-03}}$

Source: Annual Administrative Report 2004-05 of Department of Panchayats and Rural Development, Government of West Bengal.

Local Accounts for the year ending on 31st March 2004 noted that in Hooghly and Howrah districts, of the total cumulative demand of the Gram Panchayats at the end of the year 2002-03, the collection of revenue was to the extent of 44.19 and 39.73 per cent of the demands. With the expansion of the economic activities in these two districts, it is expected that the Panchayat bodies should be more interested to identify new sources. In general, the Panchayats do not take adequate initiatives to augment their own resource base. It will be relevant here to produce an excerpt, though a bit long, from a report prepared for the Government of West Bengal in the year 1993:

> The Panchayats seem to be content to remain spending agencies of money received from above. Every Panchayat that we visited prepared a performance report for own benefit. In each such report, spending achievement are proudly displayed, but resource raising was not even mentioned. Such lopsided performance negates the very idea underlying the Panchayats, for it shows that there is near-zero self-reliance, which means near-zero autonomy and correspondingly near-zero self-government. It also makes the panchayats highly vulnerable in the event of a changed political ambience. Furthermore, by failing to mobilise resources, the Panchayats have served to increase, the cost of governance at and below the district level, because now their own cost has to be added to the continuing cost of the pre-existing bureaucracy (Mukarji and Bandyopadhyay, 1993).

This trend is continuing. In conformity with the provisions in the Article 243-I, the State Government constituted the first State Finance Commission (SFC) within one year from the commencement of the 73rd Amendment to the Constitution. The purpose is to define the principles of sharing of the net proceeds of the taxes, duties, tolls and fees leviable by the State with the Panchayats at village, Block and district levels and to determine the sources of State revenue which may be assigned to the Panchayats.

Along with these two basic matters, the State Finance Commission is also advised to indicate the measures needed to improve the financial position of the Panchayats. The first SFC in West Bengal approached the issue of own resource mobilization by the local bodies in following way:

> "... raising adequate resources is a big question. The gap between what is spent in a Panchayat and what it so far has been able to raise is wide. With better efforts, its collection may improve somewhat but the amount will never reach a satisfactory level... funds came from the State Government to keep Panchayats and Municipalities going. Later on, the Union Government came forward with earmarked funding for centrally devised development programmes for these Local Self Government Institutions. This is a reality which we have to accept. Generally speaking, local governments anywhere on the globe are not self-sustaining."

The dependence of the local bodies on the centrally sponsored scheme is very heavy and the funds spent by them at different tiers are project-specific. That is, funds available for a particular scheme should be spent on the implementation of that scheme only; no diversion can be made even for meeting the local needs. Most of the funds allotted to the Panchayats at different tiers are tied in nature. As a consequence, the Panchayats have to turn into implementing agencies of the Government, it may be the State Government or the Union Government. Lack of own resources at least to meet some urgent needs in the village level makes the Panchayats completely dependent on the State Government. For sustenance of the Panchayats, it is necessary to flow some funds free from any conditionality. This fund may be termed as untied fund. For providing untied funds to the local bodies, the First SFC recommended that after tax transfers, "of the total net proceeds of taxes collected by the State in a year, 16 per cent should be transferred to districts as entitlements". According to the Second SFC, the objective of such recommendation by the First SFC was hardly met by the State Government's approach of dividing the State Plan schemes into State and district level schemes. The observation of the Second SFC on this aspect is worth-quoting here:

> "The State Government could not follow the recommendations in the manner suggested by the First SFC. The Commission was informed that arriving at a working consensus on procedures and exact methods of devolution in conformity with the First SFC recommendations required some time."

Even after accepting the Report of the First SFC and submitting Action Taken Report to the State Assembly in July 1996, in view of the Second SFC no such significant progress can be traced in the matter of devolution of sources of funds in favour of the Panchayats. The Second SFC was set up only in July 2000 by the State Government. For this reason they could not submit report in time so that the State Government can implement its recommendations with effect from 1st April, 2001. For maintaining continuity of the period, the Second SFC submitted an interim report on May 28, 2001 to cover the period from 1st April, 2001. The final report of Second SFC was submitted on 6th February 2002. In the following period, nothing significant action on the part of State Government to transfer resources to the Panchayats came out. Let us present the case of untied funds provided to the Panchayats in the next section.

SECTION II

The untied funds are required to meet the critical gap between the requirement of fund according to the felt need of the local level planning bodies (for example, the Panchayats) and the total availability of funds from various sources including the departmental and institutional sources. The Second SFC of West Bengal expressed the necessity of such funds in following words:

> "There was a general appreciation of such fund by the people because it was possible for them to take up

> schemes which helped to meet part of their felt needs. During our discussions with representatives of LSGs (Local Self Governments) in the districts, we were requested to enlarge the amount of untied grants."

In West Bengal, till 2000-01 the Panchayats did not get any untied fund from the State Government. From the year 2001-02, the Government of West Bengal in the Department of Panchayats and Rural Development took a decision to provide untied funds in favour of the Gram Panchayats. The untied funds both Plan and non-Plan were given to support and sustain the movement of decentralised planning. In Table 6.3, flow of untied fund in the year 2001-02 is presented. According to the Annual Administrative Report 2002-03 of the DPRD, "during 2001-02, the budgetary support in the shape of untied plan grants rose to Rs. 120.95 crore and the budgeted amount on this score for 2002-03 is no less than Rs. 546.15 crore against a proposed Plan expenditure of Rs. 2702.15 crore on this account during the Tenth Five Year Plan."

All these untied funds are given for the purpose of development works. If the total rural population is considered, per capita availability of funds is not that much significant. In general, thrust has been given on backward districts like Purulia, Dakshin Dinajpur, Jalpaiguri etc. As detailed expenditure report is not available, it is better to quote here the observations of Second SFC for capturing the grass-roots reality. To quote:

> "We observed that the type of schemes preferred under the untied grants were mainly construction of roads and culverts, excavation of canals for irrigation and tanks for fisheries, maintenance and repair of old buildings, construction of school buildings and Integrated Child Development Scheme (ICDS) centres, social forestry etc. LSGs were genuinely concerned about use of untied fund for creation of assets that would generate further resources for them."

Table 6.3: Availability of untied funds to the panchayats

District	*Amount of Plan fund (Rupees in Lakhs)*	*Amount of non-Plan fund (Rupees in Lakhs)*	*Total funds (Rupees in Lakhs)*	*Rural population (in Lakhs)*	*Per capita availability (in Rupees)*
Burdwan	912.50	43.73	956.23	43.47	22.00
Birbhum	594.03	30.96	624.99	27.54	22.69
Bankura	663.41	34.83	698.24	29.56	23.62
Midnapur	1653.51	82.34	1735.85	86.27	20.12
Howrah	420.53	21.82	442.35	21.20	20.86
Hooghly	620.19	31.58	651.77	33.52	19.44
North 24 Parganas	677.22	34.49	711.71	40.81	17.44
South 24 Parganas	1130.10	59.35	1189.45	58.19	20.44
Nadia	674.95	36.04	710.99	36.24	19.62
Murshidabad	1036.75	54.13	1090.88	51.31	21.26
Uttar Dinajpur	530.52	26.29	556.81	21.47	25.93
Dakshin Dinajpur	395.43	19.58	415.01	13.06	31.78
Malda	627.39	13.58	640.97	30.49	21.02
Jalpaiguri	765.35	35.50	800.85	27.99	28.61
Darjeeling	255.88	12.82	268.70	10.85	24.76
Cooch Behar	569.86	30.45	600.31	22.52	26.66
Purulia	567.38	29.46	596.84	22.79	26.19
West Bengal	12095.00	596.95	12691.95	577.34	21.98

Source: Annual Administrative Report 2002-03 of the DPRD, Government of West Bengal.

Regarding utilization of untied fund, the specific suggestion of the Second SFC is that "consideration for the poorer sections of the community, scheduled castes, scheduled tribes, minorities, women and children may be given special attention". The non-availability of data restraints us to make any firm statement regarding the benefits of these marginalized sections from the untied fund schemes. No such fund was allocated during the years 2002-03 and 2003-04. In the year 2004-05, the State Government devolved Rs. 11.59 crore as non-Plan untied funds only; no fund was provided under Plan untied fund. During the year 2005-06, the State Government has provided a fund of Rs. 278.29 crore as untied fund on the basis of the recommendations of the Second State Finance Commission. For reinforcing the resource base of the Panchayats, the State Government also devolves a portion of the entertainment tax and luxury tax collected by the concerned department. Year-wise release of untied funds on the account of the recommendations of the State Finance Commission and grants against entertainment tax and luxury tax are given in the Statement 6.1.

Statement 6.1: Release of Untied Funds for PRIs

Year	*On account of recommendation of SFC*	*On account of grants in lieu of two tax heads*	*Total*
2000-2001	100.00	0.00	100.00
2001-2002	120.95	5.97	126.92
2002-2003	0.00	0.00	0.00
2003-2004	0.00	0.00	0.00
2004-2005	0.00	11.59	11.59
2005-2006	278.29	25.34	303.63

Note: (i) Fund figures are 'Rupees in crores'.
(ii) Two taxes are entertainment tax and luxury tax.

Source: Department of Panchayats and Rural Development.

Apart from the flow of untied funds from DPRD to the Panchayats, the funds of untied nature are also placed by the State Government under the District Plan Scheme (DPS) funds to the districts. According to the Ninth Five Year Plan (1997-2002) of the

State Government, the DPS funds are placed "to meet the critical gap between the requirement of fund according to the felt need of the local level planning bodies and the total availability of funds from various sources, both department budget and institutional sources". This DPS fund for the district level schemes goes straight to the districts through District Planning Committee (DPC). The DPC was constituted in every district after the effect of the Constitution (Seventy Fourth Amendment) Act, 1992. In terms of the provisions of the West Bengal District Planning Committee Act, 1994 and the West Bengal District Planning Committee Rules, 1994, the Chairperson of a District Panchayat (Zilla Parishad) has been made the Chairperson of the DPC of the district. For non-availability of relevant data, it is difficult to ascertain the extent of devolution of funds from the District Panchayat to Block Panchayats and Village Panchayats. For the present purpose, in Table 6.4 the flow of funds for the district sector under DPS is shown for three Plan periods. This Table 6.4 will help to understand the proportion of DPS funds in total Plan outlay of the State.

Table 6.4: Outlays for District Sector Plans

Plan period	*Total outlay*	*District sector plan outlay*	*Share of District sector plans (in %)*	*Change of share (in %)*
Eighth Plan (1992-97)	993000.00	446019.17	44.92	—
Ninth Plan (1997-2002)	1690000.00	872509.78	51.63	+ 14.94
Tenth Plan (2002-2007)	2834675.32	1442812.61	50.90	–1.41

Note : All outlay figures are 'Rupees in Lakhs'.

Source : Ninth Plan and Tenth Plan documents of the Government of West Bengal, Development and Planning Department.

From Table 6.4 it can be observed that the Sate Government earmarked a quite sizable proportion of Plan outlay for the district sector schemes. For implementation, the State Sector Schemes are remained with the concerned departments and the appropriately identified District Sector Schemes are transferred to the local bodies.

It is generally felt that untied funds can give the Panchayats certain amount of flexibility in implementation of the schemes directed to the local needs. The Second State Finance Commission emphasized the need to protect the interests of the poors during utilization of the untied funds. In the words of the Second State Finance Commission, "Although the local self governments (LSGs) received only a small amount as untied entitlements ... consideration for the poorer sections of the community, scheduled castes, scheduled tribes, minorities, women and children may be given special attention". Lack of disaggregated data, however, is a major constraint in making any study relating to benefits by marginalized sections. With this discussion, let us see the utilization pattern of the own resources mobilised by the Panchayats, irrespective of the amount.

SECTION III

In Section I, we have noticed that the mobilization of own resources by the Panchayats in West Bengal is not adequate in comparison to the resources provided by the State Government. This may be evidenced by the remarks of the Department of Panchayats and Rural Development, Government of West Bengal in the Annual Administrative Report 2005-06. To quote:

> "Taxes, rates and tolls collected by the PRIs are highly inadequate for discharging their responsibilities. The State Government, therefore, provides financial support to the PRIs to meet their administrative expenditure on account of establishment cost and for discharging responsibilities entrusted with those bodies. Funds for meeting establishment cost including salary and pension of the employees of Panchayat Bodies are provided out of the budget of the Panchayat and RD Department. Grant is also provided to the Gram Panchayats to compensate for the profession tax, which the government collects. The cess grant and a share of collection of entertainment tax, as per recommendations of the State Finance Commission, are also provided to these bodies... ."

Therefore, the dependence of the Panchayats on the State Government is huge. The reluctance of the Panchayats in mobilising resources is also widely known. Through persuasion of the State Government, it is improving. In addition to this, the pattern of expenditure of own resources of the Panchayats highly influences the public to contribute for the causes of the Panchayats. If the public funds are spent for administrative expenses, like tiffin costs of the meetings or purchase of table-chairs for the Panchayat office etc., people may be disheartened to contribute on their own volition. From the Department of Panchayats and Rural Development of Government of West Bengal, we get figures of own revenue and expenditure in respect of the Gram Panchayats only. In Table 6.5, the data are presented to impress the idea that the Gram Panchayats are more interested in using a sizeable part of the own revenue for meeting contingent expenses.

Acknowledgement Table 6.5 bears the fact that the Gram Panchayats mostly do not prefer to spend own resources on priority sectors like education and health care. These two are considered as basic minimum necessities for any human being. Particularly, the rural people are at disadvantageous end to get the benefits of these two minimum needs. According to the Eleventh Schedule of the Constitution, the Panchayats have the responsibilities to ensure the benefits of these two public services to the people in their jurisdiction. The relevant matters listed in the Eleventh Schedule under these services are, drinking water, education including primary and secondary schools, adult and non-formal education, libraries, health and sanitation including hospitals, primary health centres and dispensaries and family welfare. In majority cases, the Panchayats wait for the government funds before going into any action. The field experiences tell us that even the dovetailing of own resources with the funds available from any government agency is few and far between. When the public at large see that their funds are spent by the Gram Panchayats for the purposes not otherwise endorsed by their priority they certainly express their reluctance to give money for the Panchayats, even if it is obligatory. The Panchayats have no machinery like Income Tax or Commercial Tax Departments to enforce tax or non-tax dues. There are tax

Table 6.5: Major Headwise distribution of expenditure from Gram Panchayats' own fund

District	*Expenses on Education*		*Expenses on Health Care*		*Any other Development Programmes*		*Contingent Expenses*		*Payment of Commission*	
	2003-2004	*2004-2005*	*2003-2004*	*2004-2005*	*2003-2004*	*2004-2005*	*2003-2004*	*2004-2005*	*2003-2004*	*2004-2005*
Burdwan	8.80	8.72	11.81	19.44	42.25	36.72	27.54	25.96	9.60	9.16
Birbhum	2.64	4.40	3.30	10.40	44.16	33.71	38.30	39.32	11.60	12.17
Bankura	7.70	13.32	7.23	13.12	42.43	35.66	34.50	31.46	8.14	6.44
Midnapur	7.17	7.76	4.92	8.52	50.23	45.57	29.28	27.15	8.40	11.00
Howrah	3.51	3.73	5.31	14.43	44.59	40.66	35.26	30.63	11.33	10.55
Hooghly	6.05	10.02	4.86	14.20	50.77	42.34	28.05	26.64	10.27	6.80
North 24 Parganas	5.14	6.51	5.78	15.90	45.98	32.60	33.98	34.15	9.12	10.84
South 24 Parganas	2.70	3.50	0.00	8.60	40.59	35.69	42.17	41.90	14.54	10.31
Nadia	3.07	3.87	2.60	6.80	40.17	36.68	41.64	36.47	12.52	16.18
Murshidabad	4.22	4.84	3.47	6.32	24.37	32.62	55.74	44.65	12.20	11.57
Uttar Dinajpur	5.01	7.88	4.94	11.32	32.12	42.60	47.82	29.88	10.11	8.32

Contd...

Table 6.5: *Contd. ...*

District	*Expenses on Education*		*Expenses on Health Care*		*Any other Development Programmes*		*Contingent Expenses*		*Payment of Commission*	
	2003-2004	*2004-2005*	*2003-2004*	*2004-2005*	*2003-2004*	*2004-2005*	*2003-2004*	*2004-2005*	*2003-2004*	*2004-2005*
Dakshin Dinajpur	5.90	6.85	4.93	5.73	35.03	28.13	47.00	51.62	7.14	7.67
Malda	2.30	8.80	4.16	6.93	45.10	5.10	40.84	66.91	7.60	12.26
Jalpaiguri	4.44	5.72	6.28	7.98	27.53	27.34	49.66	46.76	12.09	12.20
Darjeeling	1.07	0.00	2.52	0.00	43.66	0.00	38.32	0.00	14.43	0.00
Cooch Behar	5.23	9.10	4.72	7.12	22.25	30.55	59.10	41.47	8.70	11.76
Purulia	0.00	8.67	0.16	8.55	22.90	51.88	68.74	25.03	8.20	5.87
West Bengal	5.63	7.37	5.68	11.84	42.59	37.14	35.95	33.45	10.15	10.18

Source: Department of Panchayats and Rural Development, Government of West Bengal.

collectors in the Gram Panchayats on commission basis. They move from house to house and collect taxes. On the total amount collected, their commission is calculated and paid accordingly. As these tax collectors are not full time employees of the Gram Panchayats, often they show their unwillingness to devote sufficient time for the Panchayats. The underlying reason is that the rate of commission is not in commensurate with the labour they have to put in. Whatever be the situation, the State Government 'has felt the necessity of sensitizing the Panchayat functionaries through direct interaction and taken initiative to organise workshops with the Pradhans, Executive Assistants of all the Gram Panchayats at district level' (Department of Panchayats and Rural Development, Government of West Bengal). In view of the DPRD, the tax-payers want transparency in expenditure of public money, especially their paid tax. At the Gram Panchayat level, this transparency is still lacking. Even after the passage of the Right to Information Act, 2006, hardly the list of beneficiaries of different schemes and the amount of expenditures made are exhibited in the notice board of the Gram Panchayats. The accounts of tax collected are far off matters in this respect.

From Table 6.5, it can be seen that in 2004-05, the shares of expenditure on education and health care increased. This was possible due to constant monitoring of the activities of the Gram Panchayats. Even then, in the districts with low development profile, the share of own resource expenditure on contingent purposes is quite higher in comparison with the districts with high development profile. For example, the case of Burdwan and Hooghly can be seen *vis-à-vis* Purulia, Jalpaiguri and Dakshin Dinajpur. In developed districts, the Panchayats are seen to be better organised and quite aware of the local issues. Whereas in case of the less developed districts, the other side of the picture emerges. Shishu Siksha Karmasuchi (Child Education Programme) and community health care initiatives are in the priority areas of the State Government. The Department of Panchayats and Rural Development emphasizes the convergence of resources from different sources along with the Panchayats' own resources for enhancing the investment in education and health sectors. Infrastructural support is an essential component for effective delivery of these services. An observation of DPRD in the Annual Administrative Report 2005-06 regarding the gap in infrastructure development is quoted below to indicate the gravity of the problem:

> "... rapid increase of such institutions (SSK Centres) within a short period could not be matched by the resources available for taking up construction of adequate physical infrastructure for those schools. As a result of that, functioning of the SSKs and MSKs continued to suffer due to inadequate infrastructure. Apart from class rooms, availability of drinking water and toilet facilities were also not upto the mark in many of those centres ...".

It is, thus, desirable that the Panchayats' own revenue should supplement the allocated funds of the State Government, then the local people will see some viable things before their eyes. Similarly, in the health sector, the Gram Panchayats have been made the main agency for implementing the community health care management initiatives (CHCMI). This also calls for intertwining of the Panchayats' own initiatives (both physical and financial resources) and the activities of the Health and Family Welfare Department. The human resource support at the end of the Gram Panchayats, however, remains an unresolved issue. The recommendations of the Second State Finance Commission in respect of placing of the Government employees in the Panchayat bodies may be recalled here :

> "A considerable volume of workload of the State Government was shifted to LSGs (local self government) but the corresponding workforce continues to remain with the State. This position needs to be corrected. This can be achieved either by redeployment of the Government staff to the LSGs or by suitable reduction in the size of the State Government employees along with strengthening of administrative and technical set up in LSGs."

Devolution of functionaries is inadequate as the State Government is devolving many functions to the Panchayats at different tiers, without adequate support of the employees. Additionality to the devolution exercises, the State Government creates a number of platforms for involvement of local people in the activities of the Panchayats. In Section IV, a synoptic view of the efficacy of these forums is discussed.

SECTION IV

For harnessing active involvement of local people in the process of development in the rural areas, the State Government amended the WBP Act in the year 1994 to introduce the concept of Gram Sansad (village constituency). All persons whose names are included in the electoral roll of the West Bengal Legislative Assembly for the time being in force pertaining to the area comprised in such constituency of the Gram Panchayat are members of that Gram Sansad. Normally two meetings of the Gram Sansads are scheduled to be organised by the Gram Panchayat in a year—one in the month of May and another in the month of November. For validation of such public meetings, the WBP Act makes the provision that one tenth of the total number of members shall form a quorum for a meeting of Gram Sansad (Table 6.6.) The reality is that the attendance of local people in these meetings is not so massive than it is normally seen in the mass rally of different political parties. The Second SFC also comments on the low attendance of people in these meetings:

> "While visiting the districts, we were informed by the representatives of the GPs and some Sabhadhipatis of ZP that the attendance in the meetings of the Gram Sansad declined when the participants found that their aspirations could not be fulfilled by the GPs. It seems that a vicious circle is operating here. Because of their experience of not receiving funds promised in the past, no planning activity is undertaken till funds actually flow to the GPs."

Lack of interests among the villagers in the activities of the Panchayats is the most common deterrent factor for not coming to the Panchayats' meetings. If and only if they have some personal benefit from a scheme/programme, they feel interested to go to such meetings. It is also the fact that the Gram Panchayats do not take it seriously to convene the meetings in befitting manner. The grassroots reality is that most often cordial invitations to the local people are not made by the Gram Panchayats, as if holding of meeting of Gram Sansad is just like any other routine work. Time for holding the meetings is set in a manner which most often does not suit the villagers. Even if people come to attend, the Gram Panchayats rarely take interests to capture their voices and translate their aspirations into reality. Attendance status of Gram Sansad meetings is presented for apprehending the reality.

Table 6.6: Attendance in Gram Sansad meetings

Year	*May meeting*	*November meeting*
1996	18.64	18.05
1997	14.55	16.53
1998	19.35	16.65
1999	12.06	12.70
2000	11.00	12.10
2001	11.00	10.53
2002	12.00	11.00
2003	12.00	11.70
2004	11.80	11.85

Note: All figures are in percentage.

Source: Department of Panchayats and Rural Development, Government of West Bengal.

From the attendance figures in May and November meetings it is clear that the attendance of the members of Gram Sansads is the bare minimum required to fulfil the quorum. The State Government, however, is attaching importance to the functioning of the Gram Sansads. According to the WBP Act, "a Gram Sansad shall guide and advice the Gram Panchayat in regard to the schemes for economic development and social justice undertaken or proposed to be undertaken in its area". The WBP Act makes it mandatory for a Gram Panchayat to place in the meetings of Gram Sansad the budget and audit report of the accounts of the Gram Panchayat for deliberation, recommendations and suggestions by the Gram Sansads. When attendance of the members is so poor, the extent of people's participation in the affairs of the Gram Panchayats can easily by apprehended. For furthering the cause of making the Panchayats pro-people, the State Government amended the WBP Act in 2003 to create a provision for constitution of Gram Unnayan Samiti (GUS) in every Gram Sansad. According to the provisions of the WBP Act, GUS shall be responsible for ensuring active participation of people in implementation and equitable distribution of benefits of rural development programmes within its jurisdiction. For ensuring women participation, the State government makes a provision in the West Bengal Panchayat (Gram Panchayat Administration) Rules, 2004 that not less than one-third members of the GUS shall be women. In GUS, wide range of representations from different sections of the society are made so as to give it a representative character. It is expected that GUS in rural areas will assume the role of civil society and will be able to mobilize people around the Gram Sansad for expansion of social opportunities for the marginalised and downtrodden, in particular. In the process it can act as the linkage between the people at large, and the Gram Panchayat. Till the end of the year 2004-05 only 10,779 Gram Unnayan Samitis were formed out of 45,154 to be formed. According to the Annual Administrative Report 2005-06 of the Department of Panchayats and Rural Development, "though it will be a long journey for the GUS to play their desired role, the same has to start with the formation of the GUS".

Besides these two forums for the common people, there is a Gram Sabha in each Gram Panchayat where people have the scope to deliberate upon the activities of the Gram Panchayats. The jurisdiction of a Gram Sabha is coterminous with the area of a Gram Panchayat. In this meeting also attendance is bare minimum to satisfy the quorum, i.e. 5 per cent of the total number of persons registered in the electoral roll pertaining to the Gram Panchayat. The Gram Sabha meeting is held once in a year, ordinarily in the month of December. Low attendance in Gram Sansad and Gram

Sabha meetings, indicate that common people are not at all interested in the affairs of the Panchayats. It is also a question whether the Panchayats sincerely want to involve people. In 1984, the Minister-in-Charge, Land and Land Revenue of Government of West Bengal made a remark in the floor of the State Assembly. Here we quote it for focusing the reality:

> "People's participation *per se* has not been aimed for. What is sought after is people's participation for executing governmental work. Local Self Government is a misnomer and anachronistic. It is the local unit of the government."

Until and unless people have some purpose, say for example, getting his/her name registered for assistance under Indira Awas Yojana or for getting work in wage employment programmes, people in general do not approach Panchayats. To them a Gram Panchayat is nothing but an extension counter of the Block office. The patron-client relationship with the Gram Panchayats generally does not evoke the common villagers to pay for the Gram Panchayats. For one eighty degree turn, it is imperative that the Gram Panchayats should undo their role as mere extension agents of the State Government offices.

Conclusion

From the discussions so far made it can be asserted that the mandate given by the Constitution (Seventy Third Amendment) Act, 1992 is not appropriately respected either by the State Government or the Panchayat institutions. Many functions are assigned to the Panchayats at different levels without sufficient support of functionaries and funds. Faith has to be reposed on the Panchayats for discharging the responsibilities entrusted to them; this calls for uninterrupted flow of funds without any conditionalities. They should be allowed to spend these funds on the basis of priority of the local people; otherwise local people would not participate in the activities of the Panchayats. The question of corruption by the Panchayats may arise; but it is the fact that in our society corruption is everywhere. So what is the use in blaming the Panchayats only and crippling them through orders and guidelines from the administrative departments. Even after the recommendations of two State Finance Commissions, no significant transferring of resources was made by the State Government to the Panchayats at appropriate tier. No or very little own resources, no or insufficient untied fund, inadequate participation of people in the affairs of the Panchayats make the Panchayats excessively dependent on the State Government for their sustenance. This cannot make them institutions for Local Self Government. Rather, incomplete devolution of fund, functions and functionaries only 'induces in the Panchayats habits of sidestepping their responsibilities'. This simply widens the gap between the Panchayats and the people.

REFERENCES

Chatterji, Biswajit and Ghosh, Dilip Kumar, *Towards a District Development Report,* 2003 published by State Institute of Panchayats and Rural Development, Kalyani, West Bengal.

Government of West Bengal, *The West Bengal Panchayat Act, 1973 (as amended subsequently).*

Government of West Bengal, Finance Department, (a) *Report of First State Finance Commission, 1995;* (b) *Report of Second State Finance Commission, 2002.*

Ministry of Community Development and Cooperation, Government of India, *Report of the study team on Panchayati Raj Finances,* 1963.

Ministry of Agriculture and Irrigation Department of Rural Development Government of India, *Report of the Committee on Panchayati Raj Institutions,* 1978.

Mukarji, N. and Bandyopadhyay, *New horizons for West Bengal's Panchayats,* a report for the Government of West Bengal, published by the Department of Panchayats, Government of West Bengal, 1993.

National Institute of Rural Development, *Hyderabad, India Panchayati Raj Report* 2001, Volume 1.

Planning and Development Department, Government of West Bengal (a) *Ninth Five Year Plan* (1997-2002); (b) *Tenth Five Year Plan* (2002-2007).

7

STATUS OF PANCHAYAT FINANCE IN TAMIL NADU

G. PALANITHURAI

Introduction

In the context of globalization of economy, power is being decentralized mandatorily through the Constitution. There are open protests against globalization of economy, but the globalization process is on and activities are being carried out speedily on the other hand decentralization of power draws support from various segments of the society and yet invisible hurdles and barriers hinder the process of devolution and it takes place at a slow pace. The State government and its bureaucracy are the real barriers in the absence of political will on the part of the State government. Ever since the Panchayat Raj system came into force, questions have been raised as to what extent Panchayats are autonomous in character. The Panchayat leaders have been lamenting on the paucity of funds available at their level to fulfil the responsibilities assigned to the Panchayats.

The cry has intensified and the Panchayat leaders have been pushed to the stage of resigning their positions as they are unable to meet the basic needs of the people with the funds available with the Panchayats. Over a period of time the responsibilities of Panchayats have been increased and financial resources to them have been reduced drastically and thereby Panchayat institutions have been crippled. The State government has not enabled the Panchayats by providing the agreed resources. The financial constraints are so acute that the Panchayats have to face a volley of problems. Major achievements are made in the social development sector by the Gram Panchayat Presidents and based on their performance and achievements they submit series of petitions to the government to improve the financial status of the Panchayats but nothing moves. Against this background, it was decided to evaluate the financial position of the Panchayats thoroughly and find ways and means to strengthen the Panchayats.

Emergence of New Panchayati Raj Setup in Tamil Nadu

New Panchayat Raj system was brought into force from 1994 to ensure continuity and stability and to improve the functioning of the grassroots institutions as a system of governance in the country to achieve economic development and social justice. For this purpose, Chapter IX was newly introduced in the Constitution of India and thereby direction was given to the State governments to devolve powers and authority so as to make Panchayats as self-governing institutions. Following this direction, State governments enacted legislation on Panchayats by incorporating the salient features of the 73rd Amendment to the Constitution of India. In Tamil Nadu, the Tamil Nadu Panchayats Act, 1958 was repealed and re-enacted as the Tamil Nadu Panchayats Act, 1994. The Tamil Nadu Panchayats Act, 1994 retained almost all the sections contained in Tamil Nadu Panchayats Act, 1958 and introduced some new sections to create a three-tier Panchayat structure. District Planning Committee, Gram Sabha, Finance Commission and Election Commission and reservation of seats in the three-tier structure for SC/ST people and women were provided for. Excepting the new provisions added as mentioned above, the 1994 Act was a replica of the 1958 Act.

Devolution of Powers

Article 243G of the Constitution of India provides that "the legislature of a State, may by law endow with the Panchayats such powers as may be necessary to make them function as units of self-government". The Constitutional mandate requires devolving of powers by enacting necessary law whereas Section 257 of Tamil Nadu Panchayats Act, 1994 states, "save as otherwise provided in this Act, government may by notification and subject to such conditions and restrictions as may be prescribed therein, entrust to the Panchayats or any other committees constituted under the Act such powers and responsibilities etc." This is contrary to what is envisaged in the Constitution. But, the powers and responsibilities were not given to the Panchayats even by notification*. No doubt, some powers were given to the Panchayats by executive orders and these orders were not even communicated to the three levels of Panchayats and to the respective departments of the government properly. Certain powers relating to the 29 subjects mentioned in Schedule IV of the Tamil Nadu Panchayats Act, 1994 (Schedule XI to Constitution of India) were given to the Panchayats by issuing executive orders. The concerned sectoral departments did not act on these orders in the spirit in which they were issued. By issuing executive orders an impression is given to the officials that they need not take them into account seriously. The officials know the difference between notification and executive orders. A notification has to be published for the consumption of the public and it comes out in the gazette. But executive orders need not be published and they are only meant for officials. Thus the Government of Tamil Nadu made the devolution a non-serious affair. Many of the orders

---

* *Notification* : A notification will have more legal force and validity than an executive order issued by government. Section 257 of the Tamil Nadu Panchayats Act requires the powers to be given by notification. The courts have held that a notification issued under the Act will have the same force as the Act. Under Section 262 of the Tamil Nadu Panchayats Act, all notifications issued under this Act have to be published in the Tamil Nadu Government gazette and should be placed on the table of the Legislative Assembly. Hence the orders issued under this Act other than by way of notification will have no validity. The Supreme Court in ITC Bhadrachalam Paper Board and another *Vs* Mandal Revenue Officer, AP and others [(1996) 6 SCC 634] has held that the statutory requirement of publication of rules/orders in the official gazette is mandatory. The object of the publication in the official gazette is not merely to give information to the public also but to give final official confirmation to the rules/ orders. The orders issued by the government giving powers to the Panchayats are not published in the Tamil Nadu Government Gazette. Hence the powers given to the Panchayats in Tamil Nadu by executive orders have no legal force.

giving powers to the rural local bodies merely state that the Panchayats can assist in identification of beneficiaries, watch and advise the government in implementation of schemes. Real powers were not given to the Panchayats. Power means authority to decide things. No such decision-making powers are given to Panchayat institutions.

The fate of these Government Orders has been amply brought out by the High Level Committee on Devolution of Powers and functions to rural Local Bodies constituted under the chairmanship of Thiru M.K. Stalin, Hon'ble Minister for Rural Development and Local Governance in 2007. The committee has observed in Para 8, Chapter I as follows:

> The committee carefully examined the action taken by the government on recommendations of the first and second high level committee .... The committee is satisfied with the fact that that all departments have issued necessary orders based on the high level committees. However, the committee is constrained to point out that many of these orders have remained on paper and not much efforts has been taken in the past to implement the Government orders in letter and spirit.....

Article 243G of the Constitution clearly states that the legislature of the State may, by law, endow the Panchayats with such powers etc. Taking advantage of the word "may" in the said article, the State government considered that giving authority to the Panchayats is purely the discretion of the State government and it is not a Constitutional mandate. In this context it is pertinent to note that the observation of the National Commission to review the working of the Constitution set out in Chapter IX of its report as below, as has been quoted in "Renga Reddy District Sarpanch Association *Vs.* Government of Andhra Pradesh, 2004(1) ALT 659 (L.B.) (para 54)".

"The National Commission to review the working of the Constitution, as part of its study, took up an analysis of decentralization and devolution of powers to Panchayats. The

Commission's report records that the Union and the State Governments continue to exercise powers in planning and the Panchayats do not enjoy autonomy—financial or administrative—as institutions of Local Self Government. The Commission examined whether there has been devolution of powers and responsibility to Panchayats, *inter alia* in functional and financial spheres. The report records that Panchayats, having blossomed into institutions of self-government, have been reduced to an implementing arm of the State Government. On the financial domain the report observes, that to be an institution of self-government, a Panchayat should, as far as possible, be a viable and manageable unit. It should be capable of generating internal resources by using its own fiscal powers that include taxing power commensurate with the functions assigned to it. The Commission felt that major fiscal restructuring and financial resources are necessary to enable the Panchayats to function as viable local self-governing institutions. With regard to personnel of the Panchayati Raj Institutions, the report records that an institution of self-government must have the power to recruit and control the officers and other employees required for managing its functions. The Constitution is totally silent about this viability aspect of institutional autonomy. The failure to address the human resource issues has definitely affected the growth of Panchayats as self-governing institutions. The report also points out that since the task of assigning functions to the Panchayats was given to the State Legislature, State Governments retain the powers of the Panchayats with State Government. The conclusion of the Commission in this area is that the gap between the Constitutional hope and the reality in the area of empowerment of Panchayati Raj Institutions was on account of the inconclusiveness of the text. It recommended amendments to the provisions of Part IX and Schedule VII of the Constitution, among other provisions."

The political executive of the State did not have the will to make the Panchayats institutions of self-government. The bureaucracy also did not help in endowing the Panchayats with necessary powers intended to be given by government order. Both have joined together to see that the Local Bodies should not become a vibrant political force to challenge the State government for its omission and commission. From the perception of the political and administrative executives Panchayats are only agents of the State government.

Even though the Tamil Nadu, Panchayats Act, 1994 incorporated certain provisions of the Constitutional Amendment Act, powers, functions, functionaries and finances are not given to Panchayats in the spirit in which the Constitutional Amendment Act was enacted. In fact some of the powers given to the Panchayats that are forward looking have now been taken away. For instance, prior to 1994, Village Panchayats and Panchayat Union Councils were empowered by rules to accord administrative sanction for estimates which have been prepared and approved by competent technical authorities without any financial limit as per the rules issued under the Tamil Nadu Panchayat Act, 1958. Now under the rules relating to execution of works issued in G.O. Ms. No. 286 RD dated 31-12-1998, Village Panchayats can accord administrative sanction only to estimate up to Rs. 1 lakh. Any estimate beyond the above limit has to be sent to the District Collector for administrative sanction. If the estimate is beyond Rs. 3 lakhs it has to be sent to the Director of Rural Development for approval. Similarly, the Panchayat Union Councils can accord administrative sanction for estimates up to Rs. 5 lakhs only.* Beyond that limit, it has to go to the District Collector and the Director of Rural Development for sanction. In the name of giving power to the people through the new dispensation, the State government has taken away even the existing powers of the Panchayats granted by the Tamil Nadu Panchayat Act. It is nothing but one step forward and two steps backward. Thus, the powers already provided to Panchayats were taken away and the procedure now ordained only results in unnecessary delay and other undesirable consequences. Even simple works like black topping roads upto one km will cost more than Rs. 5 lakhs. So practically the functions of the Panchayat are crippled.

---

* *Note:* The power to accord administrative sanction for estimates has been since increased to Rs. 2 lakhs to village panchayats and Rs. 10 lakhs to Panchayat union councils in G.O.Ms. No. 203 R.D and Panchayati Raj district. 20-12-2007. However, the original position has not been restored.

The various rules issued by the State government are curtailing the powers and authority of the Panchayat. The State Government, in G.O.Ms. 57 RD dated 22-02-2001, allowed the Village Panchayats to run the fair price shops under the Public Distribution System. The Public Distribution System is one of the items to be entrusted to the Panchayats under Schedule IV to Tamil Nadu Panchayat Act (Schedule XI to Constitution of India). Initially in the above rules it was stated that Village Panchayats which are willing to run the fair price shops under the Public Distribution System located in the Panchayat village shall be identified by the District Collector and the Collector shall grant permission to run the said shop. The word in this rule "shall" was changed to "may" by an amendment made on 14-08-2001 and thus gave discretiôn to the Collector. The spirit in which the rules were issued was negated by this amendment.

Many rules issued under this Act are not positive towards Panchayats. To cite an instance, the State government, in G.O. Ms. No.108, RD dated 28-03-2001, issued the "Tamil Nadu Panchayats (determination of claim to trees growing on public roads and other property vesting in or belonging to Village Panchayats) Rules, 2001", wherein certain provisions of the rules are obnoxious and do not stand to reason. In rule 7 of the above said rules it has been stated that the Village Panchayats shall have the powers to cut down or sell by auction the live trees on road margins or in water supply sources which are considered dangerous to traffic or dangerous to life or health. But certain conditions have been imposed whereby even in that situation the Panchayats can cut the trees only with the sanction of the Revenue Divisional Officer who shall accord sanction only after getting the report of the Tahsildar. Even if the Revenue Divisional Officer who is superior to the Tahsildar finds that the trees are dangerous to the public he should not give permission without getting the report of the Tahsildhar. It is an unnecessary obstruction in the functioning of the Panchayats.

The Inspector of Panchayats District Collector has been given powers under Section 205 of the Tamil Nadu Panchayat Act to remove the elected President of a Village Panchayat. In the modern democratic set-up, the powers of the executive to remove an elected representatives is considered undesirable. This power has been often misused. There are many instances to prove this point. In a particular instance one District Collector has threatened a Panchayat President that he will initiate action under Section 205 of Tamil Nadu Panchayat Act to remove him for the simple reason that he met him with certain public grievances.

Decentralization involves devolution of functions, powers and finance to the local bodies. No real power was given and this has been brought out by the study undertaken by the National Institute of Rural Development (NIRD) as per the direction of the Ministry of Rural Development. It has been pointed out that "the Ministry of Rural Development in its memorandum to the Central Finance Commission states that the requirement of funds by the Panchayats for performing the development functions under various centrally sponsored schemes and state sponsored schemes and regulatory and maintenance needs of the Panchayats should receive special dispensation from the Commission". The Eleventh Finance Commission entrusted with the NIRD the task of studying the position of devolution of functions to the rural local bodies, the powers to raise their resources to perform the core services, namely, primary education, primary health, rural roads, drinking water supply, sanitation and street lights. The NIRD study reveals that the 73rd Amendment has not significantly altered the functions of the Panchayats at the various tiers. The Centre as well as States have sponsored schemes for rural development without associating the Panchayats in planning and implementation. This has further marginalized them (Emerging Institution for Decentralized Rural Development, Vol. I, NIRD, 2001, p. 180).

The Government of India releases more than Rs. 2000 crores every year to the rural local bodies to provide infrastructure and it is being spent and yet the people's felt needs are not met as there is no micro level planning at the grassroots which results in waste of funds and improper utilization. The Constitutional Amendment Act and the Tamil Nadu Panchayats Act, Section 240, enjoin that the Panchayats should prepare annual plans to achieve economic development and social justice. This is an important function assigned to them so that the felt needs of the people will be met through such planning. So far planning has not been done at the bottom level. Instead it has been imposed from above. The needs of the people have not been reflected in the planning exercise done above the Panchayats and, therefore, it was realized at every level as early as 1970 that planning should be done at the grassroots. The District Planning Cell has been created and the District Planning Committee has been constituted and money is being spent for it and yet there is no constant effort to initiate micro planning as per the mandate of the Constitution.

First State Finance Commission (SFC) Recommendations

In accordance with Article 243-I of the Constitution of India, the First SFC in Tamil Nadu was constituted in 1994 to make recommendations on devolution of funds to the Panchayats for five years from 1996-97 to 2001-02. It is to be noted here that the State Finance Commission started its exercise and came to the final stage before it was decided as to what powers and responsibilities have to be given to each and every tier of the three-tier Panchayat system. The First SFC submitted its report before the Committee which was constituted for making recommendations on entrusting responsibilities to the three-tier Panchayats submitted its report. The First SFC made 462 recommendations, of which 49 were common to rural and urban local bodies, 107 were related to rural local bodies and 195 were related to taxation and other issues. Of these, only 93 recommendations were accepted in principle and 97 recommendations were not accepted by the government. Even for the 93 accepted recommendations, the government had not issued orders. The details are given in Table 7.1.

The First State Finance Commission recommended devolution of State owned tax resources (other than assigned revenues) from 8 per cent to 12 per cent by increasing 1 per cent annually from 1996-97. But the State government decided to freeze it at 8 per cent of its resources for the five years period in spite of the fact that initially in the "Action Taken Report" placed before the Legislature, a commitment was made by the State government that payment will be made at the rate of 8 per cent, 9 per cent, 10 per cent, 11 per cent and 12 per cent during the period of five years starting from 1996-97. While considering the responsibilities assigned

Table 7.1: The Status of First State Finance Commission Recommendations for PRIs/ULBs

Sl. No.	*Topics*		*Accepted*	*Accepted in principle only*	*Not accepted*	*Orders not passed*	*Under examination*	*Total*
1.	Taxation and other related service		93	-	97	3	2	195
2.	Civic services	Urban Rural	- -	106 -	- -	- 26	- -	106 26
3.	Organizations	Urban Rural	- 1	5 -	- -	- 8	- -	5 9
4.	Functions	Urban Rural	- 1	1 -	- -	- -	- -	1 1
5.	Devolution of functions	Urban Rural	- 1	1 -	- -	- -	- -	1 1
6.	Staffing pattern	Urban Rural	- 2	5 -	- 2	- 1	- -	5 5
7.	Human resources development	Urban Rural	- -	11 9	- -	- 2	- -	11 11
8.	Community participation	Urban Rural	- -	6 -	- -	- 6	- -	6 6
9.	Adequacy of powers	Urban Rural	- 5	8 -	- -	- 3	- -	8 8
10.	Control system	Urban Rural	- 1	7 -	- -	- 6	- -	7 7
11.	Mechanism for performance	Urban Rural	- 2	4 -	- -	- 2	- -	4 4
12.	Database	Urban Rural	- 4	6 -	- -	- 2	- -	6 6
13.	Devolution of funds	Urban Rural	- 22	- -	- -	- -	- -	- 22
14.	Capital fund	Urban Rural	- -	- -	- 1	- -	- -	- 1
	Total		132	169	100	59	2	462

to the Panchayats, the resources devolved to Panchayats are meagre and insufficient. This poor recommendation was due to the fact that the First State Finance Commission considered the responsibilities given to the Panchayats with the 1958 Panchayat Act as a base and on that basis calculated the requirements and made recommendations.

Modifications

In some of the recommendations, the government made modifications which the First SFC had not suggested such as: (i) abolition of house tax matching grant, (ii) abolition of local cess surcharge matching grant, (iii) adoption of population as the only criterion for *inter se* distribution instead of population along with service indicators and per capita income. The modifications made by the government were detrimental to the interests of the Panchayats. The government, in its Action Taken Report placed before the Legislature in April 1997, had accepted the recommendation for direct remittance of the share of minerals and block granite to Village Panchayat account, but, subsequently, the Rural Development Department of the Government have rejected this recommendation. As a result the money goes to the treasury and it does not come to the Panchayats. To get money from the treasury a cumbersome procedure has to be followed for which officials have to take steps from the district administration and they are to be pursued at the secretariat level. At present nobody bothers about it. As a result Panchayats are not getting their due share.

Unaccepted Recommendations

Some of the major recommendations made by First State Finance Commission which have not been accepted by the government are:

(i) Calculation of local cess and local cess surcharge based on average land revenue.

(ii) Compensation for local bodies towards local cess/local cess surcharge during the period of waiver/remission of land revenue.

(iii) Water tax.

This has also affected the financial resources of the Panchayats.

Utilization of SFC Devolution

The First SFC recommended specifically that the devolution is meant to cover maintenance of assets at the time of the award period as also the assets to be created during the award period and salary and wages of the personnel of the local bodies. This has been visualized with a view to maintaining the assets created and also to avoid delay in payment of salary to the employees of local bodies. In practice, the government have set apart a sizeable sum for capital works with a view to improving basic amenities in both rural and urban areas. Further, the government have deducted the debt payable by local bodies to other institutions from the State Finance Commission grant. On the other hand, the recommendations relating to remittance of PF dues (contribution) to the respective accounts has not been implemented. Moreover the entire devolution money has been credited to general fund accounts of the local bodies. When specific orders have been issued for the maintenance of separate cash book for utilization of devolution fund in urban local bodies no specific orders have been issued in respect of rural local bodies. Experience shows that there is need for separate accounts to monitor the utilization of State Finance Commission devolution (*Source:* Second State Finance Commission Report).

Second State Finance Commission Recommendations

The Second State Finance Commission was constituted on 1-12-1999 to make recommendations on devolution of funds for five years from 2002-03 to 2007-08. The State Finance Commission made 260 recommendations of which 60 are accepted in principle as mentioned in the Action Taken Report placed before the Legislature. The Second State Finance Commission recommended devolution of 8 per cent from State owned tax resources for the first-two years and 9 per cent for the next two years and 10 per cent for last one year. But the government issued orders freezing the devolution of funds to 8 per cent for each year. When Finance Commissions are constituted a tradition has been established in Tamil Nadu that IAS officials are to be appointed Chairpersons. No doubt they have the capacity and capability to perform the job but it is a major question whether they have the needed mindset to look properly at the new paradigm. There are other experts in local body finance or public finance and they can also be appointed. With the minimum responsibilities to Panchayats the First Finance Commission recommended 8 per cent to 12 per cent for a period of five years. But in the Second Finance Commission, after fixing enormous responsibilities, the recommendation, instead of starting from 12 per cent, started from the same 8 per cent. It gives the impression that local bodies are not considered institutions of self-governance.

The government in its Action Taken Report placed before the Legislature during May 2002 indicated the extent to which the recommendations were accepted as indicated below:

Accepted in Principle	*Not Accepted*	*Accepted with Modification*
60	15	17

In respect of rural local bodies even though more than three years have lapsed after the submission of the report, the government have not passed any orders on the recommendations of the Second State Finance Commission.

Analysis of implementation of Second State Finance Commission recommendations observations of Third State Finance Commission

The Third State Finance Commission in its report (Chapter III para 2) has observed as follows:

"Even though most of the recommendations of the Second State Finance Commission have been accepted, yet *there is laxity in implementing the recommendations by the Administrative Department of the Secretariat. In fact, on the recommendations relating to improving of 'Resource Base', Casual approach is noticeable.*" The Commission has given a detailed list of recommendations accepted by the Government — but proper action not taken for implementation.

One of the major recommendations which will give some relief to rural local bodies is payment of compensation for waiver of local cess and local cess surcharge whenever land revenue is waived due to drought or flood. For Block Panchayats, local cess surcharge is the most important source of income. This recommendation for payment of compensation whenever local cess surcharge is waived was also made by the First SFC. Though the government initially stated in the Action Taken Report that the payment of the compensation will be considered, the government have not taken any decision so far. During 2003-04 the government have waived land revenue, local cess, local cess surcharge throughout Tamil Nadu. But no compensation to local bodies was thought of resulting in huge financial loss to rural local bodies roughly to the tune of Rs.33.30 crores.

Revenue Dues to Panchayats Not Settled

(i) Local Cess and Local Cess Surcharge

The Second State Finance Commission recommended in para 13.2.4 that local cess/local cess surcharge to the Panchayat/Panchayat Unions due during the period from 1997-98 to 2001-02 should be reworked and adjusted positively within two years, that is, 2002-03 and 2003-04 since local cess/local cess surcharge, which are legitimate dues of Panchayats and Panchayat Unions, are not at all being adjusted properly. This has not been done so far by the government. This results in loss of revenue to the Panchayats.

(ii) Mines and Minerals

The Second State Finance Commission in para 12 pointed out that the dues from mines and minerals have not been adjusted and it recommended that the remaining dues may be cleared by issuing suitable orders. But the government has not acted on this. Thus due share from the mines and minerals have not come to Panchayats.

(iii) Social Forestry

The Second State Finance Commission in para 8.7 stated that the share of the Village Panchayats from social forestry income from

1995-96 onwards is yet to be settled. The auctioning under social forestry is done by the Forest Department without any role assigned to the Village Panchayats. The Panchayats feel that their auction amount will be more if they are associated. Hence, the Second State Finance Commission recommended that the Village Panchayats' share may be directly credited to their own account after the conduct of auction to avoid delay. It further recommended the constitution of a committee consisting of Secretary to Government, Environment and Forest Department, Chief Conservator of Forests and DRD to monitor timely adjustment. The inaction of the government in taking steps to implement the recommendation to release the backlog dues to the Panchayats in respect of local cess/local cess surcharge, mines, social forestry has not helped the Panchayats to meet the core and basic requirements. A commitment by the government to rectify the above situation is urgently called for.

Release of State Finance Commission Devolution Fund

The Second State Finance Commission, in para 12 of Chapter XIII, pointed out that the release of SFC Devolution Fund for the first two years 1997-98 and 1998-99 was more or less regular while in subsequent two years there were erratic releases which affected any possible financial planning by the local bodies. It further pointed out that devolution has become discretionary with several local bodies finding it difficult even to pay salary to their employees.

The above instances amply make clear that the amount due to the Panchayats has not been released by the department in time even after a high level body, namely the State Finance Commission, made positive recommendations to the effect that the dues should be paid immediately. As the entitlement due to Panchayats has not been released and hence they are unable to discharge the statutory duties entrusted to them. In order to make the Panchayats functional, the State government should be made to release the dues in time. The Government is committed to releasing the State Finance Commission grant every month by modification to the Second State Finance Commission recommendations. But experience shows that the release of the State Finance Commission grant was not made every month. This has seriously affected the functioning of the

Panchayats. The State government should be made to honour its commitment and it should be watched by the Estimates Committee of the Legislature.

Unauthorized Diversion of Statutory SFC Grant due to Local Bodies by Government

The SFC grant is not being regularly released to the Panchayats. In many cases, the grant due to the Panchayats has been unauthorizedly diverted to other purposes and also paid to other departments. In some cases the grant has been adjusted at the State level towards electricity consumption charges (CC) due to the EB without verification and without any intimation to the concerned Panchayats. As this is done at the State level, the release of grant is not reflected in the accounts of the Panchayats. Nay, the Panchayats are not even aware of their entitlement and the release. This further results in the improper maintenance of accounts by the Panchayats. *"The grant released through the right hand has been snatched away by the left hand without the knowledge of the body."*

The annual entitlement of SFC grant for rural local bodies for the year 2001-02 is Rs. 416.00 crores, of which the government, in G.O.Ms.18, RD dated 26-03-2002, restricted the SFC grant to the tune of Rs. 175.00 crores for rural Panchayats in that year. Obviously, the Panchayats have been deprived of a substantial sum of Rs. 241.00 crores approximately during the year 2001-02. Even while releasing the above grant of Rs. 175.00 crores, the government have adjusted the following amounts from Village Panchayats and Panchayat Unions during the year 2001-02:

Sl. No.	*Particular*	*Amount (Rs. in crores)*
1.	CC Charges (Electricity Charges)	1.78
2.	Payment of pensionary contribution towards Panchayat Union employees	31.85
3.	Contribution for loan amount sanctioned by government to Panchayat Unions for special Self Sufficiency Programme	7.16
	Total	40.78

It is also observed that the entire equalisation and incentive grant from out of State Finance Commission funds for the year 2002-03 due to the three tier of Panchayats has been diverted for undertaking drought relief works.

Third State Finance Commission

The Third State Finance Commission submitted its report in September 2006 for the award period 2007-2012. Action taken report was placed before the Assembly in May 2007.

This is what the Commission has to say about the way in which it was treated. "Article 243(1) empowers the State Finance Commission to frame its own procedure for its functioning. But in practice the Government continue to treat the Commission as like any other department for getting that it is a constitutional body. That is especially visible when it sought the required manpower: out of 44 sanctioned posts only 20 posts could be filled up ......" (Para 40 Chapter XIV).

As for the monitoring mechanism the Commission observed "The First and Second State Finance Commissions made recommendations of which some of them were partially implemented, some have not been implemented and the remaining were under consideration of the Government. Even though the Second State Finance Commission pointed out the delay on the part of the implementing authority get its recommendations met with the same fate .... It is a reflection of the general view that the local bodies are still looked upon as the appendage of the State Government and not as a constitutionally recognized bodies. In the above context the Third State Finance Commission analysed the scenario. The Commission recommends that decisions on all recommendations of the Third State Finance Commission shall be taken within 6 months from the date of commencement of the award period. The follow-up action on the A.T.R. meets to be monitored on quarterly basis by the High Level Committee constituted for the purpose". (Para 30 Chapter XIV)

The details of recommendations made by the Third State Finance Commission, the number of recommendations accepted by the

Government and the number of recommendations not accepted etc. are furnished below:

Total number of recommendations—308

Recommendations relating to urban local bodies	-	138
Recommendations relating to rural local bodies	-	102
Common to urban and rural	-	68
Total	-	308

Recommendations accepted etc.

Common recommendations—68

Accepted	-	19
Not accepted	-	33
Accepted with modifications	-	10
Accepted in principle	-	1
Deemed to be accepted	-	1
No decision	-	4
Total	-	68

Rural Local Bodies

Total recommendations—102

Accepted	-	30
Not accepted	-	34
Accepted with modifications	-	6
Accepted in principle	-	12
Deemed to be accepted	-	5
No decision	-	15
Total	-	102

Not accepted recommendations out number the number of accepted recommendations.

The Third State Finance Commission recommended Financial devolution of 10 per cent to the local bodies for the entire award period.

The State agreed to devolved funds as follows:

2007 - 08	-	9%
2008 - 09	-	9%
2009 - 10	-	9.5%
2010 - 11	-	10%
2011 - 12	-	10%

Responsibilities of Three-Tier Panchayats

1. Village Panchayats

Onerous responsibilities are given to the Village Panchayats and they are listed as obligatory and discretionary functions in Sections 110 and 111 of Tamil Nadu Panchayat Act, 1994. The obligatory functions of Village Panchayats are:

(i) Construction, repair and maintenance of village roads.
(ii) Construction, repair and maintenance of water works for supply of water for drinking, washing and bathing purposes.
(iii) Light of public roads and public places in built up areas.
(iv) Cleaning of streets and removal of rubbish.
(v) Construction of disposal of drainage water and its maintenance.
(vi) Provision of public latrine and arrangements to clean public latrine whether public or private.
(vii) Opening and maintenance of burial and burning grounds.
(viii) Opening and maintenance of Public Distribution System.
(ix) Extension of village sites and regulation of buildings.

Apart from this, the following discretionary functions are given to Village Panchayats:

(i) Planting and preservation of trees on the public roads.
(ii) Lighting on public roads and public places in non-built up areas.
(iii) Opening and maintenance of public market.

(iv) Control of fairs and festivals.
(v) Opening and maintenance of slaughter houses.
(vi) Opening and maintenance of reading rooms.
(vii) Establishment and maintenance of TV sets etc.

2. Block Panchayats

The obligatory and discretionary functions of Block Panchayats are listed in Sections 112 and 113 to 119 of Tamil Nadu Panchayats Act, 1994. The important obligatory functions are:

(i) Construction, repair and maintenance of Panchayat Union roads.
(ii) Establishment and maintenance of rural dispensaries and payment of subsidies to rural medical practitioner.
(iii) Establishment and maintenance of maternity centres.
(iv) Maintenance and expansion of elementary school buildings.
(v) Remedial measures considered with epidemic diseases.
(vi) Control of fairs and festivals classified as Panchayat Union festivals.
(vii) Veterinary relief.
(viii) Opening and maintenance of Panchayat Union markets.
(ix) Establishment and maintenance of poultries.
(x) Improvement of agriculture.
(xi) Promotion and encouragement to cottage industries.

The discretionary functions given to Block Panchayats are:

(i) Entrustment and execution of NES and CD works.
(ii) Execution of any of the schemes or programme for economic development.
(iii) Provision and maintenance of common, burial and burning ground.
(iv) Lighting of public roads and public places in common areas of Panchayats.

(v) Maintenance of common dispensaries and child welfare centres.

(vi) Any other duty imposed by government.

3. District Panchayat

The functions of the District Panchayat as enumerated in Sections 163 and 164 of the Tamil Nadu Panchayat Act are advisory in nature. They have to advise the government on all matters relating to rural development.

Inadequate Finance and Manpower for Fulfilment of Responsibilities

Village Panchayats are given heavy and innumerable responsibilities which relate to the basic needs of the community. They have to necessarily carry out the functions. For this purpose, they are not equipped with either finance or the required technical or supporting staff. The main income of Village Panchayats is consumed by electricity charges for street lights and water supply and, even in respect of them, they are in huge arrears resulting in unauthorized adjustment at the State level from statutory grants made to them.

In respect of staff, they are provided with one part-time assistant and limited sanitary and water supply staff. More number of hamlets in Village Panchayats, expansion of population and execution of various water supply schemes with government assistance and other infrastructure development executed in the Village Panchayats require maintenance periodically and annually for which the existing staff and the funds now available are quite inadequate. Unless sufficient financial assistance and technical guidance with staff are provided, the various amenities provided at huge government cost will run into disuse and decay.

Block Panchayats were getting substantial assigned revenues during the pre-SFC period, viz., local cess surcharge matching grant, local roads grant, local education grant, minor irrigation grant, land revenue assignment etc., which are no longer in vogue and hence Block Panchayats now find it very difficult to run the administration with only the State Finance Commission grant. Though they are provided with adequate staff to carry out the above functions the increasing salary of staff and expenditure on pensionary commitments etc. have made them financially weak. The Block Panchayats should be provided with adequate financial assistance to attend to the various development schemes entrusted out of centrally sponsored schemes and State sponsored schemes besides the works carried out from their own finance in some Panchayat Unions.

As regards District Panchayats, the District Panchayats are having only an advisory role in the rural local body administration as per Section 163 of the Tamil Nadu Panchayat Act and no asset creation and maintenance are entrusted to them. Therefore, no separate allocation out of SFC grant is called for after setting apart finance towards requirement of salary for District Panchayats till additional functions are entrusted.

Reduction of Sources of Income

(i) Village Panchayats

The main sources of income of the Village Panchayats are house tax, profession tax, advertisement tax and other non-tax items like building fees, Dangerous and Offensive (D&O) trades etc., and assigned revenues, viz., surcharge on stamp duty, entertainment tax, cable TV, local cess, mines and minerals etc.*

The vehicle tax originally levied by the Panchayat as per Section 173 of the Tamil Nadu Panchayat Act, 1994 and the house tax matching grant provided as per Section 183 of the Tamil Nadu Panchayat Act were dispensed with. The surcharge on stamp duty which is the main and a substantial source of income to Village Panchayats has been drastically reduced *from 5 per cent to 2 per cent and 1 per cent in respect of mortgage of immovable*

---

* As per the recent orders issued by the Government in G.O.Ms. No. 168 R.D. district. 4-10-2007 the income from assigned revenues will be pooled at the State level and shared between the Village Panchayats, Panchayat Unions and District Panchayats in the ratio 60:32:8 after earmarking 1/3rd of the total revenue to a special fund. Though this will ensure equitable distribution of revenue between the three tires the income to the Village Panchayat will get reduced.

property resulting in more than *60 per cent loss of income* to the Panchayats from this source alone. On the introduction of cable TV the income from Entertainment Tax (ET) has been reduced to a considerable extent. Originally the tax on exhibition of cable TV was levied by Village Panchayats but Village Panchayats could not assess the volume of tax properly due to inadequate staff. As a result it was taken over by the government. But the government have not paid any compensation to the local bodies after taking over the levy of tax on cable TV.

Regarding mines and minerals, the government have to apportion the lease amount to Village Panchayats and Panchayat Unions on a 50 : 50 basis. Now, the government have taken over the mines and the quarrying of sand directly but they have not issued orders for disbursing the dues to the local bodies so far. If the income from mines and minerals are not apportioned to the local bodies they will lose heavily.

In respect of the Block Panchayat, the Act still provides for the payment of land revenue assignment grant as per Section 170 of the Tamil Nadu Panchayat Act. But this has not been paid from 1997-98 onwards. Another important source of income is local cess surcharge matching grant under Section 180 of the Tamil Nadu Panchayat Act and now it has been deleted. Likewise local roads grant paid to Block Panchayats as per Section 182 has also been deleted. Now this is supposed to be merged with State Finance Commission devolution funds except land revenue assignment which is still in the Act but is not paid.

Income and Expenditure of Rural Local Bodies

Though the 73rd Amendment Act provides for more duties and responsibilities to Village Panchayats and Block Panchayats, mobilization of resources through taxes becomes increasingly difficult due to various factors. The expectations and aspirations of the people for receiving efficient service from the local bodies are more whereas the resources mobilized through taxes and non-taxes cannot meet the demands of the people especially in providing better basic amenities like water supply, maintenance of roads, street lights etc. There is a big gap between the pre-State Finance

Commission and the post-State Finance Commission period in receipts. The expenditure has gone up.

An analysis of revenue and expenditure of Village Panchayats and Block Panchayats of the pre-SFC devolution period and the post-SFC devolution period are given below:

Village Panchayats

Source of Income for 1996-97 (Pre-SFC Devolution Period)

Sl. No.	*Particular*	*Average Amount per Panchayat (Rs. in lakhs)*	*Percentage*
1.	Tax and non-tax	0.27	21.8
2.	Assigned revenue	0.75	60.5
3.	Other grants	0.14	11.2
4.	Miscellaneous receipt	0.08	6.5
	Total	1.24	

Source of Expenditure details for 1996-97 (Pre-SFC Devolution Period)

Sl. No.	*Particular*	*Average Amount per Panchayat (Rs. in lakhs)*	*Percentage*
1.	General Administration	0.14	13.6
2.	Maintenance charge	0.69	64.14
3.	Maintenance expenditure	0.12	11.5
4.	Capital expenditure	0.11	10.15
	Total	1.06	

Break-up details for Post-SFC Devolution Period (1999-2000)

Source of Income

Sl. No.	*Particular*	*Average Amount per Panchayat (Rs. in lakhs)*	*Percentage*
1.	Own source including tax and non-tax	0.53	17.51
2.	Assigned revenue	0.82	27.17
3.	Grants	1.48	48.88
4.	Miscellaneous receipt	0.19	6.43
	Total	3.02	

Break-up details for Post-SFC Devolution Period (1999-2000)

Expenditure Details

Sl. No.	*Particulars*	*Average Amount per Panchayat (Rs. in lakhs)*	*Percentage*
1.	General administration	0.55	15.14
2.	Maintenance charge	2.08	57.29
3.	Capital expenditure	0.90	24.71
4.	Miscellaneous expenditure	0.10	2.86
	Total	3.63	
	GAP	–0.62	

Prior to the SFC devolution, the major source of income derived by Village Panchayats was assigned revenue of surcharge on stamp duty, entertainment tax etc., which constituted 61 per cent of the total income. Though there was not much resource gap between receipt and expenditure, Village Panchayats could not take up capital works (providing better infrastructure) since the major portion of expenditure was consumed on electricity charges and maintenance charges relating to streetlights and water supply which constituted 65 per cent of the total expenditure whereas the capital expenditure constituted only 12 per cent.

There is not much improvement at the receipt even though the SFC devolution passed on income to Village Panchayats at the ratio of 47 per cent of total devolution due to rural local bodies.

Block Panchayat

Break-up details for Pre-SFC Devolution Period (1996-1997)

Sl. No.	*Source of Income*	*Average Amount per Block Panchayat (Rs. in lakhs)*	*Percentage*
1.	Local cess surcharge and non-tax items	24.26	88
2.	Assigned revenue	3.20	12
3.	Miscellaneous receipt	—	—
	Total	27.56	

Expenditure Details

Sl. No.	*Particular*	*Average Amount per Block Panchayat (Rs. in lakhs)*	*Percentage*
1.	General administration	16.84	52
2.	Maintenance expenditure	11.83	36.6
3.	Miscellaneous expenditure	—	—
4.	Capital expenditure	3.61	11.2
	Total	32.28	
	GAP	–4.8	

Break-up details for Post-SFC devolution period (1999-2000)

Sl. No.	*Source of Income*	*Average Amount per Block Panchayat (Rs. in lakhs)*	*Percentage*
1.	Own source including tax and non-tax	6.52	11.99
2.	Assigned revenues	0.08	0.15
3.	Grants	47.76	87.86
4.	Miscellaneous receipt	—	—
	Total	54.36	

Break-up Details for Post-SFC devolution period (1999-2000)

Sl. No.	*Expenditure Details*	*Average Amount per Block Panchayat (Rs. in lakhs)*	*Percentage*
1.	General administration	45.05	67.56
2.	Maintenance charge	16.44	24.66
3.	Capital expenditure	5.19	7.78
4.	Miscellaneous expenditure	—	—
	Total	66.68	
	GAP	–12.32	

The above figures indicate that out of the total income derived by the Panchayat Union, local cess surcharge, local cess surcharge matching grant, local education grant, local roads grant and land revenue assignment etc., constituted 88 per cent. But in the post-SFC devolution period the financial assistance pattern has been changed and the income from local cess surcharge matching grant, local education grant, local roads grant and other statutory grants were dispensed with and assistance is given in the form of State Finance Commission devolution to Panchayat Unions. Even prior to the SFC devolution period, there was a gap of Rs. 4.80 lakhs between receipt and expenditure. This gap has widened to Rs. 12.32 lakhs per Panchayat Union in the post-devolution scenario owing to the fact that the major portion of expenditure of 52 per cent in the pre-devolution period and 68 per cent in the post-devolution period is incurred for general administration. Under general administration, an expenditure 20 per cent of salary for Panchayat employees is incurred for pensionary contributions.

The above analysis will show that while the income to the Village Panchayats has sharply declined due to reduction in the surcharge on stamp duty which is a major source of income and also due to non-adjustment of receipts legally due to the Panchayats, there has been a steep rise in the expenditure due to streetlights and drinking water supply as well as increase in the establishment cost. The electricity board charged at the rate of Rs. 1.20 paise per KWH till 15-3-2003 and it has been increased to Rs. 3.60 from 16-3-2003, which is three times the earlier rate. Due to the three fold increase, many Panchayats are facing the problem of clearing electricity charges and are now in doldrums.

EB charges have increased three fold for supplying drinking water to the inhabitants as well as water supply for other essential purposes. Water supply and street lighting are obligatory duties cast on the Panchayats and they have to necessarily maintain them. In this connection electricity supply to the agriculturalists is provided free of charges. It is a well known fact that many of the agriculturalists availing of this concession are misusing this concession for pumping water and supplying the same to others and derive substantial income from this source. When such concession is being extended to the agriculturalists who are commercially exploiting it, it is a great injustice to charge heavily the Village Panchayats who are rendering social and public obligations. Now most of the Panchayats are in arrears and whatever little grant is given by government is being adjusted towards EB charges even without the knowledge of the Village Panchayats.

It is only proper that the electricity supply to Panchayats for water supply and streetlights is charged on par with domestic consumers.

Ways and Means to Augment the Resources of Panchayats

The Panchayats face several problems in raising local tax revenue such as narrow tax base, lack of administrative machinery, staff trained in tax collection, lack of guidelines to levy new taxes. Local tax collections can be improved by improving the administrative capacity of the local bodies before levying higher tax. The existing staff at the Village Panchayat level is highly inadequate for this purpose. The staff working in other departments connected with the duty of the Panchayats may be suitably redeployed and placed at the disposal of the Panchayats.

The rate of fee levied by the Panchayats for installation of machinery and D & O trades is very low since it was fixed as early as 1960. This needs revision and a higher fee may be fixed by suitable notification by government and thereby income can be raised.

Another major source of income is levy and collection of house tax. The present law provides for levy of tax on plinth area basis and it has not been resorted to by many Panchayats. The Panchayats should be made to levy the tax on plinth area basis and they should be suitably guided and motivated to do so through incentives.

At present the implementation of the recommendations made by Finance Commission is left to the discretion of the State government. This attitude should be changed and the recommendations made by such constitutional bodies have to be accepted in all seriousness and implemented unless it is beyond the resources of the State government. We find that even accepted recommendations have not been implemented on some pretext or other. This position should be changed by making suitable amendments to the Constitution.

Summary

1. Proper devolution of function, power and funds should be made available to the Panchayats so that they can effectively discharge their duties and functions as true local self-governing institutions as contemplated in the Constitution.
2. Recommendations made by the SFC and accepted by the government in principle should be faithfully implemented and arrears due to Panchayats should be paid without delay.
3. While releasing the SFC grant deductions should not be made at the State level. The funds should be credited to the accounts of local bodies and they should be made to pay the dues so that they can watch the receipt of grants and maintain the accounts properly.
4. To improve tax collection by Village Panchayats proper staff should be given by suitable redeployment of staff working in government departments and their salary should be continued to be met by the government. The Village Panchayats which come forward to increase the rate and assessment of tax and mobilize more new sources of income may be encouraged by suitable support through incentives.
5. For maintaining the cleanliness of streets and sanitation of the Panchayats suitable personnel and recurring grant may be sanctioned to the local bodies.
6. To improve the functioning of the Panchayat, the functions, staff and finance now provided to departments dealing with the 29 subjects (as per Schedule XI to Constitution) may be transferred to the Panchayats by issuing statutory orders.
7. Maintenance cost on drinking water supply and street lights have sharply increased (to almost 70% of the income). Hence special grants may be sanctioned to Panchayats to make good the deficit.

8. The Central Finance Commission provides 29 per cent from centrally owned tax resources to State governments as CFC grant. It is recommended that one-third of the amount from out of the CFC grant released be earmarked for local bodies and directly credited to the local bodies' accounts by the Central Finance Commission itself.

8

IMPROVING FINANCES OF PANCHAYATS THROUGH CENTRAL FINANCE COMMISSION TRANSFERS

O.P. BOHRA

Introduction

The phenomenon of decentralisation is getting popular across all the developed and the developing countries. The process of strengthening of local government is welcome step accepted by all sections of the society. The decentralisation takes place through devolutions of resources and the functional responsibilities to lower level of governance. It is assumed that the local-self governance at the lowest level of decision making powers would offer socio-economic benefits and help in mobilising more resources and efficient delivery mechanism. The devolution of resources and discharging of the functional responsibilities have assumed great importance in recent past in almost all the countries. In form of two historical amendments India has also initiated the process of decentralisati n. The government has implemented the 73rd and 74th Constitutional Amendment Act (CAA) for strengthening the grassroots level of governments in rural as well as urban areas. The following section endeavour a brief discussion on revenue decentralisation across the select countries. The section third detailed the important steps initiated in the form of constitutional provisions for devolution of resources from Central Government to local bodies through Central Finance Commissions (10th, 11th and 12th). A critical review of the criterion adopted by the CFCs for transferring of grants to local bodies constitutes the fourth section. The final section presents the conclusion and the issues for the next (thirteenth) Finance Commission.

Extent of Fiscal (Revenue) Decentralisation—International Scenario

Table 8.1 presents the extent of revenue decentralisation across the select countries having federal structure of three levels of governments of Central, State/Province and the local. A close look into these figures indicates the prevailing of strong central governments in almost all the countries. The share of revenue mobilized through tax by the central governments varies from less than 50 per cent in Canada, Germany and Switzerland. In these countries the State governments are stronger. On the other hand, in the countries of Belgium, South Africa and Colombia, the predominance of the governments at the centre level exist. The tax revenue generated by the central governments in these countries goes upto more than 90 per cent of the total tax yield of all the three levels of governments. The revenue mobilized by the state governments through taxes varies from 42 per cent in Canada to lowest figure of less than 5 per cent in the countries of Belgium, Bolivia, Colombia and South Africa. The extent of revenue collected by the lowest level of governments in the total tax income shows level of taxation powers transferred to the local governments. The local government in Switzerland seems to be very strong. The revenue mobilized by the local governments was highest of 21.10 per cent. However, in the countries of Austria, Belgium, Bolivia, Colombia and Spain, the generated through tax sources were more than the State/Provincial Governments. The governments at the local level in these countries have more taxation powers than the middle level of governance. In India, the lower levels of governance have not been allocated adequate taxation powers to generate substantial resources. The GSF does not give any figure of revenue collected by local governments in India. These data are not documented by any higher level of governments in any authorised documents. The C&AG has also not been able to provide any audited figures. In the recent past only Eleventh Finance Commission endeavoured to present strong data base of local bodies. As per Rao and Singh (2005)[1] the revenue raised by the local bodies in India is almost negligible.

Table 8.1: Revenue Decentralisation in Select Countries (2000)

S. No.	*Country*	*% of Share*		
		Central	*State*	*Local*
1.	Australia	77.68	19.26	3.07
2.	Austria	70.92	11.40	17.68
3.	Belgium	90.01	3.82	6.17
4.	Bolivia	76.55	3.75	19.70
5.	Canada	48.28	41.94	9.78
6.	Colombia	83.41	5.48	11.12
7.	Germany	48.80	39.10	12.10
8.	India (1999)	62.65	37.35	NA
9.	Mexico	75.62	19.02	5.37
10.	South Africa	92.26	0.70	7.04
11.	Spain	73.47	12.12	14.41
12.	Switzerland	48.81	30.09	21.10
13.	United States	69.27	19.15	11.58

Source: Government Finance Statistics, 2005.

Tax GDP Ratio at National, State and Local Level

The tax-GDP ratios computed for different level of governments in select countries for different level of governments are discussed in Table 8.2. The total tax GDP ratio varies from highest of over

[1]Rao and Singh (2005) have shown the extent of fiscal decentralisation in the case of India for the year 1997-98 based on Eleventh Finance Commission data.

30 per cent in the countries of Australia, Belgium and Canada. The lower tax-GDP ratio was observed in the countries of Bolivia, Colombia, India and Mexico.

The extent of fiscal (revenue) decentralisation is fairly shown in the case of Canada, where the Central and State Government have mobilized about 15 per cent and 13 per cent of GDP respectively. Tax-GPD ratio at central level was more than 20 per cent in the case of Australia, Austria, Belgium, South Africa and United States. In India it was less than 10 per cent. On the other hand, barring Canada, in most of the countries, the tax-GDP ratio at the State level were less than 10 per cent. In India, it was 5.81 per cent for the year 1999-2000. The resource mobilized through taxation at the lower level of governance as, shown in Table 8.2, indicates that in the countries of Austria, Belgium, Bolivia, Colombia, South Africa, and Spain, the tax-GDP ratios were higher than the State level. However, in almost all the countries it was less than 5 per cent. The local governments in Australia and Mexico, had generated abysmally figure of less than one per cent through local taxation. Apparently, the taxation powers available with the local governments must be very less. The case of India is also not much different. Based on the data provided in the EFC report, the rural local bodies could raise only 1.40 per cent of GDP.[2]

National Perspective

The Constitution through 73rd and 74th Amendments defines 29 subject matters for rural local governments (Panchayati Raj Institutions) and 18 subjects to Urban Local Governments (Municipalities), though the local governments (bodies) were functioning for long. Presently, it has provided a composite framework delineates fiscal functions among Central, State and local governments. The Centre-State fiscal relations and its delivery mechanism were developed for long but no separate provisions existed for local governments until the recent Constitutional

[2]As per the estimates of Rao and Singh (2005), the local governments in rural areas could raise only 1.4 per cent of GDP.

Table 8.2: Tax-GDP (Central, State and local governments) Ratio, 2000

Sl. No.	*Country*	*% of Share*		
		Central	*State*	*Local*
1.	Australia	30.20	23.46	0.93
2.	Austria	27.65	19.61	4.89
3.	Belgium	30.85	27.77	1.90
4.	Bolivia	16.12	12.34	3.18
5.	Canada	31.17	15.05	3.05
6.	Colombia	16.04	13.38	1.78
7.	Germany	24.70	12.05	2.99
8.	India (1999)	15.56	9.75	NA
9.	Mexico	15.43	11.67	0.83
10.	South Africa	26.95	24.86	1.90
11.	Spain	22.31	16.39	3.21
12.	Switzerland	23.05	11.25	4.86
13.	United States	29.08	20.15	3.37

Source: Government Finance Statistics, 2005.

Amendments were made. The first generation State level finance commissions were constituted in all the States and the recommendations were made in view of identifying the resources to carry out the functions enlisted in the 11th and 12th Schedule (of 73rd and 74th Amendments) for PRIs and ULBs. A large number of States have accepted and implemented the most relevant recommendations[3]. Keeping in view the requirements of Article 243-I and 243-Y, most of the States have constituted the Second Generation State Finance Commissions and have submitted the reports. The impact of these recent developments of fiscal transfers on the State economy has not been assessed so far. It needs detail investigations of these reports. The issue of fiscal transfers has to be analysed in greater detail and perspective.

[3] See, Action Taken Report Memorandum of all the states.

Tenth Finance Commission (TFC) Approach

The Centre-State relations have been developed in India since long. Under the Constitutional provisions the Central Finance Commission was constituted to transfer the funds to the States under various constitutional provisions. Till now this exercise has been carried out for eleven times since independence. With the recent amendments in the constitutional provision the CFC has been assigned another duty to extend this exercise to local governments also. The Article 280(3) has been amended to provide for another mandatory duty to be performed by the Central Finance Commission. At the State level also, these amendments require the constitution of State Finance Commission to recommend the transfers of funds from State to local governments. Since these amendments were introduced at the time of near completion of TFC report, hence the commission could not work out transfer of funds based on any detail exercise. Therefore, it had made provisions of *ad hoc* arrangements and recommended the transfer of funds to the local bodies. The TFC has recommended that this fund would go to PRIs over and above the regular transfer of funds from State to the PRIs similarly, for the Urban Local Bodies (ULBs) the funds have been transfered for the maintenance of core civic services provided by Central Finance Commission.

Eleventh Finance Commission (EFC) Approach

Under the Terms of Reference (ToR) of EFC, for the first time the Presidential order required a Finance Commission to make recommendations regarding the transfers of fund to the States which further pass on to the local governments (PRIs and ULBs) for the augmentation of resources of these bodies. The introduction of these (73rd and 74th) amendments has given a place in the Constitution and recognized them as the institutions of self-governance. These amendments made it mandatory for holding the regular election, obligatory representation of SCs/STs and women, periodic constitution of SFCs for the devolution of financial resources to the sub-national governments at the local level, transfers of functional responsibilities to these bodies, so as to enable them to function as institutions of self-governance. The particular ToR of EFC required it to determine the transfers of resources to the local bodies on the basis of the recommendations of the SFCs. If the SFC reports were made available in that case make their own assessment in this regard.

Transfers of Resources to the Local Governments—EFC Approach

For effective functioning of the local governments the process of decentralisation needs to be speeded up. Keeping in view the strengthening of the sub-national governments at the local level, the EFC has recommended the transfers of funds for the provision and maintenance of core civic services.

Under the amended constitutional provision, the PRIs and the ULBs have to maintain the accounts and get them audited. This would reduce the charges of corruption, generally, levelled against them. Keeping this requirement in view, the EFC has recommended provision of fund to meet needs of the local bodies. Since the exercise of transfers of resources to the local governments was carried out for the first time, the EFC has faced the acute problem of database at local level. To ease out the data problem for the future commissions, the EFC has made provision in this regard also. It has made recommendations and earmarked some fund for maintenance of database at the local level, in the standard format suggested by it.

Grants for the Local Bodies

As a measure of augmenting of Consolidated Fund of States to supplement the resources of local bodies, the EFC has made recommendations considering the availability of resources and the limits prescribed for the overall transfers of funds of these bodies. This would help local governments for provision/maintenance of core civic services to the local citizens. The EFC has recommended a grant of Rs.1600 crore for the Panchayats and Rs. 400 crore for the Municipalities (ULBs) for the period of five years (2000-01 to 2004-05).

Principle for Inter Se Distribution

The transfers from the national to State governments are generally guided by four basic principles, namely, equity, autonomy, efficiency, and fiscal discipline. In the case of local governments, the EFC has selected five factors for the distribution of funds to the local governments. These are population, index of decentralisation, distance from highest per capita income, revenue efforts and geographical area. In this formula, the equity aspect is taken care of by population factor, therefore, the EFC has assigned maximum weightage of 40 per cent to this factor. Next important factor is that which should speed up the process of decentralisation at the third level of governance. The EFC has worked out an index of decentralisation by taking care of all the important factors envisaged in the provisions made in the recent amendments introduced for decentralisation. The revenue effort made by the local bodies has been assigned 10 per cent weight. The States with low SDP have been duly compensated by the weight of 10 per cent assigned to the factor of distance from highest per capita income. The geographical area has been given the weighable of 10 per cent. This would take care of the differentials in the cost of provision of basic services in sparsely populated area, where the cost is relatively high.

Equity vs. Performance

While estimating the devolution to local bodies the TFC and EFC both have given more importance to the equity aspects. In determination of share of each State the population has played a pivotal role. The TFC has made the allocation on the basis of per capita grants to the PRIs on the basis of 1971 population. For the ULBs the ratio of slum to urban population has been used. We have ranked the States according to their share in the total for PRIs and ULBs and computed the rank correlation. The populous States occupied the higher places in PRIs, and in the case of ULBs the developed States with higher level of urbanization and industrial growth got the high position. The EFC have used the population of 1991 census (rural and urban) for assigning the weights to the different determinants. In addition to the population and geographical criteria, the other

Contd. ...

> *determinants such as distance from highest per capita income, revenue efforts of PRIs with respect to own revenue of the State and with respect to GSDP (primary sector excluding Mining and Quarrying), and the index of decentralisation have been used in computation of composite index for each State's share. The States have been ranked on the basis of proportion of each share in the total. On examination of these results, it is noticed that highly populated States got the more share and the high ranks whereas the performing States with less population were deprived of their due shares and ranked at low levels.*
> ***Source :** EFC Report.*

Twelfth Finance Commission (TFC) Resource Transfers to Local Bodies

While making its recommendation for the augmentation of own resources of the local bodies, the TFC has recommended a share of 20 per cent to the local bodies in the urban areas. The factors such as taxable capacity and the need of resources has duly considered in the case of urban local bodies. For the rural bodies (Panchayats), an amount of Rs. 20,000 crores (80 per cent of the total grant to local bodies) has been recommended for the period of five years from 2005-06. It was assumed that the level of standard of civic services provided by these local bodies would enhance in future.

Grants Utilisation

The basic purpose of the devolution of grant to rural local bodies was to improve the level of services in respect of water supply and sanitation. On the other hand, in the case of local bodies in urban areas, the commission emphasised that there is need to encourage the concept of public-private partnership for improving the mechanism of service delivery with respect to solid waste management. The ULBs should be assigned the task of collection, segregation and transportation of solid waste. Accordingly, it has recommended that the 50 per cent of the grants allocated for the ULBs should be utilized for the scheme of solid waste management in urban areas.

Database

The commission has suggested that the priority areas such as creation of database and maintenance of accounts should be given due consideration. Therefore, is has recommended that 50 per cent of the grants should be earmarked for this purpose. This would be applicable for both, the RLBs and the ULBs.

Criteria of Devolution

While making its recommendations for *interse* distribution across the States, the commission has endorsed almost all the criteria except one. The EFC has stressed on strengthening the aspect of decentralisation and recommended 20 per cent weightage. On the other hand the TFC has emphasized on reduction in the disparities with respect to provisions of core services of drinking water supply and the sanitation. Accordingly, it has recommended a weightage of 10 per cent assigned to index of deprivation. Besides the equity aspect, there is greater need to push the performance upward. Another important criterion is revenue effort with respect to States' own revenue and the GSDP. This criterion of revenue effort was used by both, EFC and TFC for judging the performance of local bodies across the States. In comparison to EFC, TFC has stressed on revenue effort and assigned 20 per cent weightage (see Table 8.3)

Table 8.3 : Criterion and Weightage used by EFC and TFC report for *inter se* Distribution

Sl. No.	*Criteria*	*Weight*	
		EFC	*TFC*
1.	Population	40	40
2.	Geographical Areas	10	10
3.	Distance from highest per capita income	20	20
4.	Index of Decentralisation/Deprivation	20	10
5.	Revenue Effort (a) with respect to States own revenue (b) With respect to GSDP	10 5 5	20 10 10

Source: EFC and TFC Reports.

A Comparison of Allocation of Grants to Local Bodies through 10th, 11th and 12th Central Finance Commissions and *inter se* Distribution

In absolute term, the 10th FC has recommended an amount of Rs. 5,380.93 crores for the local bodies. The ULBs share was Rs. 1,000 crore while Panchayats have received larger amount of Rs. 4,380.93 crore. The allocation was based on Rs. 100 per capita in rural areas and for ULBs, the criteria was ratio of slum population to urban population. The major shares have gone to populous and developed States. The industrialiesd and urbanized States claimed large chunk in total kitty. The State with less number of people and less developed was major sufferer. On similar count, the States in north-east region too were deprived required resources. The States are ranked as per their share in total grants. Of the total grants, more than 50 per cent grants have gone to first five States, in both, rural and urban areas. In rural side the States ranked in first-five places were: Uttar Pradesh, Bihar, Andhra Pradesh, Madhya Pradesh and Maharashtra. On the urban side two States of Tamil Nadu and West Bengal have replaced Bihar and Madhya Pradesh (see Table 8.4).

Table 8.4 : Allocation of Grants and Ranks of the States—Tenth Finance Commission

PRIs			*ULBs*		
State	*Share (%)*	*Rank*	*State*	*Share (%)*	*Rank*
Uttar Pradesh	17.34	1	Maharashtra	13.3	1
Bihar	11.58	2	Uttar Pradesh	12.12	2
Andhra Pradesh	8.01	3	West Bengal	12.03	3
Madhya Pradesh	7.96	4	Tamil Nadu	11.55	4
Maharashtra	7.92	5	Andhra Pradesh	7.39	5
Total Five States	52.81		Total Five States	56.39	

Source: TFC Report.

Eleventh Finance Commission

It has recommended Rs. 8000 crore for PRIs and Rs. 2,000 crore for ULBs. The *inter se* distribution was made on the basis of criteria such as population (40%), geographical areas (10%) per capita income distance (20%), decentralisation (20%) and tax effort (10%). The States were ranked as per their share in the total allocation for PRIs and ULBs. Similar to 10th FC, the first five states of Uttar Pradesh, Maharashtra, Madhya Pradesh, Bihar and Andhra Pradesh received a little less than 50 per cent of the total grants allocated for the PRIs. In the case of ULBs, the 50 per cent share was accounted for the States of Maharashtra, Tamil Nadu, Uttar Pradesh, Gujarat and West Bengal. They occupied first-five places (Table 8.5).

Table 8.5 : Allocation of Grants and Ranks of the States—Eleventh Finance Commission

PRIs			*ULBs*		
State	*Share (%)*	*Rank*	*State*	*Share (%)*	*Rank*
Uttar Pradesh	16.489	1	Maharashtra	15.813	1
Bihar	9.813	2	Uttar Pradesh	12.582	2
Andhra Pradesh	9.503	3	West Bengal	9.874	3
Madhya Pradesh	8.943	4	Tamil Nadu	9.668	4
Maharashtra	8.209	5	Andhra Pradesh	8.233	5
Total Five States	52.958		Total Five States	56.17	

Source: EFC Report.

Twelfth Finance Commission

In absolute term, the TFC has recommended more than double the grants allocated by EFC for the local bodies. It has recommended Rs. 20,000 crore for the rural local bodies and Rs. 100 crore for the local bodies in urban areas. In other words 80 per cent went to Panchayats and 20 per cent to the municipalities for the period of five years beginning from 2005-06. The criterion adopted by the

TFC was same as used by EFC except the index of deprivation was used in place of index of decentralisation. Another minor difference in the weight was done in case of revenue effort. The weight increased from 10 per cent to 20 per cent. More stress was placed on the resource mobilization at the local level. As indicated in Table 8.6, in case of PRIs, the first-five ranks occupied by the States of Uttar Pradesh, Maharashtra, Madhya Pradesh, Bihar and Andhra Pradesh. The scenario was slightly different than the RLBs. Other than Maharashtra and Uttar Pradesh (Common States), the States of Tamil Nadu, Gujarat and West Bengal got the place in the band of first-five States (see Table 8.6).

Table 8.6 : Allocation of Grants and Ranks of the States—Twelfth Finance Commission

PRIs			*ULBs*		
State	*Share (%)*	*Rank*	*State*	*Share (%)*	*Rank*
Uttar Pradesh	14.64	1	Maharashtra	15.82	1
Maharashtra	9.915	2	Tamil Nadu	11.44	2
Madhya Pradesh	8.315	3	Uttar Pradesh	10.34	3
Bihar	8.12	4	Gujarat	8.28	4
Andhra Pradesh	7.935	5	West Bengal	7.86	5
Total Five States	48.925		Total Five States	53.74	

Source: Twelfth Finance Commission Report.

Allocation of Grants to Local Bodies—Gain/Loss over the Previous Finance Commission

(a) Rural Local Bodies

The State-wise allocation (in terms of percentage) to the Rural Local Bodies as recommended by the 10th Finance Commission depicted in Appendix I. The gain or loss (in terms of percentage share) over the previous Commission was computed. A close look into the figures indicate that as many as 11 States incurred losses in their allocation from 10th Finance Commission to 11th Finance Commission. The 14 States were gainers. On the other hand in the case of 11th Finance Commission to 12th Finance Commission, more number of States (15 States) have lost in their allocation in comparison to previous Commission. Only 10 states were happy with the more allocation.

	10th-11th Finance Commissions		*11th-12th Finance Commissions*	
PRIs	Loss	11	Loss	15
	Gain	14	Gain	10

(b) Urban Local Bodies

In the case of allocation to ULBs from 10th Finance Commission to 11th Finance Commission, the picture is not much different from the Rural local bodies. The 12 States incurred losses in their allocation while 13 States received more grants. Whereas in the grants recommended by 11th Finance Commission and 12th Finance Commission, the scenarios were more pleasant for 15 States. Only 10 States contented with low share in allocation in comparison to previous Commission.

	10th - 11th Finance Commissions		*11th - 12th Finance Commissions*	
ULBs	Loss	12	Loss	10
	Gain	13	Gain	15

Conclusions

From the above discussion, it is difficult to draw any firm conclusion with respect to decentralisation started before more than a decade. However, many attempts were made to strengthen the various aspects of decentralisation at Central as well as State level. The Constitutional provisions make it mandatory for the Central Finance Commission to recommend measures for the augmentation of resources of the lowest level of governance. The criteria used by Central Finance Commission for the devolution of grants to local bodies seem to be ineffective. Only five major States (in terms of population and development) claimed the lion's share of resources from the Central Finance Commission allocation, irrespective of any criteria used for the *inter se* distribution. For the future Central Finance Commission (Thirteenth Finance Commission) a greater need would be to select the criteria very carefully so that an unbiased and balanced devolution should take place.

APPENDIX—I

Allocation of Grants and Ranks of the States, Tenth Finance Commission

PRIs			*ULBs*		
State	*Share (%)*	*Rank*	*State*	*Share (%)*	*Rank*
Uttar Pradesh	17.34	1	Maharashtra	13.30	1
Bihar	11.58	2	Uttar Pradesh	12.12	2
Andhra Pradesh	8.01	3	West Bengal	12.03	3
Madhya Pradesh	7.96	4	Tamil Nadu	11.55	4
Maharashtra	7.92	5	Andhra Pradesh	7.39	5
Total Five States	**52.82**		**Total Five States**	**56.39**	
West Bengal	7.61	6	Karnataka	7.02	6
Tamil Nadu	6.56	7	Gujarat	6.75	7
Karnataka	5.05	8	Bihar	6.71	8
Rajasthan	4.84	9	Madhya Pradesh	6.17	9
Orissa	4.59	10	Rajasthan	4.32	10
Gujarat	4.38	11	Punjab	3.06	11
Kerala	4.08	12	Kerala	2.54	12
Assam	3.04	13	Orissa	1.91	13
Punjab	2.36	14	Haryana	1.66	14
Haryana	1.89	15	Assam	1.42	15
Jammu & Kashmir	0.86	16	Jammu & Kashmir	1.21	16
Himachal Pradesh	0.73	17	Manipur	0.22	17
Tripura	0.32	18	Himachal Pradesh	0.21	18
Manipur	0.21	19	Meghalaya	0.15	19
Meghalaya	0.20	20	Tripura	0.10	20
Goa	0.13	21	Sikkim	0.06	21
Nagaland	0.11	22	Nagaland	0.06	22
Arunachal Pradesh	0.10	23	Mizoram	0.04	23
Mizoram	0.07	24	Arunachal Pradesh	0.01	24
Sikkim	0.04	25	Goa	0.00	25

APPENDIX—II

Allocation of Grants and Ranks of the States Eleventh Finance Commission

PRIs			***ULBs***		
State	*Share (%)*	*Rank*	*State*	*Share (%)*	*Rank*
Uttar Pradesh	16.489	1	Maharashtra	15.813	1
Bihar	9.813	2	Uttar Pradesh	12.582	2
Andhra Pradesh	9.503	3	West Bengal	9.874	3
Madhya Pradesh	8.943	4	Tamil Nadu	9.668	4
Maharashtra	8.209	5	Andhra Pradesh	8.233	5
Total Five States	**52.958**		**Total Five States**	**56.170**	
West Bengal	7.222	6	Madhya Pradesh	7.801	6
Rajasthan	6.137	7	Gujarat	6.626	7
Tamil Nadu	5.826	8	Karnataka	6.241	8
Karnataka	4.926	9	Rajasthan	4.971	9
Gujarat	4.351	10	Bihar	4.695	10
Orissa	4.320	11	Kerala	3.762	11
Kerala	4.120	12	Punjb	2.736	12
Assam	2.918	13	Orissa	1.998	13
Punjab	1.933	14	Haryana	1.832	14
Haryana	1.839	15	Assam	1.077	15
Jammu & Kashmir	0.930	16	Jammu & Kashmir	0.783	16
Himachal Pradesh	0.821	17	Goa	0.232	17
Tripura	0.356	18	Manipur	0.220	18
Arunachal Pradesh	0.348	19	Tripura	0.201	19
Meghalaya	0.320	20	Himachal Pradesh	0.195	20
Manipur	0.235	21	Mizoram	0.192	21
Nagaland	0.161	22	Meghalaya	0.135	22
Goa	0.116	23	Nagaland	0.089	23
Mizoram	0.098	24	Arunachal Pradesh	0.034	24
Sikkim	0.066	25	Sikkim	0.010	25

APPENDIX—III

Allocation of Grants and Ranks of the States Twelfth Finance Commission

PRIs			*ULBs*		
State	*Share (%)*	*Rank*	*State*	*Share (%)*	*Rank*
Uttar Pradesh	14.640	1	Maharashtra	15.820	1
Maharashtra	9.915	2	Tamil Nadu	11.440	2
Madhya Pradesh	8.315	3	Uttar Pradesh	10.340	3
Bihar	8.120	4	Gujarat	8.280	4
Andhra Pradesh	7.935	5	West Bengal	7.860	5
First Five States	**48.925**		**First Five States**	**53.740**	
West Bengal	6.355	6	Andhra Pradesh	7.480	6
Rajasthan	6.150	7	Madhya Pradesh	7.220	7
Kerala	4.925	8	Karnataka	6.460	8
Gujarat	4.655	9	Rajasthan	4.400	9
Karnataka	4.440	10	Punjab	3.420	10
Tamil Nadu	4.350	11	Kerala	2.980	11
Orissa	4.015	12	Bihar	2.840	12
Chhattisgarh	3.075	13	Orissa	2.080	13
Assam	2.630	14	Jharkhand	1.960	14
Jharkhand	2.410	15	Haryana	1.820	15
Haryana	1.940	16	Chhattisgarh	1.760	16
Punjab	1.620	17	Assam	1.100	17
Jammu & Kashmir	1.405	18	Jammu & Kashmir	0.760	18
Uttaranchal	0.810	19	Uttaranchal	0.680	19
Himachal Pradesh	0.735	20	Goa	0.240	20
Arunachal Pradesh	0.340	21	Mizoram	0.200	21
Tripura	0.285	22	Manipur	0.180	22
Meghalaya	0.250	23	Himachal Pradesh	0.160	23
Manipur	0.230	24	Meghalaya	0.160	24
Nagaland	0.200	25	Tripura	0.160	25
Mizoram	0.100	26	Nagaland	0.120	26
Goa	0.090	27	Arunachal Pradesh	0.060	27
Sikkim	0.065	28	Sikkim	0.020	28

APPENDIX—IV

State-wise Gain/Loss in allocation of Resources to Panchayats during 10th, 11th and 12th Finance Commissions

S.No.	*State*	*10th FC*	*11th FC*	*12th FC*	*Diff 11th-10th FC*	*Diff 12th-11th FC*
1.	Andhra Pradesh	8.01	9.503	7.935	1.491	–1.568
2.	Arunachal Pradesh	0.010	0.348	0.340	0.245	–0.008
3.	Assam	3.04	2.918	2.630	–0.126	–0.288
4.	Bihar	11.58	9.813	8.120	–1.764	0.717
5.	Chhattisgarh			3.075		
6.	Goa	0.13	0.116	0.090	–0.019	–0.026
7.	Gujarat	4.38	4.351	4.655	–0.032	0.304
8.	Haryana	1.89	1.839	1.940	–0.048	0.101
9.	Himachal Pradesh	0.73	0.821	0.735	0.086	–0.086
10.	Jammu & Kashmir	0.86	0.930	1.405	0.072	0.475
11.	Jharkhand			2.410		
12.	Karnataka	5.06	4.926	4.440	–0.136	–0.486
13.	Kerala	4.08	4.120	4.925	0.039	0.805
14.	Madhya Pradesh	7.96	8.943	8.315	0.984	2.447
15.	Maharashtra	7.92	8.209	9.915	0.288	1.706
16.	Manipur	0.21	0.235	0.230	0.022	–0.005
17.	Meghalaya	0.20	0.320	0.250	0.123	–0.070
18.	Mizoram	0.07	0.098	0.100	0.031	0.002
19.	Nagaland	0.11	0.161	0.200	0.055	0.039
20.	Orissa	4.59	4.320	4.015	–0.268	–0.305
21.	Punjab	2.36	1.933	1.620	–0.426	–0.313
22.	Rajasthan	4.84	6.137	6.150	1.293	0.013
23.	Sikkim	0.04	0.066	0.065	0.023	–0.001
24.	Tamil Nadu	6.56	5.826	4.350	–0.732	–1.476
25.	Tripura	0.32	0.356	0.285	0.038	–0.071
26.	Uttar Pradesh	17.34	16.489	14.640	–0.848	–1.039
27.	Uttaranchal			0.810		
28.	West Bengal	7.61	7.222	6.355	–0.390	–0.867

APPENDIX—IV Contd. ...

	11th - 10th Finance Commission		*12th - 11th Finance Commission*	
PRIs	Loss	11	Loss	15
	Gain	14	Gain	10

Loser States (10th FC to 11th FC)	*Loser States (11th FC to 12th FC)*
1. Assam	1. Andhra Pradesh
2. Bihar	2. Arunachal Pradesh
3. Goa	3. Assam
4. Gujarat	4. Goa
5. Haryana	5. Himachal Pradesh
6. Karnataka	6. Karnataka
7. Orissa	7. Manipur
8. Punjab	8. Meghalaya
9. Tamil Nadu	9. Orissa
10. Uttar Pradesh	10. Punjab
11. West Bengal	11. Sikkim
	12. Tamil Nadu
	13. Tripura
	14. Uttar Pradesh
	15. West Bengal

APPENDIX—V

State-wise Gain/Loss in Allocation of Resources to Urban Local Bodies during 10th FC, 11th FC and 12th FC

S.No.	*State*	*10th FC*	*11th FC*	*12th FC*	*Diff 11th-10th FC*	*Diff 12th-11th FC*
1.	Andhra Pradesh	7.39	8.233	7.480	0.839	–0.753
2.	Arunachal Pradesh	0.01	0.034	0.060	0.022	0.026
3.	Assam	1.42	1.077	1.100	–0.343	0.023
4.	Bihar	6.71	4.695	2.850	–2.014	0.105
5.	Chhattisgarh			1.760		
6.	Goa	0.00	0.232	0.240	0.232	0.008
7.	Gujarat	6.75	6.626	8.280	–0.120	1.654
8.	Haryana	1.66	1.832	1.820	0.174	–0.012
9.	Himachal Pradesh	0.21	0.195	0.160	–0.010	–0.035
10.	Jammu & Kashmir	1.21	0.783	0.760	–0.426	–0.023
11.	Jharkhand			1.960		
12.	Karnataka	7.02	6.241	6.460	–0.778	0.219
13.	Kerala	2.54	3.762	2.980	1.219	–0.782
14.	Madhya Pradesh	6.17	7.801	7.220	1.627	1.179
15.	Maharashtra	13.30	15.813	15.820	2.518	0.007
16.	Manipur	0.22	0.220	0.180	–0.003	–0.040
17.	Meghalaya	0.15	0.135	0.160	–0.012	0.025
18.	Mizoram	0.04	0.192	0.200	0.154	0.008
19.	Nagaland	0.06	0.089	0.120	0.033	0.031
20.	Orissa	1.91	1.998	2.080	0.087	0.082
21.	Punjab	3.06	2.736	3.420	–0.324	0.684
22.	Rajasthan	4.32	4.971	4.400	0.653	–0.571
23.	Sikkim	0.06	0.010	0.020	–0.048	0.010
24.	Tamil Nadu	11.55	9.668	11.440	–1.884	1.772
25.	Tripura	0.10	0.201	0.160	0.098	–0.041
26.	Uttar Pradesh	12.12	12.582	10.340	0.464	–1.562
27.	Uttaranchal			0.680		
28.	West Bengal	12.03	9.874	7.860	–2.158	–2.014

APPENDIX—V Contd. ...

	10th - 11th Finance Commission		*11th - 12th Finance Commission*	
ULBs	Loss	12	Loss	10
	Gain	13	Gain	15

Loser State (10th FC - 11th FC)	*Loser States (11th FC - 12th FC)*
1. Assam	1. Andhra Pradesh
2. Bihar	2. Haryana
3. Gujarat	3. Himachal Pradesh
4. Himachal Pradesh	4. Jammu & Kashmir
5. Jammu & Kashmir	5. Kerala
6. Karnataka	6. Manipur
7. Manipur	7. Rajasthan
8. Meghalaya	8. Tripura
9. Punjab	9. Uttar Pradesh
10. Sikkim	10. West Bengal
11. Tamil Nadu	
12. West Bengal	

REFERENCES

Bajaj, J.L. (1995), *Administrative Reforms and Decentralisation,* Report submitted to Government of Uttar Pradesh.

Besley, Timothy, Rohini Pande and Vijendra Rao (2007), Political Economy of Panchayats in South India, *Economic and Political Weekly,* 24th February.

Bohra, O.P. (2007), *Rural Decentralisation and Participatory Planning for Poverty Reduction*—Rajasthan State Report, NIPFP, New Delhi, Mimeo.

------ (1996), *State-Local Fiscal Relations in India,* Delhi, National Book Shop with collaboration of Dolphin Publishing House.

------ (2006), Fiscal Decentralisation and Local Governments in the North-East States, *Manpower Journal,* Vol. XXXXI, No.2, April-June 2006 (Special issue on North-East).

Chattopadhyay, Raghvendra and Esther Duflo (2007), Impact of Reservation in Panchayati Raj—Evidence from Nation-wide randomized experiment, *Economic and Political Weekly,* 28th February.

Government of India (1994), *Report of the Tenth Finance Commission,* New Delhi.

------ (2000), *Report of the Eleventh Finance Commission,* New Delhi.

------ (2004), *Report of the Twelfth Finance Commission Report,* New Delhi.

Kadekodi, Gopal, Ravi Kanbur and Vijendra Rao (2007), Governance and the Karnataka Model, *Economic and Political Weekly,* 28th February.

Prud'homme Remy (1996), The Economics of Decentralisation in very low income Countries, *Revue Region et Development.*

Rao, M. Govinda (2000), *Fiscal Decentralisation in India Federalism,* Bangalore, Institute for Social and Economical Change, mimeo, September.

Rao, M. Govinda and Singh, Nirvikar (2005), *Political Economy of Federalism in India,* Oxford University Press.

The World Bank (2004), *Fiscal Decentralisation to Rural Governments in India,* Oxford University Press.

Rajaraman, Indira and O.P. Bohra (2006), Redesigning Job Guarantee Scheme, *Economic Times,* Page 14, October 6.

Rajaraman, Indira, O.P. Bohra and V.S. Renganathan (1996), Augmentation of Panchayati Raj Resources, *Economic and Political Weekly,* XXXI, 18th May.

Rondinelli, Dennis A. and Others (1983), *Decentralisation in Developing Countries: A Review of Recent Experience,* Washington: The World Bank. (World Bank Staff Working Paper No. 581).

Woo, Sik Kee (1975), *Fiscal Decentralisation and Economic Development,* Washington: World Bank (World Bank Studies in Domestic Finance No.10).

9

GUIDING ROLE OF CENTRAL FINANCE COMMISSION REGARDING STATE COUNTERPARTS

D. BANDYOPADHYAY

The 73rd Constitutional Amendment was enacted to restore power to where it belonged. Devolution of powers, functions, authority at the substate level was the objective of this amendment. Thus, theoretically, the 73rd Amendment conceived of a six-layered polity starting from the Gram Sabha, through the Gram Panchayat, Block/ Tehsil Panchayat and Zilla Parishad to the State and the Centre. The idea could really take shape if the finances could be correspondingly devolved for all the tiers of the Panchayat bodies in an appropriate manner. For this purpose, the Constitution provided for the creation of the State Finance Commissions (SFCs) every five years under Article 243-I for the devolution of finance from the State level to the three tiers of Panchayats. The Constitution also amended Article 280 regarding the Central Finance Commission (CFC) adding sub-clause (bb) to clause (3) of the same article. The CFC was mandated to suggest "measures needed to augment the consolidated fund of a State to supplement the resources of the Panchayats in the State on the basis of the recommendations made by the Finance Commission of the State".

Link between CFC and SFC

By mandating the CFC to base its recommendations to augment the resources of the Panchayat on the basis of the recommendations made by the SFC, the Constitution established an "organic" link between the CFC and the SFCs. The Eleventh Finance Commission (EFC) accepted this linkage by observing in para 8.11 "the determination by us of the measures needed for augmentation of the consolidated funds of the States for supplementing the resources of Panchayats and municipalities has to be done on the basis of the reports of the SFCs. In fact SFCs' recommendations should have been the basis of our report but it could not be so in full measure for several reasons" (Government of India 2000). The EFC also listed these reasons. These were: (i) the non-synchronisation of the period of recommendations of the SFCs and the CFCs; (ii) the lack of clarity with respect to the assignment of powers, authority and responsibilities to Panchayati Raj Institutions (PRIs); (iii) the absence of a time frame within which the State governments are required to take action on the recommendation of SFCs; and (iv) the non-availability of the reports of the SFCs (GoI 2004).

The Parliament enacted the Finance Commission (Miscellaneous Provisions) Act, 1951, which prescribed the qualifications a person must have to be appointed as the chairman or a member of the CFC. In spite of the provisions under Article 243-I (2), only a few States had enacted laws similar to the Central Act. This had led to a wide diversity in the matter of qualifications of the chairman/members of the SFCs. "For instance in some States, serving government officers are appointed as chairperson and members of the SFC and that too in *ex-officio* capacities. This puts limitations on the ability of the SFC to act as an autonomous body to make recommendations in a free and independent manner, as has been envisioned in the Constitution" (GoI 2000). The EFC recommended appropriate legislation to the States to ensure that chairperson and members of SFCs should be drawn from amongst experts in specific disciplines such as economics, law, public administration and public finance (*ibid.*). Thus, willynilly, the EFC gave itself the role of a guide though it provided for no mechanism for the monitoring and enforcement of its guidelines and non-fiscal recommendations. In view of the various constraints which prevented the EFC to base its advice on the recommendations made by the SFCs, it suggested an amendment to the Constitution by deleting the words "on the basis of the recommendations made by the finance commissions of the State". Though one could sympathise with the EFC, in their total exasperation and annoyance about the SFCs in making this recommendation, it was good that the Central Government did not accept the suggestion, otherwise this organic link would have snapped, perpetuating the existing confusion. It must be said to the credit of the EFC that it did perform its oversight role though it made no attempt to formalize and institutionalise it. EFC's three areas of concern related to preservation of civic services, maintenance of accounts and audit and a very weak database. The EFC did not stop by only expressing its concern. To remedy the situation, it provided for an *ad hoc* annual grant of Rs. 1,600 crore for panchayats primarily for "maintenance of accounts, development of a database and audit to be the first charge of this grant. The amount remaining thereafter was to be utilised by the local bodies for maintenance of core civic services" (GoI 2004). Since there was no monitoring and supervisory agency, the result was that out of Rs. 200 crore set apart by the EFC for the creation of the database, States could spend only Rs. 93 crore. Worse still was that out of allocation of Rs. 483 crore for maintenance of accounts only Rs. 113 crore was utilised. This is a poor reflection on the priorities of the States. Equally disturbing is the fact that although the Controller and Auditor General prepared budget and accounting formats for PRIs and urban local bodies with a view to rationalising them, only six States have issued formal orders to implement them (Oommen, 2005).

States and their Finance Commissions

How did the States treat their own finance commission reports? It is a tale of gross disregard, utter disdain and total inaction. One feels constrained to believe it but the brazen and ugly facts fly in one's face. The TFC commissioned a study which was conducted by the National Institution of Rural Development on this issue. The TFC summarized findings of the study in the following terms: "With regard to implementation of SFC reports, which were accepted the following issues were highlighted: (a) several States did not take follow-up action in terms of legislative/administrative measures; (b) recommendations marked 'under examination' met with 'natural death'; (c) very few States have honoured their commitment for the release of additional resources against these recommendations; and (d) budgetary provisions regarding these recommendations have 'fallen short' ."

The study has admitted that it could not succeed in assessing the net additional resource flow from the States to the Panchayats consequent to the implementation of the SFC recommendation (GoI 2004). Thus, States treated the recommendations of their own SFCs with utter contempt and disrespect. No further comment is called for.

Augmentation of the consolidated fund of a State to supplement the resources of the Panchayats is required when Panchayats have been endowed with functions and activities as indicated in the 11th Schedule to the Constitution. With the devolution of functions budgeted funds and functionaries, Panchayats would require additional funds to implement their basic function to put into effect plans prepared for economic development and social justice. Intensity of activities would be much higher and deeper with local level planning as mentioned in Article 243G of the Constitution. Hence, to be fair and transparent, the CFC should have an objective indicator of the real devolution of powers, functions and activities. Thus, an objective "devolution index" (DI) properly constructed with appropriate ingredients would have been greatly helpful. The EFC did try to approach the issue rationally. It devised the following 10 parameters for the purpose of arriving at the index of decentralisation: (i) enactment/amendment of the State Panchayat Legislation; (ii) intervention/restriction in the functioning of PRIs; (iii) assignment of functions to PRIs by State legislation; (iv) actual transfer of functions to PRIs by way of rules, notification and orders; (v) assignment of power of taxation to PRIs; (vi) extent of exercise of taxation powers; (vii) constitution of the SFCs and submission of action taken on their reports; (viii) action taken on the major recommendations of the SFC; (ix) regular elections to PRIs; and (x) constitution of the district planning committees as per the letter and spirit of the Article 243ZD (*ibid.*).

One may agree or disagree with these 10-point parameters for the construction of the DI. There was undoubtedly a scope for further refinement to make the DI more realistic and effective. In spite of that, one has to appreciate that the EFC tried to create an objective set of criteria for recommending additionality of funds. Since there has not been any real devolution of functions and activities except in Kerala the preparation of such an index could have been politically embarrassing. This is probably why having set the parameters, the EFC did not proceed further.

Role of 13th Finance Commission

The TFC having acknowledged the work done by the EFC could not, perhaps, muster the courage to proceed with the issue. Sensing its grave political awkwardness, with superb bureaucratic timidity, it dropped the idea. Thus, it chose the role of the proverbial blind man searching for an elusive and mute black cat in a totally dark room. One could question both the rationality and objectivity of their recommendations under Article 280(3)(bb).

The 13th Finance Commission (13th FC) has the opportunity to set right many acts of omission and commission of its worthy precursors, not on the grounds of the usual predecessor-successor complex but to strengthen the financial base of the PRIs on sound objective and rational foundations.

In the first place, it should openly and explicitly assume the role of overseeing the functioning of the SFC from a technical angle without, in any way, trying to influence their judgment as implicitly laid down in Article 280(3)(bb) of the Constitution. This should include, *inter alia,* a standard formatting of the structure of the report, commonality of database and the methodology of interpreting both the required financial and economic data and information that would go into the substantive part of the report.

Second, it should review the quantitative and qualitative aspects of the expenditure of monies granted by the EFC and TFC for administrative upgradation, etc. Unjustified failures should be sharply brought out followed by some degree of disciplining activity. For instance, since only 30 per cent of monies granted by the EFC was spent on creating a database and preparation and maintenance of accounts of the PRI, any further grant in this regard would be subject to the State's own effort to fill the gap out of its own resources before fresh money could be released.

Third, the 13th FC should develop a workable, objective and rational DI, which should be the basis of augmenting the consolidated fund of a State to supplement the resources of the PRI. If significant devolution had occurred after more than a decade and a half of constitutionally mandated PRIs Started functioning, why should the consolidated fund of the state be augmented to supplement the resources of PRIs? If they do not have any worthwhile function, why should they require additional resources?

Fourth, under the constant pressure of the Ministry of Panchayati Raj Institutions (MoPRI) of the Government of India (GoI), many State governments have completed activity mapping for the three tiers of Panchayat bodies but some of them are unfortunately glossy public relations materials containing hardly any real activity. The 13th FC should go beyond the shining façade and try to find out the reality. A study on activity mapping by Ghosh and Sircar (2007) shows how hollow are some of the so-called "activity maps". They observe "the activity mapping exercise undertaken so far by some State governments, including West Bengal Government have been largely unsatisfactory. Most of them have approached the issue from the angle of transferring various ongoing schemes sponsored by the government at the Centre or States. This is an erroneous approach because the objective of activity mapping is not to transfer schemes but to transfer certain functional responsibilities from one level of a government to another. In fact, after a specific activity is transferred, a Panchayat should have the right to determine whether an ongoing scheme of a higher level of government should be continued or not for an organisation to which certain responsibilities are transferred should also have the authority to determine how such responsibilities should be discharged." Thus, completion of activity mapping for the three tiers would not mean that devolution has occurred in any real sense. Mapping could be completed without any devolution. The 13th FC should perhaps be careful about it and try to pierce the glittering veneer to get at the substance.

Fifth, as mentioned earlier, most of the State governments treat their own SFCs with utter disdain and contempt. Even after formally accepting the recommendations, they refuse to follow them up and do not release the recommended funds. While they are far too eager to augment their own consolidated funds under Article 280(3)(bb), they tend to deprive their own PRIs of required resources, ignoring the recommendations of their own SFCs. In its new proactive guiding role, the CFC should bring home to the States that such double standard amounting to chicanery would not be acceptable. The 13th FC should withhold the grant of funds to augment the consolidated fund of a State till such time the States do not make good all the withheld funds recommended by their SFC and accepted by them in their Action Taken Report to the legislature out of their own resources.

Sixth, for the conditional release of funds as suggested above, the Ministry of Finance has neither the charter nor the monitoring system to operationalise. This is the task of the subject matter of the ministry. Hence, it is suggested that the transfer of funds under Article 280(3)(bb) should be handled by the MoPRI. Bulk allotment of funds should be placed with the MoPRI for the five-year period.

Seventh, external technical assistance and guidance might help the SFCs to upgrade the quality of their own reports. That many of these reports were not accepted among academia was mainly due to their uneven quality. Devolution of resources recommended by the SFCs ranged from 2.5 per cent in Rajasthan, through 16 per cent in West Bengal to 40 per cent in Karnataka. A mere look at this statement would make some of the recommendations rather suspect. Moreover, style, language and the manner of presentation also varied widely. As an irreverent person quipped, "the quality of these reports oscillated between scribblings of neo-literates and undergraduate dissertations". In practice, things might not be as bad as made out but it depicted the wide divergence in quality, which requires to be remedied.

Eighth, the EFC was taking a proactive leadership role regarding the SFC. It went ahead for a while, then it faltered. The TFC lacked the courage and tenacity to pursue the line. It deliberately opted for a soft option. The 13th FC, consisting of persons of high technical competence and proven probity, it is hoped, will have both the courage and skill to give appropriate guidance that the SFCs require, which is so vital for financial devolution.

Ninth, any guideline that the 13th FC would issue should evolve out of mutual consultations, which might be put into effect through exchange of letters between the 13th FC and SFC. A better option would be to bring in a short amendment to the Finance Commission (Miscellaneous Provisions) Act, 1951 giving this power to the CFC in such a manner so as not to offend the sensitivities of the States. SFCs came into existence precisely four decades after the above-mentioned central law was enacted. It requires to be updated by appropriate amendments at this stage.

A long way to go lastly, though we have been talking rather loudly about decentralisation of power since the 73rd Constitutional Amendment, in reality, we have been practising a bit of political fraud. One unmistakable indicator of real devolution is the percentage of expenditure of local bodies to the combined Central and State expenditure. This figure worked out to be only 4.7 per cent in India. It is important to recall that in advanced countries, local governments normally account for 20-35 per cent of total government expenditure. It is as high as 45 per cent in Denmark and 41 per cent in Finland (Oommen, 2005). Thus, we have a long way to go. The 13th FC could be a pathfinder.

REFERENCES

Ghosh, B.D. and A.K. Sircar (2007): 'A Note on Functional Devolution to Panchayats', Kolkata (not yet published).

Government of India (2000): *Report of the Eleventh Finance Commission, 2000-2005,* Ministry of Finance.

Government of India (2000), (2004): *Report of the Twelfth Finance Commission, 2005-2010,* Ministry of Finance.

Oommen, M.A. (2005): 'Twelfth Finance Commission and Local Bodies', *Economic & Political Weekly,* Vol. 40, No. 20, pp. 2022-26.

BIBLIOGRAPHY

Agarwal, Amba, *Fiscal Decentralisation: Financing of Panchayati Raj Institutions in India*, New Delhi: Serial Publications, 2005.

Aziz, Abdul, *Decentralised Planning: The Karnataka Experience*, New Delhi: Sage Publications, 1993.

Babu, M. Devendra, "Eleventh Finance Commission's Recommendations and the Local Bodies: Impact Across the States", *Management in Government*, Vol. XXXIV, No. 2, 2002.

Babu, M. Devendra, "Report of the Karnataka State Finance Commission: Status and Implications", *The Indian Journal of Economics*, Vol. LXXXII, No. 326, 2002.

Babu, M. Devendra, *Functional and Financial Devolution to PRIs: A Study in Karnataka* (Mimeo), Bangalore: Institute for Social and Economic Change, 1999.

Bagchi, Amaresh and Nicholas Stern, *Tax Policy and Planning in Developing Countries*, New Delhi: Oxford University Press, 1994.

Bardhan, P. and D. Mookerjee (eds), *Decentralization and Local Governance in Developing Countries: A Comparative Perspective*, New Delhi: Oxford University Publications, 2007.

Chandrashekar, P.K. (ed.) *Panchayat Raj in India—A Status Report 1999*, New Delhi: Rajiv Gandhi Foundation, 2000.

Chaubey, P.K. (ed.), *Fiscal Federalism in India*, New Delhi: Deep & Deep Publications Pvt. Limited, 2003.

Debroy, Bibek, and P.D. Kaushik, *Energising Rural Development Through Panchayats*, New Delhi: Academic Foundation, 2005.

Finance Department, *Karnataka Taxation Review Committee, (Part-II, Report on Local Finances)*, Government of Karnataka, 1983.

Finance Department, *Report of the Taxation Enquiry and Resource Committee*, Government of Punjab, 1971.

Government of India, *Report of the Taxation Enquiry Commission, 1953-54,* Vol. I, 1954.

Government of India, *Report of the Twelfth Finance Commission*, 2005.

Government of India, *Report of the Eleventh Finance Commission*, 2000.

Government of India, *The Study Team on Panchayat Raj Finances,* 1963.

Government of Karnataka, *District Governments and Decentralised Planning,* 1988.

Government of Karnataka, *Report of the State Finance Commission Relating to Rural Local Bodies*, 1996.

Government of Karnataka, *Salary Amount Allocated to Zilla Panchayats, Appendix Table-B, (Staff)*, 1999-2000.

Government of Karnataka, *The Karnataka Panchayat Raj Act, 1993*, 1993.

Govinda Rao, M. and Tapas, K. Sen, *Fiscal Federalism in India: Theory and Practice*, New Delhi: Concept Publishing Company, 1996.

Gulati, I.S., *Central-State Budgetary Transfers*, Bombay: Oxford University Press, 1987.

Harold D. Smith, *The Management of Your Governance*, London: McGraw-Hill Book Company, 1945.

Issac, Thomas and Richard W. Franke, *Local Democracy and Development*, New Delhi: Left World, 2000.

Jain, L.C. (ed), *Decentralisation and Local Governance*, Hyderabad: Orient Longman Private Limtied, 2005.

Jha, S.N and Mathur (ed.), *Decentralisation and Local Politics*, New Delhi: Sage Publications, 1999.

Joshi, R.P. and Narwani, G.S., *Panchayat Raj in India: Emerging Trends across the States*, New Delhi: Rawat Publications, 2002.

Konrad Adenauer Foundation, *Local Government Finance in India*, New Delhi: Manohar, 1998.

Mandal, Amal, *Rural Development in West Bengal*, New Delhi, Eastern Book Corporation, 2005.

Mathew, George (ed.), *Status of Panchayati Raj in the States and Union Territories of India-2000*, New Delhi: Institute of Social Sciences and Concept Publishing Co., 2000.

Ministry of Rural Development, *Report of the Committee on Panchayati Raj Institutions, 1977-78*, Government of India, 1998.

Misra, S.N., Anil Dutta Misra and Sweta Misra (ed.), *Public Governance and Decentralisation*, New Delhi: Mittal Publications, 2003.

Oommen, M.A. in Jha, S.N and Mathur, P.C. (ed.), *Decentralisation and Local Politics*, New Delhi: Sage Publications, 1999.

Pal, Mahi, *Panchayati Raj: The Experiences of a Decade and Task Ahead, Public Governance and Decentralisation*, New Delhi: Mittal Publications, 2003.

Palanithurai, G. (ed.), *New Panchayati Raj System: Status and Prospects*, New Delhi, Kanishka Publishers, 1996.

Pattanayak, Raimann (ed.), *Financial Administration and Management*, New Delhi, Anmol Publications Pvt. Limited, 1994.

Rajaraman, Indira, *A Fiscal Domain for Panchayats*, New Delhi, Oxford University Press, 2003.

Rao, Hemlata, *Federal State Financial Relations*, New Delhi, Ashish Publishing House, 1994.

Richard M. Bird and Francois Vaillancourt (ed.), *Fiscal Decentralisation in Developing Countries*, Cambridge, Cambridge University Press, 1998.

Robert W. Johnson, *Financial Management*, Boston: Allyn and Bacon Inc., 1962.

Roy, Bahl, *The Rules of Fiscal Decentralisation*, Georgia, Georgia State University, 1999.

Rural Development and Panchayat Raj Department,`*Annual Report-2003-04*, Government of Karnataka, 2004.

Second Administrative Reform Commission, *Local Governance: An Inspiring Journey into the Future*, New Delhi, Government of India, 2007.

Sethi, Geetha, *Fiscal Decentralisation to Rural Governments in India*, New Delhi: Oxford University Press, 2005.

Singh, Surat, *Problems and Prospects of Panchayat Finances*, New Delhi: Mittal Publications, 2001.

Singh, Udai Bhan, *Fiscal Federalism in Indian Union*, New Delhi, Concept Publishing Company, 2003.

Singh, Raj (ed.), *New Panchayati Raj : A Functional Analysis*, New Delhi: Anmol Publications Pvt. Ltd., 2000.

Teresa Ter-Minassian, *Fiscal Federalism in Theory and Practice*, Washington, International Monetary Fund, 1997.

The World Bank, *Overview of Rural Decentralisation in India*, Vol. I, II and III, Washington D.C., The World Bank, 2000.

Thimmaiah, G., *Local Government Finance : Some Issues*, New Delhi: Manohar Publishers and Distributors, 1998.

Index